THE FALL OF THE FACULTY

The Fall of the Faculty

The Rise of the All-Administrative University and Why It Matters

Benjamin Ginsberg

OXFORD
UNIVERSITY PRESS

OXFORD
UNIVERSITY PRESS

Oxford University Press, Inc., publishes works that further
Oxford University's objective of excellence
in research, scholarship, and education.

Oxford   New York
Auckland   Cape Town   Dar es Salaam   Hong Kong   Karachi
Kuala Lumpur   Madrid   Melbourne   Mexico City   Nairobi
New Delhi   Shanghai   Taipei   Toronto

With offices in
Argentina   Austria   Brazil   Chile   Czech Republic   France   Greece
Guatemala   Hungary   Italy   Japan   Poland   Portugal   Singapore
South Korea   Switzerland   Thailand   Turkey   Ukraine   Vietnam

Published by Oxford University Press, Inc.
198 Madison Avenue, New York, NY 10016
www.oup.com

Oxford is a registered trademark of Oxford University Press

Library of Congress Cataloging-in-Publication Data
Ginsberg, Benjamin.
The fall of the faculty : the rise of the all-administrative university
and why it matters / Benjamin Ginsberg.
p.   cm.
Includes bibliographical references and index.
ISBN 978-0-19-978244-4 (hardback : alk. paper)
1. Universities and colleges—United States—Administration.
2. Organizational behavior—United States. 3. Education, Higher—Aims and
objectives—United States. 4. Education, Higher—Social aspects—United States.
5. Academic freedom—United States. I. Title.
LB2341.G496   2011
378.1′010973—dc22   2010049033

5 7 9 8 6

Printed in the United States of America
on acid-free paper

To Sandy

Woodson

Contents

Preface

I BEGAN MY ACADEMIC career in 1968 as a graduate student at the University of Chicago, joined the Cornell faculty in 1973 as an assistant professor of government, and moved in 1992 to Johns Hopkins, where I was appointed and remain the David Bernstein Professor in the Department of Political Science. I have always felt fortunate to be associated with great universities where I have been surrounded by excellent colleagues and interesting students. Hence, I was saddened to learn from a recently published study that my own university ranks fourth in the nation in terms of the expansion of administrative and support personnel between 1997 and 2007.[1] This finding, unfortunately, coincides with the personal observations that were among the factors prompting me to write this book.

My book sounds a warning and offers a prescription designed to slow if not halt the spread of administrative blight. The prescribed medication will come too late for some victims, but others may yet recover. That, at least, is my hope.

In writing this book I profited greatly from conversations with a number of my Hopkins colleagues, particularly Matthew A. Crenson and Robert Kargon. I am very grateful to my colleague Steve Teles for recommending the book to Oxford University Press and to the readers commissioned by Oxford for their many excellent suggestions. David McBride has been an outstanding editor. I must also thank the many colleagues at schools around the nation who shared their stories with me.

One caveat is very much in order. As I wrote the book, I thought about several administrators with whom I work at Hopkins who are intelligent, talented, and dedicated individuals. I wish all university administrators were like them. Sarah and Judy—this book is not about you.

Benjamin Ginsberg
Potomac, Maryland
June 2010

THE FALL OF THE FACULTY

1

The Growth of Administration

DURING MY NEARLY five decades in the academic world, the character of the university has changed, and not entirely for the better. As recently as the 1960s and 1970s, America's universities were heavily influenced, if not completely driven, by faculty ideas and concerns. Today, institutions of higher education are mainly controlled by administrators and staffers who make the rules and set more and more of the priorities of academic life.

Of course, universities have always employed administrators. When I was a graduate student in the 1960s and a young professor in the 1970s, though, top administrators were generally drawn from the faculty, and even midlevel managerial tasks were directed by faculty members. These moonlighting academics typically occupied administrative slots on a part-time or temporary basis and planned in due course to return to full-time teaching and research. Because so much of the management of the university was in the hands of professors, presidents and provosts could do little without faculty support and could seldom afford to ignore the faculty's views.

Many faculty members proved to be excellent managers. Through their intelligence, energy and entrepreneurship, faculty administrators, essentially working in their spare time, helped to build a number of the world's premier institutions of higher education. One important reason for their success was that faculty administrators never forgot that the purpose of the university was the promotion of education and research. Their own short-term managerial endeavors did not distract them from their long-term academic commitments.

Alas, today's full-time professional administrators tend to view management as an end in and of itself. Most have no faculty experience, and even those who spent time in a classroom or laboratory hope to make administration their life's work and have no plan to return to the faculty. For many of these career managers, promoting teaching and research is less important than expanding their own administrative domains. Under their supervision, the means have become the end.

Every year, hosts of administrators and staffers are added to college and university payrolls, even as schools claim to be battling budget crises that are forcing them to reduce the size of their full-time faculties. As a result, universities are filled with armies of functionaries—the vice presidents, associate vice presidents, assistant vice presidents, provosts, associate provosts, vice provosts, assistant provosts, deans, deanlets, deanlings, each commanding staffers and assistants—who, more and more, direct the operations of every school. Backed by their administrative legions, university presidents and other senior administrators have been able, at most schools, to dispense with faculty involvement in campus management and, thereby to reduce the faculty's influence in university affairs.

At some schools, the faculty has already surrendered and is hoping that the Geneva Convention will protect it from water boarding. This seemed to be the upshot of a conference on academic freedom and shared governance held in 2009 by the American Association of University Professors.[1] At other institutions, the faculty continues to fight what are increasingly rearguard actions. There is hardly a university today that is not suffering from rampant administrative blight. In battles with the faculty, administrators sometimes win because they are clever. More often they win because there are so many of them and, having little to do, they are free to focus on bureaucratic struggle while the faculty is occupied in its classrooms, libraries, and laboratories and refuses to commit its time to the effort.

Some readers may wonder why they should care about the decline of faculty influence on university campuses. This might, after all, be an issue mainly of concern to the professorate and of little moment to the more general public. The general public, however, has a stake in the quality of America's colleges and universities, and the question of who controls the university has a direct and immediate impact on institutional quality. Former Harvard dean Henry Rosovsky once observed that the quality of a school is likely to be "negatively correlated with the unrestrained power of administrators."[2] As we shall see, Rosovsky was correct. Controlled by its faculty, the university is capable of producing not only new knowledge but new visions of society. The university can be a subversive institution in the best sense of that word, showing by its teaching and scholarship that new ways of thinking and acting are possible. Controlled by administrators, on the other hand, the university can never be more than what Stanley Aronowitz has aptly termed a knowledge factory, offering more or less sophisticated forms of vocational training to meet the needs of other established institutions in the public and private sectors. There is nothing wrong with vocational education, but it is a shame when that is all that the university offers. Though the for-profit University of Phoenix may offer good career training, contrary to its ubiquitous television commercials, we should not all become Phoenixes.

Professors and Administrators

College students generally view professors as individuals who exercise a good deal of power. Members of the faculty, after all, direct the lectures, labs, studios, and discussions around which academic life is organized. Professors also control the grades and recommendations that help to determine students' graduate school and career prospects. Students are often aware, too, that some of their professors are movers and shakers beyond the walls of the campus. Academics are visible in the worlds of science, literature, the arts, finance, and especially politics, where they serve as analysts, commentators, advisors, and high-level policy makers.

But, whatever standing they may have in the eyes of under-graduates or even in the corridors of national power, most profes-sors possess surprisingly little influence in their own schools' decision-making processes. At most, though perhaps not all, of America's thousands of colleges and universities, the faculty has been shunted to the sidelines. Faculty members will learn about major new programs and initiatives from official announcements or from the campus newspaper. Power on campus is wielded mainly by administrators whose names and faces are seldom even recognized by students or recalled by alumni.

At most schools to be sure, faculty members control the content of their own classes and, for the most part, their own research agendas. The faculty, collectively, plays a recognized though not exclusive role in the hiring and promotion of its members. Out-side these two areas, though, administrators seldom bother to consult the faculty. And, should faculty members have the temer-ity to offer unsolicited views, these will be more or less politely ignored. Thus, there are few schools whose faculty members have a voice in business or investment decisions. Hardly any faculties are consulted about the renovation or construction of buildings and other aspects of the school's physical plant. Virtually every-where, student issues, including the size of the student body, tui-tion, financial aid, and admissions policies are controlled by administrators. At most schools, fund-raising and alumni rela-tions are administrative matters, though faculty members are often asked to entertain alumni gatherings by giving talks and presentations.

Most professors, perhaps, have only a passing interest in the university's physical plant or its investment strategies. Particularly at research universities many faculty members normally pay little attention to their school's undergraduate admissions policies. But, professors lack much power even in areas in which they have a strong interest, such as the appointment of senior administrators, the development of new programs and curricula, and the definition of budgetary priorities.

As to appointments, on most campuses, presidential searches are controlled by the trustees or regents, while provosts, deans, and other senior administrators are appointed by the president with varying degrees of faculty input. Professors, to be sure, often do serve on administrative or presidential search committees, alongside administrators, students, and college staffers. These searches, however, are usually organized and overseen by corporate search firms employed by trustees, in the case of presidential searches, or the school's administration for other searches. Before the 1960s, such firms were seldom retained by universities. Today, however, as college administrators imitate the practices of their corporate counterparts, search firms are a fixture of academic life. In recent years, two-thirds of the presidential searches conducted by large universities have been directed by professional head hunters.[3] In consultation with their employers, these firms identify most of the candidates whom the committee will be able to meet and consider. Generally speaking, search firms rule out candidates about whom anything at all negative is said when they investigate candidates' backgrounds. This practice introduces a marked bias in favor of the most boring and conventional candidates. And, even the constrained choice given the committee is seldom final. Search committees are generally empowered only to recommend two or three candidates for review by the president or trustees who actually make the final decision. Many schools, of course, do not bother with even the pretense of faculty participation in administrative searches. The faculty learns the name of a new president or provost when the trustees issue a press release.

Once appointed, presidents serve at the pleasure of the trus-tees and can only be removed by them. Other administrators serve at the pleasure of the president. Every school employs a great many administrators whom the faculty regard as foolish or incompetent. But, so long as these individuals retain the support of their administrative superiors, the faculty is usually power-less to remove them. At one school, Pennsylvania's Albright Col-lege, the faculty were dismayed to learn in 1999 that the resume of their newly appointed president was filled with fraudulent claims—books never published, positions never held, and so on. Yet, while the facts of the matter could not be disputed, most trustees continued to support the president for nearly five years before he finally agreed to step down.[4] Much of the Boston Uni-versity faculty loathed and feared the dictatorial president John Silber during his twenty-five years in office but, given Silber's solid base of support among powerful members of the board of trustees, faculty opposition came to naught. In a similar vein, the trustees stood by the president of West Virginia University in the face of a faculty no-confidence vote when it was revealed that the university had awarded the daughter of the state's gov-ernor an MBA degree she had not actually earned. Conversely, faculty support will certainly not protect an administrator's job if she or he runs afoul of the board. In 2005, for example, Cor-nell's Jeffrey Lehman, a president whose work was generally approved by the faculty, was summarily fired by the board, apparently in the wake of a personnel dispute. The board neither consulted with nor informed the faculty before determining that Lehman should go.[5]

Occasionally, to be sure, just as riots and disturbances in a third world country can bring about the regime's downfall, severe faculty unrest may bring about the sudden ouster of an unpopular or inept administrator. In 2006, for example, vehement faculty protest forced the resignation of Harvard's Larry Summers and Case Western's Edward Hundert. Yet, not unlike third world peasants, disgruntled professors are seldom able to convert their brief paroxysm of rage into any form of sustained influence. In the university as in the third world, after the jubilant celebrations marking the ouster of the hated old regime end, an imperious new leadership cadre arrives to grasp the reins of power. Confined to an occasional uprising, the faculty exercises little more power over administrative tenure than the students, another campus group that can occasionally overthrow a college president but almost never governs. Thus, in 2006, apparently a difficult year for college leaders, several weeks of protests by Gallaudet College students forced the resignation of president-elect Jane Fernandez. At last report, however, students were not running the college. As often as not, faculty protests have little effect. Thus, for example, at New York's New School for Social Research, several years of faculty rebellion, including a 271 to 8 vote of no confidence in December 2008, did not result in the ouster of despised president, Bob Kerrey.[6]

The views of the faculty play a similarly limited role when it comes to new programs and spending priorities. For example, in 1998, faculty at the University of Texas at Austin were surprised to learn that the university administration had decided to spend nearly $200 million to expand the school's athletic facilities. This plan included renovation of the football stadium as well as construction of an air conditioned practice field, a new track-and-field stadium, and a new athletic center. Not only did this involve a diversion of funds from other potential uses, but it would come at the expense of badly needed classroom and laboratory space, The faculty's objections were ignored.[7]

In a similar vein, early in 2005, Florida State University professors were startled to learn from press accounts that their school's administration planned to build a school of chiropractic medicine on the Tallahassee campus. Indeed, before the faculty had even read about the idea, the university's president had already hired an administrator to oversee planning for the new school and advertised for a dean to direct its programs.[8] University administrators boasted that theirs would be the first chiropractic school formally affiliated with an American university, making FSU the nation's leader in this realm. Administrators apparently were not bothered by the fact that chiropractic theories, claims, and therapies, beyond simple massage, are universally dismissed by the medical and scientific communities as having no scientific basis. In essence, FSU administrators aspired to a lead role in the promotion of quackery. Fortunately, the state legislature cut off funds for the chiropractic school before the administration's visionary plans could be implemented.

In 2008, Virginia Commonwealth University faculty were astonished to discover that their administration had signed a secret agreement with the Philip Morris tobacco company that prohibited professors from publishing or even discussing the results of their research without the company's permission. Under the agreement, queries from third parties, such as news organizations, were to be directed to the company and university officials were to decline to comment. The school's vice president for research asserted that the contract, which violated the university's own rules, struck a reasonable balance between the university's need for openness and Philip Morris's need for confidentiality.[9]

At my own university, a 2006 press release informed the faculty that the school's administration had decided to establish a graduate school of business and would soon begin a search for a dean. The announcement came as a complete surprise to the faculty. Even professors in such fields as economics, who would be expected to contribute to the new school's efforts, were not consulted about or even informed of the plan before it was made public. Most faculty members were dubious about the administration's objectives, particularly when it became evident that fund-raising for the business school, which would require tens of millions of dollars from the university, would take precedence over other, more pressing, development priorities. Oblivious to faculty concerns, the school's former president and former provost blithely declared that they hoped professors would direct graduating seniors with business interests to the new and even now unaccredited school.

Particularly aggressive administrators are prepared to confront and silence faculty resistance to their plans to establish new programs or reorganize old ones. One favorite administrative tactic is the claim that some fiscal or other emergency requires them to act with lightning speed—and without consulting the faculty—to save the university. For example, in 1999, the president of the University of Dubuque informed the faculty that because of a financial shortfall, the administration was eliminating or consolidating more than half the school's majors and programs.[10] For the most part, liberal arts programs were to be cut in favor of the business curriculum favored by the administration and the school's trustees. No faculty were consulted before the president made his announcement, nor was evidence of the supposed financial crisis presented to the faculty.

More recently, in the wake of the 2005 Hurricane Katrina disaster, administrators at several New Orleans schools declared states of emergency. These administrators asserted, with some legal justification, that in times of emergency they possessed the power to reorganize programs, drastically change the college curriculum, eliminate course offerings, and indeed close entire departments without consulting the faculty. At Loyola University of New Orleans, according to a report commissioned by the American Association of University Professors (AAUP), President Kevin Wildes surprised the faculty by releasing a document entitled "Pathways toward Our Second Century," which presented a blueprint for a complete reorganization of the university, including the elimination of several programs, consolidation of others, and the suspension of eleven degree programs. The president conceded that his administration had begun work on "Pathways" before the hurricane. Katrina, though, "may have forced us to accomplish this undertaking much earlier than expected."[11] In other words, the hurricane provided the administration with an opportunity to bring about a complete reorganization of the school's teaching and research programs without faculty involvement.

Similarly, under the cover of a declaration of fiscal exigency, Tulane's president, Scott Cowen, proffered a "Plan for Renewal," which included reorganization or elimination of academic programs and major changes in the curriculum. Some faculty members charged that the plan was an opportunistic effort to implement proposals that had been presented to the faculty and defeated before Katrina. Tulane's administration rejected this interpretation of events, but President Cowen conceded that the hurricane had allowed him to take "bold" actions that could not have succeeded under normal circumstances. "Out of every disaster comes an opportunity," Cowen said.[12] As we shall see below, the financial crisis of 2009 gave administrators new opportunities to take bold actions.

Even in matters of curriculum planning, an area usually seen as the province of the faculty, some college administrators and trustees have been encroaching on professorial power. In 1999, for example, faculty at the State University of New York (SUNY) charged that the system's trustees were mandating a new systemwide general education curriculum without so much as consulting the SUNY faculty.[13] In 2005, Delaware State University administrators relieved the faculty of the burden of curriculum planning when they informed professors that the university would be developing a new degree program without any faculty involvement at all. The university had contracted with a New York company called "Sessions.edu" which would design and staff a new online Delaware State Master's degree program in graphic arts and Web design.[14] The school's administration dismissed faculty objections to its curricular outsourcing plan.

In many instances, when they declare the need to reform the undergraduate curriculum, administrators have no actual interest in the curriculum's content. Their real goal is to reduce the centrality of the traditional curriculum and to partially supplant it with what might be called a "student life" curriculum consisting of activities, seminars, and even courses led by administrative staff rather than faculty. The traditional curriculum gives the faculty a privileged claim on university resources and decision-making priorities while the new curriculum enhances the power of administrators and justifies hiring more administrators and fewer faculty. Administrators usually seek to justify their school's shift in emphasis by explaining that a good deal of learning takes place outside the classroom or involves subjects beyond the realm of the faculty's traditional sphere of competence.

A former assistant dean—or perhaps deanlet or deanling might be a better title—at my university explained that students need to learn more than academic skills.[15] They also must be taught, "the universal life skills that everyone needs to know." And what might be an example of one of these all-important proficiencies? According to this deanling, a premier example is event planning. "For many students, the biggest event they've ever planned is a dinner at home." But, planning an event on campus might require, "reserving the room, notifying Security, arranging transportation and lodging for out-of-town speakers, ordering food."[16] Armed with training in a subject as important and intellectually challenging as event planning, students would hardly need to know anything about physics or calculus or literature or any of those other inconsequential topics taught by the stodgy faculty.

An instrument often used by administrators to gain control over the curriculum is the study commission. Many universities, in recent years, have established commissions or committees to study the undergraduate curriculum and make recommendations for reform. Though the precise reasons for reform may not be clear, Americans generally believe that reform is a good thing and find it difficult to deny the desirability of considering reform proposals. Thus, even when the faculty is dubious about the need for such a commission, it is hard pressed to argue against its creation. At some schools: Berkeley, Chicago, Harvard, and Stanford for example, professors were able to gain control of reform committees, asserting plausibly that they knew more about curricular needs than other groups on campus. More often, though, the makeup of the committee is designed to dilute or diminish faculty influence, and the committee's subsequent recommendations are often designed to create new budgetary priorities that will enhance administrators' power and prerogatives.

One example of this phenomenon is the Commission on Undergraduate Education (CUE) established by my university in 2002. This commission, whose announced goal was to improve the quality of undergraduate education, seemed to be modeled after similar commissions that had been established at Berkeley and Stanford. This sort of "borrowing" is common in administrative circles, where original ideas are usually in short supply. Administrators often hide their mimicry under the rubric of adherence to "best practices." They can seldom offer any real evidence that the practice in question is even good, much less best. The Hopkins president who launched the committee had once been a Stanford faculty member, while the Hopkins provost, formerly a Berkeley professor, had actually served on Berkeley's undergraduate education commission. Perhaps it was only natural that they should copy concepts from campuses with which they were familiar. While Hopkins borrowed the name CUE from its sister schools, the Hopkins commission functioned quite differently from its namesakes. At Berkeley and Stanford faculty members had seized control of their undergraduate commissions and had largely beaten back administrative incursions into curricular matters. Hopkins's faculty, however, was caught off guard and watched as the committee became an administrative tool.

Administrative designs were evident from the outset when the president charged the commission with the task of improving undergraduate education, "both inside and outside the classroom." The phrase *outside the classroom* usually signals an effort by administrators to shift budgetary priorities from teaching, which the faculty controls, to other activities where, as noted above, faculty claims of expertise are weaker and administrators have an opportunity to expand their own bureaucratic domains. The role the administration expected the committee to play became even more clear when its make-up was announced. At

Berkeley and Stanford most CUE members had been drawn from the faculty. At Hopkins, though, only eight of the forty individuals named to the commission were full-time professors. Twelve were administrators and staffers, and the remainder were students and alumni. Of the eight faculty commissioners, two were untenured and, thus, concerned not to make waves, and some of the others were individuals frequently appointed to university committees because they could be trusted by the administration to refrain from making trouble.

Named to chair Hopkins's CUE was a freshly appointed vice provost for undergraduate education, a former medical school professor who had little or no experience with undergraduate education. This lack of acquaintance on the part of its chair with the subject of the commission's inquiry would presumably be no hindrance to its efforts to improve education *outside the classroom*. Before the commission could complete its work, this worthy left the university to become the provost of a small college. The inaugural chair was soon replaced by a new vice provost for undergraduate education, also an individual with no experience inside the classroom.

For at least some of the faculty committee members, service was a mind-numbing experience. On many occasions the CUE chair scheduled presentations by counselors and consultants—presumably experts in education outside the classroom—who led the commissioners in incomprehensible role-playing exercises. One professor told me that he thought he had been transported to an alternative universe whose official language was psychobabble. Administrators on the commission, though, were reported to enjoy their work. Like their bureaucratic counterparts everywhere they welcomed time out of the office, particularly if lunch was provided.

CUE submitted its report in 2003. Only a handful of the report's recommendations actually focused on undergraduate education, the committee's nominal topic. For the most part, these recommendations took the form of vague and platitudinous exhortations.

Recommendation 5, for example, declared that the university should, "Expand the opportunities available to first-year students for intellectually engaging academic experiences in a small group format." Presumably, implementation of this bold proposal would require overcoming fierce opposition from the many groups on campus committed to blocking student exposure to intellectually engaging experiences. Other recommendations were trivial. Number 12, for example, called on professors to, "give final examinations only during the final examination period." This would end the common practice of offering exams on the last day of class, a custom that had undoubtedly diminished the quality of American higher education for more than a century. Equally bold was Recommendation 33, which prodded the university to, "improve food quality and service."

If CUE had little to offer on the topic of undergraduate education inside the classroom, it had much to say about what should happen outside the classroom. Recommendation 1 called on each college within the university to appoint a "senior level administrator" to assure the quality of undergraduate education. Recommendation 12 affirmed the need for a new administrator to, "develop networking and internship opportunities for undergraduates." Recommendation 26 demanded that more minority administrators be hired. Other recommendations called for expansion of administrative supervision of most aspects of campus life.

One might have thought that improving undergraduate education would begin by enlarging the faculty to allow a larger number and greater variety of courses. Perhaps the committee might have considered changes in the undergraduate curriculum to address emerging fields in the sciences or new concepts in the humanities. But, apparently the idea that at least the first steps in improving undergraduate education should have something to do with faculty and courses is an old fashioned and overly professorial perspective. Created and led by administrators, the commission found that the undergraduate experience could be most effectively improved if the university hired more administrators! Several years later, many committee recommendations, including those pertaining to the quality of student life, had not been fulfilled, according to the school's student newspaper.[17] Those proposals calling for the appointment of more administrators, however, had been quickly implemented.

Shared Governance?

Of course, virtually every college and university boasts institutions through which the views of the faculty are formally articulated. In some instances these assemblies, senates, councils, and the like are representative institutions whose members are elected by the faculty. In other cases these bodies are meetings of the entire college faculty. Some schools possess both representative bodies and assemblages of the entire faculty, each institution exercising specified powers. Under the principle of "shared governance" which is supposed to characterize academic decision making, university administrators share power over important decisions with these faculty institutions.

The actual power of faculty assemblies varies from school to school. At some universities, these bodies have formal power in a number of areas, most notably faculty appointments, degree requirements, and the creation of new degree programs. At the University of California, Berkeley, for example, university rules give the Academic Senate a veto over many sorts of administrative decisions.[18] At most schools, however, faculty senates and assemblies have little power. They resemble the old Supreme Soviet more than the U.S. Congress or British Parliament. One recent study of these institutions concludes that, on the whole, faculty senates and assemblies are not particularly important decision-making bodies. "Their input is advisory in character, and not binding on the administration."[19]

When administrators do not like the advice they receive from faculty senates and assemblies they typically ignore it. In 2006, the

Brandeis faculty senate protested ineffectually that the president had appointed a new dean without consulting the senate as specified by university rules.[20] In the same year, the Kent State faculty senate complained that it had not been consulted when the university's president signed a partnership agreement with Ohio University creating a joint degree program. The administration told the senate it had no role to play in this plan.[21]

If faculty senates press their cases too vigorously, administrators at some universities are prepared to discard the pretense of shared governance in favor of more direct rule. This is precisely what occurred at Rensselaer Polytechnic Institute (RPI) in 2007, when the administration disbanded the faculty senate. For a number of years, segments of the RPI faculty had been sharply critical of the school's president, Shirley Ann Jackson. In 2006, Jackson narrowly survived a faculty no confidence vote by a margin of 155–149 in her favor.[22] In 2007, one of the leaders of faculty resistance to Jackson was elected vice president of the senate. Facing the prospect of heightened faculty opposition to the administration, RPI Provost Robert E. Palazzo switched from shared to third-world governance. Seizing on a pretext, the provost ordered the dissolution of the faculty senate, saying it had "lost credibility."[23] At least the provost did not aver that radical faculty senators had set fire to the *Reichstag*.

Professors usually have little recourse when the administration decides to ignore or even to disband faculty governance institutions. Generally, speaking, the courts have not shown much understanding of or sympathy toward the concept of shared governance except where state law requires state colleges to establish faculty senates or similar institutions and outline their duties and powers. Absent such legislation, faculty senates have been said to be "dependent bodies" granted power through the "grace" of the administration.[24] In a recent case, the National Labor Relations Board went so far as to say that faculty participation in shared governance is no more than a, "sophisticated version of the familiar suggestion box."[25]

Who Are the Administrators?

Perhaps if we could be confident that administrators were more able than typical faculty members and better qualified to manage university affairs, there would be no reason to object to their dominant place in institutional decision making. The fact of the matter, though, is that most administrators are not especially talented, nor are most especially qualified for their leadership positions. Obviously, excellent administrators can be found on college and university campuses. Over the years, I have had the pleasure of working with several outstanding administrators at Johns Hopkins and Cornell. Many administrators, however, are individuals who earned advanced degrees and, perhaps, intended to pursue academic careers, but failed to secure faculty posts or progress along the academic track. Many others began their careers as staffers, earned degrees in applied fields, and were promoted to positions of academic responsibility despite having no academic background. In the world of university administration, lack of academic credentials or actual experience in the realms of teaching and research is no disqualification for a career as a professional manager.

Until recent years, as I noted above, most senior academic administrators were drawn from the ranks of the faculty, and most expected to return to teaching and research when their administrative duties ended. From time to time a university might recruit a celebrity president to enhance its visibility. Shortly after World War II, for example, General Dwight D. Eisenhower was named president of Columbia. Finding that the duties of a university president required little time or energy, Ike used his Columbia stint to prepare for a national presidential campaign.[26] But despite notable exceptions like Eisenhower, presidents, provosts, and deans were typically former senior faculty members, albeit sometimes recruited from other schools.[27] Some planned to return to the faculty after a term or two as administrators, while others viewed administration as a respectable way to end an academic career that had begun in the laboratory or classroom. Many other senior administrators, the vice provosts and associate deans, were often part-timers, that is, senior faculty members who found administrative work interesting (or whose arms had been twisted vigorously by the dean or provost) but were not prepared permanently to abandon their academic projects.

In general, these faculty members turned administrators had a good understanding of the culture of the university and, more important, had respect for research and teaching. When professors who demonstrated intelligence and a strong work ethic in the academic realm turned to administration, they generally brought these same qualities into their new administrative suites. I remember that when I was a student at the University of Chicago in the 1960s, the presidents included a Nobel Prize–winning geneticist, George Wells Beadle, and one of the nation's most prominent law professors, Edward Levi. Not surprisingly, both were excellent managers and fund raisers. In a similar vein, when I was a faculty member at Cornell in the 1970s and 1980s, three distinguished senior faculty members in succession were appointed to the deanship of the College of Arts and Sciences—a nationally known economist, a well-regarded professor of Romance languages, and a noted musicologist. The college prospered during their regimes.

At my current university, Johns Hopkins, the president and several of the top administrators have perfectly respectable faculty credentials, though they might view themselves as having made permanent career changes and have no plans to return to the laboratory or classroom. But, consistent with national trends, more and more of the school's other senior academic managers are professional administrators with little or no academic background. Even some of the academic deans in recent years have been younger individuals, frustrated in their scholarly efforts, who sought new leases on life in administration. For these individuals a deanship was less an opportunity to serve the school than a potential stepping stone to higher administrative offices.

While some administrative posts continue to be held by senior professors on a part-time basis, their ranks are gradually dwindling as their jobs are taken over by full-time managers. This shift, too, is consistent with national trends. College administrations frequently tout the fiscal advantages of using part-time, "adjunct" faculty to teach courses. They fail, however, to apply the same logic to their own ranks. Over the past thirty years, the percentage of faculty members who are hired on a part-time basis has increased dramatically so that today almost half the nation's professors work only part time. The percentage of administrators who are part-time employees has fallen during the same time period (see Table 1).

The old-style college administrators were not all perfect, and the new professional administrators are not all bad. Again, I have personally enjoyed working with several excellent professional administrators. On average, though, the new administrators are not as good as the people they have supplanted. They do not understand the character of the university or its purposes. To make matters worse, many of the new administrators would like to redefine—dumb down might be an appropriate term—the mission of the university to enhance the centrality of their own roles. Shouldn't "event planning" be as important as physics? Perhaps if you understand event planning but not physics you might wish to make that argument. But that is why the physicists, and not the event planners, should fill the university's leadership positions. If the event planners take charge, the quality of the university will

TABLE 1. Change in Percentage of Part-Timers, 1976–2005

	1976	2005
Faculty	31%	48%
Administrators	4%	3%

Source: National Center for Education Statistics (NCES), "Digest of Education Statistics, 2006," Tables 227 and 228.

almost inevitably suffer as they redefine educational goals to coincide more fully with their own level of understanding and ability.

This point was brought home to me when I served as one of the few faculty members of a search committee organized to find a new director of admissions. The dean who chaired the committee, one of our administrators with a recent doctorate in education but no academic experience, informed us that while some people might think that the admissions process entailed bringing students to the campus to work with the faculty, this was a mistaken notion. There were, he intoned, many "stakeholders" in the admissions process who should have a voice in admissions decisions and the selection of an admissions director. When I inquired who these might be besides, of course, the coach of our often-national-championship lacrosse team, he mentioned the counseling staff, the librarians, the residence hall staff, the dining hall staff, and many others. A good deal of education occurred "outside the classroom," he declared, repeating the phrase that had become an administrative mantra. I suggested that students did not come to Hopkins to work with our dining services personnel, our counselors, or even our distinguished administrators, but my objection was dismissed. This dean was determined to redefine the purposes of the university in terms that inflated the importance of his own place in it.

The Growth of Administration

To nonacademics, and even sometimes to academics, the administrative organization of a typical university can seem quite confusing. The managerial ranks include a bewildering array of vice presidents, provosts, vice provosts, associate provosts, deans, vice deans, associate deans, and assistant deans. To make matters more confusing, the structure of ranks is not the same at all schools. A title that indicates substantial authority at one school may denote a low place in the administrative hierarchy at another. For example, at most schools the dean of the college is the chief administrative officer of a unit within the university. At Brown, though, this official is called the dean of the faculty while the dean of the college occupies a lower rung on the administrative ladder that at other schools would be called dean of students. It might be useful to review the basic administrative structure of the university, recognizing that each campus will vary to some degree from the model presented below.

Almost always, a college or university's chief administrator holds the title president or chancellor, though at some institutions like the University of California, the president is the head of the university system while the leader of each quasi-autonomous campus is called the chancellor. Most, but not all, presidents have an academic background. About three-fourths of current college and university presidents hold doctoral degrees and about two-thirds held faculty positions before becoming administrators.[28] The president reports to a board of trustees in the case of private schools or board of regents in the case of public institutions. College or university trustees are usually prominent individuals drawn from the business community, politics, and the arts. Many, though not all, are likely to be alumni of the institution. Membership on the board is almost always by invitation, and there is some expectation that wealthy invitees, especially if they are alumni, will make a substantial contribution to the school in return for the honor of serving.

Usually, the college president and the board's leadership work together to select new members who are deemed likely to be sympathetic to the existing board's policies and to the school's administration. Potential troublemakers are almost always avoided. At a small number of schools, Dartmouth for example, some board members are elected by the alumni-at-large. Elected trustees are more likely than their carefully chosen colleagues to bring ideas to board meetings that are inconsistent with the school's current programs and policies. At Dartmouth, where half the trustees were traditionally chosen by the alumni, several of the elected trustees vehemently opposed what they saw as efforts by the president and board to change the school's character. The administration and majority faction among the trustees responded by increasing the board's size so that, in the future, only one-third of its members would be chosen by the alumni.[29] At public colleges and universities, regents are generally appointed by the state governor in consultation with the school's president and existing board members. Most regents, like their private school counterparts, are prominent individuals, generally with ties to the school.

Reporting directly to the president are usually several vice presidents. These officials manage the school's business affairs, including finance, human resources, information technology, and so forth, and are more likely to have business than academic backgrounds. At larger schools, the vice presidents often have many assistants who, in turn, have their own assistants. The University of Maryland at College Park, for example, employs six vice presidents, six associate vice presidents, five assistant vice presidents, six assistants to the president, and six assistants to the vice presidents.[30]

Also reporting to the president at larger colleges and most universities is the provost, who may also hold the title vice president for academic affairs. The provost is the school's chief academic officer. Provosts almost always have academic backgrounds and oversee university activities relating to teaching, research, scholarship, and other elements of the university's core mission. At some schools, the provost manages campus matters while the president focuses on fund-raising and relations with external constituencies such as alumni, donors, state legislators, and the federal government. Some presidents, however, prefer to oversee campus as well as external matters, and cede little discretionary authority to the provost. At larger schools, the provost is assisted by vice provosts, associate provosts, and assistant provosts, who have a variety of responsibilities. Cornell, according to its Web site, employs eight vice provosts on its Ithaca, New York, campus. The University of Michigan, an enormous school, boasts eleven vice, associate, and assistant provosts, whose stated responsibilities include academic affairs, information, faculty affairs, academic human resources, multicultural affairs, and planning.

Within a university or larger college, there are typically several colleges or schools, each with its own administrative structure led by a dean. There may be a dean of the college of arts and sciences, a dean of the law school, as well as deans of the medical school, the engineering school, the business school, and so on. Deans report to the provost, though on some campuses individual deans have considerable autonomy. It will come as no surprise that deans are supported by phalanxes of vice deans, associate deans, and assistant deans plus other officials who hold the title "dean" but rank below the college dean. These might include the dean of students and dean of admissions. For example, at the University of Southern California (USC), a school with nineteen college deans, each dean is assisted by a sizable body of assistants and associates. The dean of arts and sciences oversees eight helpers. These include an executive vice dean for academic affairs, a senior associate dean for administration and planning, a senior associate dean for business and finance, a senior associate dean for advancement, a vice dean for faculty affairs, a vice dean for graduate programs, a vice dean for research advancement, and, last but not least, a vice dean for undergraduate programs. And, of course, every provost, vice provost, associate provost, dean, vice dean, associate dean, and so forth employs a huge body of staffers and assistants whose titles and job descriptions can fill hundreds of pages in a university's human resources manual.

Administrators are not only well staffed, they are also well paid. Vice presidents at the University of Maryland, for example, earn well over $200,000, and deans earn nearly as much. Both groups saw their salaries increase as much as 50 percent between 1998 and 2003, a period of financial retrenchment and sharp tuition increases at the university.[31] The University of Maryland has long been noted for its bloated and extortionate bureaucracy but it actually does not seem to be much of an exception.[32] Administrative salaries are on the rise everywhere in the nation.[33] By 2007, the median salary paid to the president of a doctoral degree–granting institution was $325,000.[34] Eighty-one presidents earned more than $500,000, and twelve earned over $1 million. The highest paid presidents were the leaders of Northeastern University ($2.9 million), Philadelphia University ($2.6 million), and Johns Hopkins ($1.9 million).[35] As is often true in the corporate world, the relationship between salary and institutional performance is unclear. Some of the best paid presidents lead undistinguished schools, while the presidents of some of the nation's leading universities earn relatively moderate salaries. The presidents of Harvard, Princeton, and Stanford, for example, are nowhere near the pinnacle of executive compensation.[36] Presidents, at least, might perform important services for their schools.[37] Somewhat more difficult to explain is the fact that by 2010, even some of the ubiquitous and largely interchangeable deanlets and deanlings earned six-figure salaries.

Laboring beneath (some would say crushed under) this administrative superstructure are the faculty members, organized into departments, who actually undertake the activities that are the university's nominal mission. They teach the courses, organize the research projects, run the laboratories, conceive and supervise the academic programs that nominally represent the core mission of institutions of higher education. Administrators and staffers actually outnumber full-time faculty members at America's colleges and universities. In 2005, colleges and universities employed more than 675,000 full-time faculty members. This number may seem large but, in the same year, America's colleges and universities employed more than 190,000 individuals classified by the federal government as, "executive, administrative and managerial employees." Another 566,405 college and university employees were classified as "other professional."[38] This category includes information technology specialists, counselors, auditors, accountants, admission officers, development officers, alumni relations officials, human resources staffers, editors and writers for school publications, attorneys, and a slew of others.

These "other professionals" are not administrators, but they work for the administration and serve as its arms, legs, eyes, ears, and mouthpieces. Administrative staffers do not work for or, in many cases, even share information with the faculty.[39] This army of professional staffers is the bulwark of administrative power in the contemporary university. Before they employed an army of staffers, administrators were forced to rely on the cooperation of the faculty to carry out tasks ranging from admissions through planning.[40] An administration that lost the confidence of the faculty might find itself unable to function. Today, its army of staffers makes the administration "relatively autonomous" in the language of political science, and marginalizes the faculty.

Forty years ago, America's colleges actually employed more professors than administrators. The efforts of 446,830 professors were supported by 268,952 administrators and staffers. Over the past four decades, though, as the number of full-time professors increased slightly more than 50 percent—a percentage comparable to the growth in student enrollments during the same time period—the number of administrators and administrative staffers employed by those schools increased by an astonishing 85 percent and 240 percent, respectively (see Table 2).

The significance of these numbers comes into particularly sharp focus if viewed in terms of college and university spending priorities. Between 1975 and 2005, total spending by American

TABLE 2. Changes in Staff Size, 1975–2005

	1975	2005	%Change
Full-Time Faculty	446,830	675,624	+51%
Administrators	102,465	190,078	+85%
Other Professionals	166,487	566,405	+240%

Source: 1975 data, *Academe*, November/December, 1971, 22. 2005 data, NCES, "Digest," 2006, Table 228.

educational institutions, stated in constant dollars, tripled to more than $325 billion per year.[41] To what use was this money put? It is often said that schools are concerned with their faculty to student ratios. This ratio is generally seen by students, parents, and publications that rank colleges as one measure of educational quality. A large number of students per faculty member is viewed negatively while a small number of students per faculty member is universally taken to suggest an environment conducive to learning. If America's institutions of higher education were primarily concerned with educating students we might expect that increased levels of spending would be associated with expansion of the size of the faculty and some drop in the number of students per college and university faculty member.

What we find, instead, is that even as higher education spending has increased, the faculty to student ratio has remained fairly constant over the past thirty years at approximately fifteen or sixteen students per instructor. What has changed dramatically, though, is the administrator and staffer per student ratio. In 1975, colleges employed one administrator for every 84 students and one professional staffer for every 50 students. By 2005, the administrator to student ratio had dropped to 1 administrator for every 58 students while the professional staffer to student ratio had dropped to 1 for every 21 students (see Table 3). Apparently, as colleges and universities had more money to spend they chose

TABLE 3. Full Time Equivalent (FTE) Students Per FTE Staff, 1975–2005

	1975	1995	2005
Faculty	16	15	15
Administrators	84	71	68
Professional Staff	50	25	21

Source: NCES, "Digest," 2006, Table 227.

not to spend it on expanding their instructional resources, i.e., faculty. They chose, instead, to enhance their administrative and staff resources. A 2009 study reported similar findings.[42] A comprehensive study published by the Delta Cost Project in 2010 reported that between 1998 and 2008 America's private colleges increased spending on instruction by 22 percent while increasing spending on administration and staff support by 36 percent.[43] Parents who wonder why college tuition is so high and increases so much each year should be pleased to learn that their sons and daughters will have an opportunity to interact with more deanlets and staffers, though not more professors. Well, you can't have everything. The recommendations of the Hopkins CUE, which seemed so peculiar, appear to reflect the prevailing view among university administrators—the university's chief priority should be the recruitment of more administrators!

It is worth noting that in spring 2010, an external review committee created by the Hopkins administration to evaluate the School of Arts and Sciences and to make recommendations for improvements issued its report. The committee, consisting of five experienced academic administrators and chaired by former Columbia provost Jonathan Cole evaluated the school's research and teaching efforts and concluded that these could be enhanced by—you guessed it—an expansion of administrative authority at Hopkins. The faculty suggested that administrators neither do research nor teach students, but what do we know?[44]

Why Administration Has Grown

Three main explanations are often adduced for the sharp growth in the number of university administrators over the past thirty years. One common explanation is growth in demand for administrative services. In this view, the expansion of administrative and staff ranks has been an inevitable result of the ongoing expansion of the number of students, faculty members, and even the number of

28 THE FALL OF THE FACULTY

educational institutions in the United States.[45] There is, no doubt, some truth to this explanation. In recent years, student enrollments, faculty size, and the sheer number of colleges and universities in the United States have all increased, producing more need for the services of educational administrators. Growth in demand for administrative services, however, cannot tell the whole story. The fact is that over the past thirty years, administrative and staff growth has outstripped by a considerable margin virtually all other dimensions of the expansion of American higher education (see Table 4). Between 1975 and 2005, the number of colleges, professors, students, and BA degrees granted all increased in the neighborhood of 50 percent. During the same time period, as we saw earlier, the number of administrators increased 85 percent, and the number of administrative staffers employed by America's schools increased by a whopping 240 percent. These numbers do not seem to be explained by underlying growth in the sources of demand for administrative services.

Perhaps it could be argued that in recent years, there have been new sorts of demands for administrative services that require more managers per student or faculty member than was true in the past. Universities today have an elaborate information technology infrastructure, enhanced student services, a more extensive fund-raising and lobbying apparatus, and so on, than was

TABLE 4. Changes in the Supply of and Demand for Administrative Services, 1985–2005

Staff	+240%
Administrators	+85%
Student Enrollments	+56%
Faculty	+50%
No. of Degree-Granting Institutions	+50%
No. of BA Degrees Granted	+47%

Source: Calculated from NCES, "Digest," 2006.

common thirty years ago.[46] Yet, it might also be said that during this same time period, whole new fields of teaching and research opened in such areas as computer science, genetics, chemical biology, and physics. Other new research and teaching fields were opened by ongoing changes in the world economy and international order. And yet, faculty growth between 1975 and 2005 simply kept pace with growth in enrollments and substantially lagged administrative and staff growth. When push came to shove, colleges obviously chose to invest in management rather than teaching and research.

A second common explanation given for the expansion of administration in recent years is the ever-increasing need to respond to mandates and record-keeping demands from federal and state governments as well as numerous licensure and accreditation bodies. It is certainly true that large numbers of administrators spend a good deal of time preparing reports and collecting data for these and other agencies. The federal government requires the reporting of mountains of data on everything from affirmative action through campus crime and the treatment of laboratory animals in university research facilities. Boards that accredit and license educational institutions require reams of reports and often make time-consuming site visits to inspect campus facilities. A variety of state agencies demand data and, in the case of public institutions, conduct extensive audits, reviews, surveys, and inspections.

But, as burdensome as this paperwork blizzard might be, it is not clear that it explains the growth in administrative personnel that we have observed. Often, affirmative action reporting is cited as the most time consuming of the various governmental mandates. As Barbara Bergmann has pointed out, though, across the nation only a handful of administrators and staffers are employed in this endeavor.[47] More generally, we would expect that if administrative growth were mainly a response to external mandates, growth should be greater at state schools, which are more exposed to government obligations, than at private institutions, which are freer to manage their own affairs in their own way. Yet, when we examine the data, precisely the opposite seems to be the case. Between 1975 and 2005, the number of administrators and managers employed by public institutions increased by 66 percent. During the same time period, though, the number of administrators employed by private colleges and universities grew by 135 percent (see Table 5). These numbers seem inconsistent with the idea that external mandates have been the forces driving administrative growth at America's institutions of higher education.

It should also be noted that while mandates from government agencies or accrediting bodies are conventionally viewed as external forces acting on a school, this is not entirely true. Often, administrators welcome and even encourage the intervention of external agencies because these can help administrators gain the upper hand over the faculty in course planning and curricular matters. After all, if a particular course of action is required by a licensing or accrediting agency, how can the faculty refuse? I once resisted efforts by administrators to change the class times of courses within a program I directed. Finally, I was informed that the change sought by the administration was required by the licensing body that nominally exercised authority over this area. Since this particular licensing board was known for the somewhat lackadaisical manner with which it approached its responsibilities, I was surprised that it had taken an interest in my class schedules.

TABLE 5. Administrative Growth at Public and Private Institutions, 1975–2005

	1975	1995	2005	Change
Administrators and Managers at Public Colleges	60,733	82,396	101,011	+66%
Administrators and Managers at Private Colleges	40,530	65,049	95,313	+135%

Source: Calculated from NCES, "Digest," 2006.

I learned later that the contact between the licensing board and school administrators had been initiated by the latter. In essence, the university was compelled to respond to an external mandate that its own administrators had helped to initiate.

A similar phenomenon is apparent in administrators' reactions to the report of the so-called Spellings Commission, the Commission on the Future of Higher Education, launched by the former education secretary Margaret Spellings in 2005. One of the main recommendations of the Spellings report was the development and publication of "accountability measures" that would permit comparisons of student performance across schools. Many critics question whether such measures applied across different types of schools have much validity, and the fact that the testing industry was rather well represented in drafting a federal report recommending more testing, raised questions and more than a few eyebrows. Eventually, in response to opposition from America's premier universities, the proposal was tabled. Initially, though, the idea of accountability measures was welcomed by administrators at hundreds of colleges and universities as well as their colleagues at regional accreditation bodies who moved to implement the idea even before the Department of Education could begin to act on it.[48]

For several years, some administrators have been aware of the potential value of externally mandated performance criteria as instruments through which to wrest control of the curriculum from the faculty. Accountability measures allow administrators to require the faculty to "teach to the test," rather than devise the curriculum according to its own judgment. In this way, college professors can be reduced to the same subordinate status to which elementary and secondary school teachers have already been relegated.[49] One university administrator eagerly called on his colleagues to meet the "major challenge" of getting a skeptical faculty "on board" for accountability measures.[50] At many schools this challenge has already been met by requiring faculty to match their course content to some set of standardized evaluation tools.[51]

The Spellings mandate was not imposed on colleges, but even as a proposal it was seized by administrators as an opportunity to advance their own interests. After all, professors have long used their control of testing to exert authority over the conduct of students. Why should it be surprising that administrators would seek control of testing as a way of exerting authority over the faculty?

A third explanation often suggested for administrative growth in higher education has to do with the conduct of the faculty. Many faculty members, it is often said, regard administrative activities as obnoxious chores and are content to allow these to be undertaken by others. Relatedly, some have suggested that professors also contribute to administrative bloat by pressing schools to create positions for their spouses and partners.

There is no doubt that some members of the faculty have been complicit in the expansion of college and university bureaucracies. Almost every professor would prefer to spend time in the laboratory, library, or classroom than to attend committee meetings and, indeed, virtually every school employs some staffers and administrators who owe their positions to the efforts of faculty spouses.

But, while there is some truth to the assertion that the faculty has contributed to its own downfall, this is certainly not the whole story. Often enough, professors who are willing to undertake administrative tasks lose interest when they find that the committees, councils, and assemblies through which the faculty nominally acts have lost much if not all their power to administrators. And, as to faculty demands for spousal positions in the bureaucracy, this was more common in previous generations when (usually) male PhDs were typically married to non-PhD spouses. More common in the university today is the dual-PhD couple seeking two faculty positions.

If growth-driven demand, governmental mandates, and faculty preferences are not sufficient explanations for administrative expansion, an alternative explanation might be found in the nature of university bureaucracies themselves. In particular, administrative growth may be seen primarily as a result of efforts by administrators to aggrandize their own roles in academic life. Students of bureaucracy have frequently observed that administrators have a strong incentive to maximize the power and prestige of whatever office they hold by working to increase its staff and budget.[52] To justify such increases, they often invent new functions to perform or seek to capture functions currently performed by others.[53]

This model may help to explain why between 1947 and 1995 (the last year for which the relevant data were published) administrative costs increased from barely 9 to nearly 15 percent of college and university budgets. More recent data, though not strictly comparable, follow a similar pattern.[54] During this same time period, stated in constant dollars, overall university spending increased 148 percent. Administrative spending, though increased by a whopping 235 percent. Instructional spending, by contrast, increased only 128 percent, 20 points less than the overall rate of spending increase.[55] In essence, administrators have increased their level of activity more rapidly than university budgets have grown and so have gradually increased their share of the budget to pay for it. Much of this increase in spending has come at the expense of the instructional budget possibly as administrators have revised university priorities or taken over functions previously controlled by members of the faculty.

Most academics are familiar with the creativity often shown by administrators in inventing new tasks for themselves and the diligence they can demonstrate when endeavoring to capture established functions. In some instances, to be sure, the tasks that administrators invent may be useful ones. As they pursue their own interests, they may also advance the more general interest. To the extent, for example, that administrators create new offices and staff positions designed to promote equal opportunity, their efforts can only be commended. Often enough, though, administrators advance their interests by inventing activities that cost money or take up staff time without doing much to further the university's educational or research goals. At one school, an inventive group of administrators created a "committee on traditions," whose mission seemed to be the identification and restoration of forgotten university traditions or, failing that, the creation of new traditions. Another group of deans constituted themselves as the "War Zones Task Force." This group recruited staffers, held many meetings, and prepared a number of reports whose upshot seemed to be that students should be discouraged from traveling to war zones unless, of course, their homes were in war zones.

Similarly, in 2006, administrators at my university mobilized furiously to combat campus racism. Responding to racially insensitive material disseminated by a campus fraternity, the university's former president issued a set of guidelines on equal treatment of minorities and created a campuswide commission to implement them. Racial sensitivity training was organized for faculty and students (but not administrators). In addition, every incoming freshman was assigned a book dealing with racial issues that would be discussed in special orientation seminars led by university administrators. The faculty, which includes some of America's leading authorities on issues of race, was not consulted or invited to become involved as the administration seized a new opportunity to expand its range of endeavors.

And, if the struggle against campus racism was not enough to occupy administrative time, another group of administrators at my university established the Office of Critical Event Preparedness and Response (CEPAR), whose staff promised to protect the university from nuclear chemical and biological attack. Perhaps the administration feared that our frustrated lacrosse rivals were working in secret to devise new tactics to use against Hopkins. Navy, one of our chief foes, does after all possess a nuclear capability.

Administrators everywhere seem to be incredibly creative when it comes to fashioning positions that appear to be less than essential to the proper functioning of the university. The administrative and staff jobs listed in the "careers" section of a recent issue of the *Chronicle of Higher Education* include many whose descriptions suggest a bureaucracy gone wild. For example, one Tennessee community college hoped to hire a "Director of Institutional Effectiveness," whose job it would be to monitor the "campus-wide institutional effectiveness process."[56] A Texas college was eager to hire a "Dual Credit Coordinator,' whose services were needed to help students through the apparent complexities of dual credit enrollments.[57] But, perhaps the expansion of university bureaucracies is best illustrated by an ad placed by a Colorado school, which sought a "Coordinator of College Liaisons."[58] This is definitely an area in which students do not need administrative assistance.

When administrators are not devising ambitious new tasks, they often can be found attempting to take control of established programs, usually by wresting them from the hands of the faculty. Administrative imperialists, like their counterparts in other realms, may claim that their intervention is needed to rescue faltering enterprises. This claim, however, is usually no more than a pretext for territorial expansion. I will cite an example from my own experience. Several years ago, I was visited by an assistant dean who informed me that, with the support of the dean, he would be taking administrative responsibility for a popular undergraduate program that I had created and had successfully managed for more than a decade with little or no administrative assistance or supervision. We would work together, he said, to strengthen the program. I politely suggested that he look elsewhere for administrative opportunities. I suppose that in the interest of full disclosure I should admit that I was not polite. Contrary to campus gossip, though, I did not physically attack him. After several days of bureaucratic skirmishing, this assistant dean was driven off, and the program continued to be sufficiently successful that it was often touted to prospective students by the college admissions people. Some time later, administrators did manage to take control of another undergraduate program similar to mine but less aggressively defended by its faculty sponsors. Within a year the program had virtually no students and had to be closed.

The foregoing is not an unusual outcome. College administrators are usually better at inventing or seizing control of activities than managing them effectively. When administrators take control of a program from the faculty they often ruin it, since they typically know far less about the program and have less commitment to it than its original faculty directors. For example, at one university, individual departments had, for many years, developed exchange agreements with their counterparts at foreign universities. The Political Science department, according to a colleague who related the story to me, exchanged one or two graduate students every year with a European university, providing a useful experience for both groups of students. Recently, however, a provost took control of international programs. What was once done easily and simply at the departmental level now required elaborate forms and procedures and the approval of administrators and staffers who knew next to nothing about the institutions with which the faculty thought it might be useful to develop exchange programs.

Some time after this administrative shift, the Political Science department was approached by faculty from an excellent university in South America which hoped to establish a tie to the American school. The department chair struggled for months with the approval process now required and finally gave up. It was too complex and cumbersome. He said life was too short. Now that the school had a provost for international programs it might soon have no international programs. But, of course, in the administrative world titles often count for more than substance.

These examples illustrate the fact that administrative growth in American colleges and universities is an internally generated phenomenon more than a response to external forces. Administrators everywhere have been eager to invent or take control of activities that would expand their influence and provide them with an opportunity to hire more subordinates and staffers. This sort of administrative aggrandizement, as Anthony Downs pointed out, is most often associated with officials who have a strong stake in the positions they hold.[59] Administrators drawn from the faculty, particularly senior faculty members temporarily taking on administrative assignments, perhaps on a part-time basis, have no particular reason to endeavor to enhance the power and prerogatives associated with their administrative slots. They expect, in due course, to return to the faculty. Professional administrators, though, lack the academic credentials that would allow them to secure faculty posts and have every reason to aggrandize the administrative positions on which they depend. The increasing prevalence of nonfaculty administrators may explain why the growth of professional staff at America's colleges and universities is accelerating (see Table 6).

Many college administrators often seem to assign more weight to increasing the size of their staffs than to actually performing the tasks for which they are nominally responsible. One administrator told me that administrative prominence was defined in terms of the number of "direct reports," that is the number of individuals who reported to a particular administrator. I recently encountered an amusing example of this phenomenon. For many years, one school with which I am acquainted had sponsored a successful precollege summer program that drew several hundred secondary school students to the campus for classes and other activities. The program generated substantial tuition and dormitory revenues and operated at an extremely low cost. In fact, the entire program was run by one full-time staff person with the assistance of a group of part-time student helpers during the busy season. When this summer session staffer unfortunately departed, the program was assigned to an assistant dean. He quite properly met with interested faculty members and was advised to begin immediately calling and, where possible, visiting the secondary

TABLE 6. Growth of Professional Staff, 1989–1995

1989–2005	1995–1999	1999–2005
+12%	+16%	+25%

Source: NCES, "Digest," various years.

school teachers and counselors who had, over the years, sent students to the program. Professors with some experience in this area said personal contact was a very important mechanism for maintaining the loyalty of feeder schools in the face of competition from other colleges. It was also suggested that he quickly update brochures and catalogs and make certain that these were sent to the secondary schools on which the program depended.

The dean listened carefully and politely to this advice and agreed that these were good ideas. Nevertheless, he said, his first priority would be to hire a new summer session director and staff which would, in turn, move to implement these and other suggestions he had received. The staff selection process took some time, but after a few months the dean had hired a director who, in turn, hired several staff people. Now the university had a whole group to do what once was done by one person. This group always seemed to be very busy, sending out many notices to alert the campus to its activities and accomplishments. Unfortunately, though, the new summer session staff appeared not to have directed enough of its energy to student recruitment. Under the new summer regime, precollege enrollments fell dramatically. To the consternation of the faculty, however, the collapse of these enrollments and their associated revenue stream did not seem to bother either the assistant dean in charge or the higher ranking administrators to whom he reported. The assistant dean had been able to increase the size and prominence of his own staff as well as the administrative domain controlled by his bosses. This seemed to be enough of an achievement.

The Onward March of the All-Administrative University

The power and size of college and university administrations varies from school to school. According to data recently reported by the *Chronicle of Higher Education*, in the nation as a whole, between 1997 and 2007 the ratio of administrators for every one hundred students increased by about 30 percent at private colleges. During the same period, however, some universities—Yeshiva and Wake Forest, in particular—experienced more than 300 percent growth in the size of their managerial and support staffs.[60]

Numbers, of course, are not the whole story. As we shall see in the coming chapters, large numbers of managers and deanlets do very little besides collecting checks and engaging in make-work activities that siphon off resources from potentially more productive uses. Numbers, however, create possibilities. Given large numbers of deanlets and deanlings, more ambitious presidents and provosts have an opportunity to marginalize the faculty and to expand their own power on campus. On a firm foundation of bureaucratic bloat, the all-administrative university can be built. In the concluding chapter, I will offer a number of suggestions for halting or reversing these developments. Some colleges and universities may be saved, but I fear that it may be too late at most schools.

What Administrators Do

THE NUMBER OF administrators and staffers on university campuses has increased so rapidly in recent years that often there is simply not enough work to keep all of them busy. I have spent time in university administrative suites and in the corridors of public agencies. In both settings I am always struck by the fact that so many well-paid individuals have so little to do. To fill their time, administrators engage in a number of make-work activities. They attend meetings and conferences, they organize and attend administrative and staff retreats, and they participate in the strategic planning processes that have become commonplace on many campuses.

While these activities are time consuming, their actual contribution to the core research and teaching missions of the university is questionable. Little would be lost if all pending administrative retreats and conferences, as well as four of every five staff meetings (these could be selected at random), were canceled tomorrow. And, as to the ubiquitous campus planning exercises, as we shall see below, the planning process functions mainly to enhance the power of senior managers. The actual plans produced after the investment of thousands of hours of staff time are usually filed away and quickly forgotten.

There is, to be sure, one realm in which administrators as-a-class have proven extraordinarily adept. This is the general domain of fund-raising. College and university administrators have built a massive fund-raising apparatus that, every year, collects hundreds of millions of dollars in gifts and bequests mainly, though not exclusively, from alumni whose sense of nostalgia or obligation make them easy marks for fund-raisers' finely-honed tactics. Even during the depths of the recession in 2009, schools were able to raise money. On the one hand, the donors who give selflessly to their schools deserve to be commended for their beneficence. At the same time, it should still be noted that, as is so often the case in the not-for-profit world, university administrators appropriate much of this money to support—what else?—more administration.

Meetings, Retreats, and Conferences

One activity with which underworked administrators can and do busy themselves is talk. In fact, administrators spend a good part of every day talking to one another in a variety of informal and formal contexts. For example, most administrators and staffers attend several meetings every day, usually with other administrators and staffers. Of course, in any bureaucracy, a certain number of meetings to exchange information and plan future courses of action is unavoidable. In academic bureaucracies, though, many meetings seem to have little purpose. Indeed, the major agenda item at many administrative meetings consists of reports from and plans for other meetings.

For example, at a recent "President's Staff Meeting," eleven of the eighteen agenda items discussed by administrators at one Ohio community college involved plans for future meetings or discussions of other recently held meetings.[1] In a similar vein, at a meeting of the "Administrative and Professional Staff Advisory Committee" at a large midwestern university, ten of approximately twenty-four agenda items concerned other meetings.[2] And, at a meeting of the "Process Management Steering Committee" of a midwestern community college, virtually the entire meeting was devoted to planning subsequent meetings by process management teams including the "search committee training team," the "faculty advising and mentoring team," and the "culture team," which was said to be meeting with "renewed energy." The culture team was also said to be close to making a recommendation on the composition of a "Culture Committee."[3] Since culture is a notoriously abstruse issue, this committee may need to meet for years, if not decades, to unravel its complexities. These examples conjure up a nightmarish vision of administrative life in which staffers and managers spend much of the day meeting to discuss meetings where other meetings are discussed at which still other meetings have been discussed. This vision may seem bizarre, but unfortunately it is not far from the truth.

When they face particularly challenging problems, academic administrators sometimes find that ordinary meetings in campus offices do not allow them the freedom from distraction they require. To allow them to focus fully and without interruption, administrators sometimes find it necessary to schedule off-campus administrative retreats where they can work without fear that the day-to-day concerns of the campus will disturb their deliberations. Some retreats are simply extended off-campus meetings organized for the discussion of serious issues. Other retreats are more elaborate and include athletic and role-playing activities that are supposed to help improve the staff's spirit of camaraderie and ability to function as a team. Some retreats feature arts and crafts activities that are somehow related to team-building. For example, at a 2007 professional development retreat, Michigan Tech staffers broke into teams and spent several hours building furniture from pieces of cardboard and duct tape. Similarly, at a 2006 retreat, Georgia Southern College of Education staffers were divided into teams to build plastic bubbles into which all team members could fit. This bubble-building exercise was followed by an extended discussion of the strengths and weaknesses of each team's efforts. Many staff retreats also include presentations by professional speakers who appear to specialize in psychobabble. Topics at recent retreats included, "Do You Want to Succeed?" "Reflective Resensitizing," and "Waking Up the Inner World." In all likelihood, the administrators and staffers privileged to attend these important talks spent the next several weeks reporting on them at meetings with colleagues who had been deprived of the opportunity to learn firsthand how to make certain that their inner worlds remained on alert. In this way, retreats can help to provide material for administrative meetings, which can, in turn, be used to plan subsequent retreats, and so forth.

Some staff retreats are planned and led by professional facilitators. Several West Coast schools including Pepperdine, for example, have employed the "Boojum Institute" to organize their administrative retreats. Boojum specializes in experiential education, leading groups of retreating administrators in such activities as rock climbing, back packing, river canoeing, hiking, and kayaking. The institute refers to these activities as "transformational outdoor adventures." Corporate executives generally view this sort of retreat as a subsidized vacation. We can, however, be confident that college administrators would never spend even a dime of tuition revenue on selfish pursuits. They force themselves to hike, canoe, and kayak solely to sharpen their managerial skills and ability to work as a team for the betterment of the college.

These professionally staffed team-building retreats have become quite popular in the administrative world. Take, for example, a recent two-day administrative retreat organized by the president of Chicago State University. At the time of the retreat, the school faced substantial funding cutbacks and a large budget deficit. How to deal with these fiscal problems was one of the major questions to be considered by the retreating administrators. Other problems also threatened the university. According to its president, these included, "student retention and graduation rates, calls for greater accountability . . . escalating conflict among staff, administrators, faculty and students . . . [and] . . . unrelenting student complaints about customer service issues."[4] Given all these problems, it hardly seems surprising that the university's administrators would need uninterrupted time to develop solutions. The school's president, however, thought more was required. "In effort to place major focus on the issues cited," he said, "I contracted with the Hayes Group to engage us in the team building process as a method of developing an action plan to assist us with meeting the aforementioned challenges."[5] The Hayes Group is a North Carolina consulting firm that, like Boojum, specializes in organizing corporate retreats and training sessions. According to the firm's Web site, Hayes's trainers can help an organization promote team development, motivation, communication, and stress management. This last skill presumably became especially relevant when Hayes's hefty fee added to the budget deficit that prompted the retreat in the first place.

In addition to meeting and retreating with one another, administrators often believe that they can benefit from interacting with their counterparts at other schools. One mechanism for bringing this about is the "joint administrative retreat" in which the administrators and staffers from two or more schools retreat together. In 2006, for example, administrators from the Northern Ohio University College of Pharmacy went on retreat with their counterparts from the East Tennessee State University College of Pharmacy. Both groups seem to have enjoyed the experience though it is not clear what concrete benefits they derived from it.[6]

Another common forum for administrative interaction is the conference. Administrators and staffers with an urge to travel and a desire to network with their counterparts at other schools can choose from among dozens of conferences held every month in almost every part of the nation. According to recent notices posted in the *Chronicle of Higher Education*, those interested in

fund-raising could travel to San Diego to participate in a conference entitled "Incorporating Data Mining into Your Annual Giving Strategy." Those interested in gender issues might travel to
Fond du Lac, Wisconsin, to attend the conference "Gender and
Education: Honoring Differences, Exploring Equity." More quantitative staffers might have to choose between "Data for Informed
Decisions: Who Is in the Driver's Seat?" and "Data Driven: What's
Our Direction?" Those who saw themselves as future college presidents also had a choice of two conferences. In Washington, DC,
the American Personnel Association sponsored a conference entitled "Our Place at the Table—Cabinet and Presidential Dynamics:
How to Build Trusting, Collaborative and Win-Win Relationships." A few miles south in Virginia, ambitious administrators
could find themselves "On the Road to the Presidency: Meeting
Today's Fiscal, Legal and Academic Challenges." And those who
felt that they should learn to cooperate more effectively with
administrators in other fields might have journeyed to Savannah,
Georgia, to attend "Sharing Responsibility for Essential Learning
Outcomes: New Partnerships across Departments, Academic
Affairs and Student Affairs."

Administrators and staffers whose schools refused to fund their
travel could still participate in online conferences. Several were
available in November, including "Understanding Sustainable
Dining Options," "Developing Student Engagement through Pod-
casting to Reach Students," "Creating and Managing a Successful Admissions Blogging Program," and "Expanding Recruitment
Efforts to Students' Family Members." Curiously, an international
conference on asynchronous learning networks, "The Power of
Online Learning: Mobilizing to Expand Community," was held in
Orlando, Florida, rather than online. Apparently community can
be more fully expanded near Disney World.

Senior and even midlevel administrators are typically able to
travel to conferences at their school's expense. Administrative
budgets frequently include travel funds, on the theory that conference participation will hone administrators' skills and provide

them with new information and ideas that will ultimately serve their school's interests. We can be absolutely certain that this would be the only reason administrators would even consider dragging themselves to Maui during the winter for a series of workshops sponsored by the North American Association of Summer Sessions. Given the expense and hardship usually occasioned by travel to Hawaii, it is entirely appropriate for colleges to foot the bills. When colleges cannot or will not pay, other third-party payers can sometimes be found. For example, the May 2007 meeting of the Florida Association of Financial Aid Administrators was heavily subsidized by private lenders who presumably hoped that grateful administrators would steer business to their companies—something that has become an all-too-common practice. Sallie Mae, Student Loan Xpress, and others contributed $128,000 toward the meeting's expenses.[7]

Planning

Given the enormous burden of attending meetings, retreats, and conferences, to say nothing of the need to devote at least some attention to their normal college duties, it might seem unlikely that administrators and staffers have time to undertake any other assignments. This perception, however, is false because it ignores a form of administrative activity that can occupy managers and staffers for years at a time. This is, of course, the development and continual revision of the school's strategic plan.

Until recent years, colleges engaged in little formal planning. Today, however, virtually every college and university in the nation has an elaborate strategic plan.[8] Indeed, whenever a school hires a new president, his or her first priority is usually the crafting of a new strategic plan. In a macabre imitation of Orwell's *1984*, all mention of the previous administration's plan, which probably had been introduced with great fanfare only a few year's earlier, is instantly erased from all college publications and Web sites. The college president's first commandment seems to be, "Thou shall have no other plan before mine."

The strategic plan is a lengthy document—some are one hundred pages long or more—that purports to articulate the school's mission, its leadership's vision of the future and the various steps that are needed to achieve the school's goals. The typical plan takes six months to two years to write and is often subject to annual revision to take account of changing circumstances. A variety of university constituencies are usually involved in the planning process—administrators, faculty members, staffers, trustees, alumni, and even students. Most of the work, though, falls to senior administrators and their staffs as well as to outside consultants who may assist in the planning process. The final document is usually submitted to the trustees or regents for their approval. A flurry of news releases and articles in college publications herald the new plan as a guide to an ever brighter future for the school. Hence, as one journalist noted, most strategic plans could be entitled "Vision for Excellence."[9]

The growth of planning has a number of origins. University trustees are generally drawn from a business background and are accustomed to corporate plans. Accreditors and government agencies, for their part, are enamored of planning, which they associate with transparency and accountability. Florida, in fact, requires publicly supported schools to develop strategic plans. More generally, though, the growth of planning is closely tied to the expansion of college and university administrations. Their growing administrative and staff resources have given schools the capacity to devote the thousands of person-hours generally required to develop and formulate strategic plans. Before 1955, only ten of the very largest universities could afford to allocate staff time to institutional research and planning, but by the late 1960s, several hundred schools possessed adequate staff resources for this purpose.[10]

At the same time, the strategic plan serves several important purposes for administrators. First, when they organize a planning process and later trumpet their new strategic plan, senior administrators are signaling to the faculty, to the trustees, and to the general community that they are in charge. The plan is an assertion of leadership and a claim to control university resources and priorities. This function of planning helps to explain why new presidents and sometimes new deans usually develop new strategic plans. We would not expect newly elected presidents of the United States simply to affirm their predecessors' inaugural addresses. In order to demonstrate leadership to the nation, they must present their own bold initiatives and vision for the future. For college leaders, the strategic plan serves this purpose.

A second and related purpose served by planning is co-optation. A good deal of evidence suggests that the opportunity to participate in institutional decision-making processes affords many individuals enormous psychic gratification. For this reason, clever administrators see periodic consultation as a means of inducing employees to be more cooperative and to work harder.[11] Virtually everyone has encountered this management technique at one time or another. Some years ago, a former president of my university called to ask my advice before he appointed a new dean of the College of Arts and Sciences. I was pleased to be consulted, and later neither I nor other senior faculty who felt that the new dean was insufficiently experienced voiced so much as a word of opposition when the president announced his appointment.

In a similar vein, the university planning process entails months of committee meetings, discussions, and deliberations during which the views of large segments of the faculty and staff are elicited. For the most part, those involved in the process, even if only peripherally, tend to buy into the outcome and, more important, tend to develop a more positive perception of the administration's ideas, priorities, and leadership. I can recall being greeted with hostile silence at the faculty club when I asserted that our college's strategic plan was a waste of paper. I was completely correct. The plan was a waste of paper and within a year was forgotten. Nevertheless, my colleagues who had participated in the planning process had been co-opted by it.

Still another way in which strategic planning serves administrators' interests is as a substitute for action. Many senior administrators are smooth and glib in the manner of politicians. These qualities are sure to impress the corporate headhunters who direct contemporary administrative searches and help such administrators secure many job interviews. But, like some of their counterparts in the realm of national electoral politics, university leaders' political dexterity and job-hunting skills are often somewhat stronger than their managerial and administrative capabilities, inevitably leading to disappointment on the campus after they take charge. Indeed, the disparity between their office-seeking savvy and actual leadership ability probably explains why many college and university presidents move frequently from school to school.[12] By the time the campus has become fully aware of their strengths and weaknesses, they have moved on to another college. Thus, for many administrators, eighteen months devoted to strategic planning can create a useful impression of feverish activity and progress and may mask the fact that they are frequently away from campus seeking better positions at other schools.

An individual of my acquaintance was appointed to the position of dean of arts and sciences at an important university. Soon after his appointment, he launched a year-long strategic planning process telling all who would listen that the college's first priority should be the development of a sound plan of action. During this period, the dean delayed undertaking any new programs and initiatives because, he said, all the school's major activities should comport with the soon-to-be-announced strategic plan. After a year the plan was ready, but the dean informed the campus that he was leaving to become the president of a small college. Apparently the school was too engrossed in planning to notice that the dean was sometimes away on job interviews. Not surprisingly, as soon as he arrived at his new campus, this individual announced that he would lead the school in—what else?—the formulation of a strategic plan.

It would be incorrect to assert that strategic plans are never what they purport to be—blueprints for the future. Occasionally a college or university plan does, in fact, present a grand design for the next decade. A plan actually designed to guide an organization's efforts to achieve future objectives, as it might be promulgated by a corporation or a military agency, contains several characteristic elements. Such a plan typically presents concrete objectives, a timetable for their realization, an outline of the tactics that will be employed, a precise assignment of staff responsibilities, and a budget. Some university plans approach this model. The 2007 strategic plan of the University of Illinois, for example, puts forward explicit objectives along with precise metrics, bench marks, timetables, and budgets. The school's leadership hoped to equal or exceed the performance of several other large public institutions along a number of concrete dimensions.[13] Whether one agrees or disagrees with the goals stated by the plan, there could be little disagreement about the character of the plan, itself. It resembles a corporate plan for expanding market share or a military plan choreographing the movement of troops and supplies.

The documents promulgated by most colleges and universities, however, lack a number of these fundamental elements of planning. Their goals tend to be vague and their means left undefined. Often there is no budget based on actual or projected resources. Instead, the plan sets out a number of fund-raising goals. These plans are, for the most part, simply expanded "vision statements." As one college president said at the culmination of a year-long planning process that engaged the energies of faculty, administrators, and staffers, "The plan is not a specific blueprint, but a set of goals the college hopes to meet. The college has not yet determined how the initiatives will be implemented and the plan is subject to change."[14]

Obviously what was important here was not the plan but the process. The president, a new appointee, asserted his leadership, involved the campus community, and created an impression of feverish activity and forward movement. The ultimate plan, itself, was indistinguishable from dozens of other college plans and could have been scribbled on the back of an envelope or copied from some other school's planning document. As I noticed while reading dozens of strategic plans, plagiarism in planning is not uncommon. Similar phrases and paragraphs can be found in many plans. In 2006, the chancellor of Southern Illinois University's (SIU) Carbondale campus was forced to resign after it was discovered that much of the school's new strategic plan, "Southern at 150," had been copied from Texas A&M's (TAMU) strategic plan, "Vision 2020." SIU's chancellor had previously served as vice chancellor at TAMU, where he had coordinated work on the strategic plan.[15] In a similar vein, the president of Edward Waters College was forced to resign when it was noticed that his new "Quality Enhancement Plan" seemed to have been copied from Alabama A&M's strategic plan.[16]

This interchangeability of visions for the future underscores the fact that the precise content of most school's strategic plans is pretty much irrelevant. Plans are usually forgotten soon after they are promulgated. My university has presented two systemwide strategic plans and one arts and sciences strategic plan in the last fifteen years. No one can remember much about any of these plans but another one is currently in the works. The plan is not a blueprint for the future. It is, instead a management tool for the present. The ubiquity of planning at America's colleges and universities is another reflection and reinforcement of the ongoing growth of administrative power.

Image Polishing and Fund-Raising

There are two dimensions of university life in which administrators have performed quite well in recent years. These are the related fields of image polishing and fund-raising. As to the first of these, virtually all of America's colleges and universities engage in extensive efforts to cultivate favorable public images on both an individual and industry-wide basis. Large universities typically employ dozens of media specialists to produce a host of university publications and broadcasts aimed at prospective students, alumni, and other potential donors, and the more general public. These might include a "view book" aimed at attracting new students, dozens of newsletters and periodicals trumpeting the school's achievements, and a glossy alumni magazine designed to evoke feelings of nostalgia and a spirit of generosity among the school's graduates. At some schools, a senior official, usually called the vice president or vice provost for public affairs, coordinates the organization's overall media strategy and articulates the school's official position on important matters.

A university's media specialists are expected to work diligently to garner favorable publicity for the school by sending out press releases and contacting journalists to alert the news media to important new campus developments that might bolster the school's image or, alternatively, to counter negative publicity by presenting the school's version of potentially unflattering developments. Media staffers also maintain lists of faculty experts in a variety of fields to whom writers and reporters may be directed for comments on political developments, scientific discoveries, economic crises, or other matters. Such expert commentary is seen as an excellent form of publicity, strengthening the school's reputation as a repository of wisdom. In recent years, university media relations staffers, like their counterparts everywhere, have increasingly turned to podcasts, webcasts, and other electronic instruments to disseminate their school's messages. A well-crafted print and electronic public relations strategy is seen by university officials as an essential tool for boosting the flow of student applications and alumni donations.

Paralleling the individual efforts of the nation's five thousand colleges and universities is an industry-wide lobbying and public relations operation. American colleges and universities are represented in Washington by more than fifty lobby groups led by the American Council on Education (ACE), which was founded in 1918. Building on Americans' respect for education, the industry's public relations efforts emphasize the importance of providing access to higher education to all citizens, regardless of their financial means. The key to access, according to industry lobbyists and spin doctors, is a steady increase in federal subsidies to schools and students, particularly through the federally guaranteed student loan program, to make it possible for every American to afford college tuition. This approach, of course, is highly beneficial to the interests of the schools who are guaranteed a steady stream of federally funded customers for their services. Typically, when the government allows students and parents to borrow more, colleges raise their tuitions to take advantage of the customers' increased ability to pay. The equally obvious solution to the problem of access—slashing universities' lofty tuition costs and trimming their bloated managerial ranks, is certainly not presented as an option by industry spokespersons.

For the most part, Americans seem to support the education industry's viewpoint. Most Americans (roughly 70 percent) think Congress and the states should make more money available to the financially healthy higher education industry.[17] By contrast, fewer than half favor providing federal support to prevent the nation's struggling passenger rail system from collapsing.[18] The difference reflects both the value Americans place on education and the effects of a century of successful image polishing. Taken together, these have given the higher education industry a strong base of popular approval on which it can draw in the political arena.

Indeed, thanks in part to industry image-polishing efforts, most Americans do not even regard colleges and universities as businesses. Viewed objectively, most of America's thousands of colleges and universities could be seen as successful firms of varying sizes selling services at a very high price. Before various discounts are applied, private college tuition can be as much as $40,000 per year with dormitory charges, books, and fees adding nearly another $12,000 to each student's annual bill. College faculty and staff members are not lavishly compensated. But, like their counterparts in other businesses, successful college administrators and managers, and even many mediocre ones, are handsomely paid as we have seen, with some university presidents earning seven-figure salaries in addition to the usual perks of the corporate world including houses, drivers, club memberships, and paid service on corporate boards. Universities may be not-for-profit entities according to the tax code, but as is true of their counterparts in the charity business, this definitely does not mean that they are not run for the enrichment of their bosses.

Most Americans, however, have a much more favorable view of colleges than other enterprises. A survey published in a recent issue of the *Chronicle of Higher Education* revealed that while only 9 percent of Americans expressed a "great deal" of confidence in large corporations taken as a whole, more than 48 percent indicated a great deal of confidence in colleges and universities. This figure was comparable to the 44 percent proclaiming a great deal of confidence in churches and considerably more than the 26 percent who had a great deal of confidence in the health care profession.[19] What accounts for this relatively positive public perception of institutions of higher learning? Obviously, Americans view education as the ticket to success for their children and are inclined to have a favorable view of the institutions that provide that ticket. The higher education industry, however, does not rely simply on spontaneous good will to bolster its cause. Instead, the industry has built a substantial lobbying and public relations apparatus to tout its virtues and its frequently self-proclaimed determination to make higher education available to all.

Fund-Raising

The success of institutional and industry-wide image-polishing efforts is seen not only in the polls but, more importantly, in university fund-raising. Building on the base of good feeling created by their image polishing activities, America's colleges and universities raised nearly $30 billion in 2007 in gifts from alumni, foundations, and other benefactors.[20] Of course, fund-raising became more difficult in 2008 and 2009 as falling investment values forced many donors to tighten their purse strings. Yet, as the economy improves, college fund-raising activities are expected to shift back into high gear.

To be sure, a substantial percentage of the money raised by America's institutions of higher education consists of donations to America's elite schools—Harvard, Yale, Princeton, and so forth—which regularly conduct multimillion- and even multibillion-dollar fund-raising campaigns and boast endowments worth tens of billions. Harvard alone has averaged more than $600 million per year in gifts in recent years.[21] Even small and obscure colleges, though, strive to raise a few million or even a few hundred thousand dollars every year to help them meet current expenses and gradually build an endowment. In recent years, four-year nonprofit schools have relied on fund-raising for an average of 12 percent of their total revenues. The presidents of private schools are expected to devote most of their time and energy to fund-raising, and an otherwise effective president who is thought to be a poor fund-raiser is likely to be handed his or her walking papers by the school's trustees.

Colleges and universities have sought financial support from alumni and friends since the seventeenth century. And, of course, many private universities such as Stanford, Vanderbilt, Duke, Cornell, and Hopkins were established with large gifts from the wealthy benefactors for whom these schools are named. Until the nineteenth century, colleges generally depended on the largesse of tiny cliques of affluent donors. Often, indeed, when schools ran short of funds their presidents would depend on the continuing generosity of the institution's founding family. Thus, when William Rainey Harper needed more money to support his fledgling University of Chicago, Harper's fund-raising plan consisted mainly of asking the school's fabulously wealthy founding patron, John D. Rockefeller, for another contribution.[22] This form of fund-raising could be effective, but left schools at the mercy of a small number of sometimes fickle potentates who could use their financial leverage to interfere with the operations of the university. The entrepreneurial "captains of erudition" who rose to power on America's campuses in the late nineteenth and early twentieth centuries were anxious to find new ways of raising money that would reduce their dependence on their founders or small cliques of patrons. This desire led them to adopt what came to be called the "Ward method" of fund-raising, which remains the basis of contemporary fund-raising efforts.

Charles Sumner Ward was a YMCA executive from Chicago who came to be quite well known as fund-raiser in the early 1900s.[23] Ward emphasized the use of publicity, organization, careful record keeping, competition among teams of volunteers recruited from among the institution's supporters, a definite dollar goal, and constant measurement of progress by a heavily publicized campaign clock or thermometer. Ward also declared that fund-raising was a continuous process requiring the long-term cultivation of large numbers of prospects rather than occasional visits, hat-in-hand, to the homes of a few fat cats. Indeed, as Ward saw it, individuals persuaded to make small donations might, over time, provide ever larger gifts as they grew older and wealthier, and became habituated to the process of giving.

Ward's methods, in sum, were designed to expand an institution's donor pool and to secure smaller donations from large numbers of individuals in addition to large gifts from small numbers of donors. Ward certainly sought and welcomed large gifts. Even today, 80 percent of the funds raised by universities come from 10 percent of the donors.[24] Ward, however, saw large donations as the beginning rather than the end of a fund-raising effort. Ward liked to use a heavily publicized major gift as a challenge grant, with the major donor promising to match all other contributions on a dollar for dollar or other basis up to the stated amount of the initial gift. In this way, large donors' contributions could be used to increase the overall number of donors, simultaneously leveraging and diluting—though certainly never eliminating—the influence of the small number of wealthy contributors on whom the institution had customarily depended. Ward demonstrated the value of his methods by helping the University of Pittsburgh raise the then-enormous sum of $3 million in 1914.

Ward and several of his disciples established fund-raising consultancies, which spread the Ward method throughout the academic community. Within a few years, most colleges and universities sought the services of these and similar advisors to plan their fund-raising campaigns. Ward, however, had taught that fund-raising should be a continuous rather than an episodic effort. And, following the logic of this argument, schools began to employ full-time fund-raisers to manage the day-to-day work of identifying and cultivating prospects. By the 1960s, full-time fund-raisers employed by the schools, themselves, had begun to supplant the outside consultants who had dominated fund-raising for the previous half century.[25] Today, every college and university in the United States, whether public or private, employs full-time fund-raisers, who are euphemistically known as "development officers." The development offices of large universities are staffed by dozens, or even several hundred of these development officers, who usually report to a senior university official, typically a vice president for development. Top development officers often earn six-figure salaries and are frequently courted by rival schools.

At large schools, development officers are usually organized both geographically and functionally. Officers are responsible for specific regions and particular types of prospects—older alumni, recent graduates, major gift prospects, and so on. Within their specified domains, development officers are responsible for maintaining lists of prospects, befriending the school's alumni and supporters, and organizing events, such as talks by touring faculty members, designed to build ties between potential donors and the school. Consistent with Ward's teachings, development has become a long-term and continuous enterprise, punctuated by occasional special campaigns.

Fund-raising does not produce as much income as tuition. In recent years, student tuitions and fees have amounted to nearly $50 billion in annual revenues, or about $20 billion more than was

generated by college and university fund-raising. From the perspective of university administrators, though, fund-raising represents a more attractive income source than tuition. For an
established institution, generating additional tuition revenue is
likely to require increasing the size of the student body and making a substantial investment in facilities, faculty, and programs.
For some schools, these overhead costs may approach or even
exceed anticipated tuition revenues.[26] Generally speaking, tuition
revenues are difficult to increase without an increase in enrollments because price competition among all but the most prestigious colleges means that even if a school increases its nominal
tuition or "sticker price," its tuition net of discounts (scholarships)
cannot easily be increased without losing students to the competition. Indeed, an investment in facilities and programs may not
guarantee that substantial new tuition dollars will actually be
earned, since all but the top tier of schools must constantly compete with one another in an uncertain effort to attract new students. A school might invest in expensive new dormitories and
classrooms only to find itself with empty beds and seats.

From an administrator's viewpoint, moreover, another draw-
back to the idea of earning additional tuition revenue is that this
often requires negotiating with the faculty. Professors must be
persuaded to teach more students, offer new courses, and develop
new programs. Faculty members are usually willing to undertake
these activities, but insist on extensive consultations and a substantial voice, through faculty senates, academic councils, and
other faculty institutions, in shaping whatever initiatives might
be required. In essence, administrators who seek to increase tuition revenues may, by their actions, empower the faculty or, at the
very least, stimulate faculty organization and action in response
to the administration's plans. For example, efforts by University
of Chicago administrators in the 1990s to recruit more students
required the faculty's cooperation in changing the school's curriculum. The faculty agreed but only after a series of "bruising sessions" with administrators.[27] The conflict both energized the

faculty and soured its relationship with the school's president, who was compelled to resign soon thereafter.

Hence, to administrators anxious to generate new revenues, an increased emphasis on fund-raising usually seems a far more attractive strategy than seeking additional tuition dollars. Fund-raising is almost entirely under the control of the administration and requires minimal, if any, faculty involvement. Indeed, the purposes for which funds are raised are generally determined by senior administrators, often in consultation with donors. The faculty is, for the most part, out of the loop. Reliance on the development office has helped senior administrators marginalize the faculty just as the advent of modern development techniques helped administrators gain some measure of independence from their schools' founders or other potentates. As to the staff of the development office, these functionaries work exclusively for the administration. Faculty members who approach the development office with ideas generally receive a polite brush-off. Fund-raising, moreover, can be quite cost-effective. On average, schools spend sixteen cents for every dollar raised, with some especially efficient development operations spending as little as eight cents per dollar.[28] Why bother with expensive students or the annoying faculty?

For these reasons, colleges and universities have placed an ever-growing emphasis on development. From the 1920s through the 1970s, gift income to institutions of higher education generally amounted to less than 20 percent of the tuition income earned by these schools. Today, thanks to schools' major emphasis on development, gifts to colleges and universities total about 40 percent of their tuition income, and given the logic of the situation, we can only assume that this percentage will grow.

Endowment Income

The growth of gift income has also given a number of schools the opportunity to build sizable endowments, whose earnings collectively totaled more than $30 billion in 2007. Harvard's endowment, the academic world's largest, was valued at $34 billion in mid-2008. Yale, with the second-largest endowment, boasted more than $22 billion in assets. More than seventy schools reported endowments over $1 billion before the nation's 2008–09 financial crisis reduced the values of most investment portfolios by 30 percent or more.[29] These still-sizable endowments continue to generate substantial annual income for wealthier schools. Harvard alone earned more than $6.7 billion in 2007. Viewed on a national basis, endowment income plus gift income now exceed annual tuition revenues for America's four-year nonprofit schools by several billion dollars.

Even more than gift income, earnings from university endowments enhance administrative autonomy. Endowments produce revenue that is dependent neither on faculty cooperation nor even on the good will of alumni and other donors. Endowment income does not even require administrators to do much besides hope that the school's investment committee knows what it's doing. Endowment income is an administrator's dream come true. One might argue that the larger the endowment, the greater the power and independence of the school's administration. Perhaps this notion helps to explain why many schools—particularly the wealthiest— hoard the earnings from their endowments, reinvesting a large fraction of their annual endowment income so that their endowment and future income will grow.

In point of fact, many schools follow a recommendation made in 1969 by the Ford Foundation, which suggested that the spending rate from endowment income be set at 5 percent.[30] This recommendation was based on the then-prevailing yield from long-term bonds, but the foundation also recommended that universities shift their investment portfolios mainly to equities. Most did so and, as a result, have earned an average endowment income of more than 10 percent per year, tax free, over the past several decades.[31] In recent years, the rate of return has been substantially higher for some endowments. During the 2007 fiscal year, for example, Harvard's endowment which had already been $29.2

billion, earned a whopping 23 percent, or more than $6.7 billion. The difference between a school's 5 percent spending rate and its actual annual return on its investments is generally retained to increase the size of its endowment. Thus, in FY 2007, Harvard spent roughly $1.1 billion of its endowment earnings and retained the remaining $5.6 billion to increase its total endowment to about $34.9 billion.

No one would wish to encourage universities to engage in profligate spending. During economic downturns a healthy endowment can be a vitally important asset. At the same time, however, college and university endowment practices also raise a number of questions. The first of these concerns the public interest. As is true for most other charitable and philanthropic organizations, under the U.S. tax code, donations to colleges are tax deductible and school's earnings from their endowments and educational enterprises are tax exempt. This tax exemption is worth nearly $20 billion per year to America's colleges and universities. The basis for their favorable tax treatment is the presumption that colleges and universities serve the public interest by spending their revenues for educational and other worthy purposes.

Their high rate of taxpayer-subsidized saving, however, seems inconsistent with the presumption that colleges and universities should receive favorable tax treatment for their earnings because they will subsequently spend the money in a manner designed to promote the public interest. To the extent that universities spend their revenues to enhance their educational programs, to promote research, or to subsidize students' tuitions, the public interest is clearly being served and schools are justifying their tax-exempt status. And, of course, to some extent, America's colleges and universities do all these things. When, however, universities add billions of dollars to their endowments they are, in effect, spending tax-exempt dollars on themselves rather than the public-spirited activities anticipated by the tax code.

It is worth noting that private foundations are required, under the tax law to justify their favorable tax status by spending at least 5 percent of their net worth each year on the charitable or philanthropic activities that they are nominally created to undertake. This requirement is designed to ensure that such organizations will actually carry out their social responsibilities and not simply hoard their earnings. In 2008, Iowa's Republican senator Charles Grassley proposed applying the same requirement to colleges and universities or, alternatively, taxing their endowment income. Grassley and other lawmakers found it especially difficult to understand how colleges could justify hefty annual tuition increases while they were simultaneously retaining billions of dollars in endowment income. The proposal, however, was dropped after the education industry mounted an intense lobbying campaign against it.[32]

In testifying before Congress against the Grassley proposal, college and university presidents defended their institutions' uniquely favorable tax treatment by pointing to the enormous amounts of money needed to maintain educational quality, scholarship assistance, university facilities, and the cutting-edge academic research from which America has benefited in recent decades. College presidents also asserted that endowment growth provided schools with a measure of financial protection against economic downturns that might undermine college's abilities to provide educational benefits to future students.[33] No doubt, all these points have some validity.

The presidents who testified, however, neglected to mention several other matters. They failed to mention that endowment income sheltered their institutions from being forced to develop intellectually exciting programs that might interest more students—a point made by Adam Smith three hundred years ago when he observed that the quality of a college's curriculum seemed to decline as the size of its endowment increased.[34] The presidents failed to mention that endowment income helped to free them from having to consult their faculties regarding university programs and priorities. The presidents also failed to mention that a large fraction of the endowment income they actually spent helped to pay for the enormous and ongoing expansion of the size of university administrations that has been among the most rapidly growing areas of higher education spending over the past decade. In short, the presidents forgot to tell the senators that a large endowment was needed to sustain the all-administrative university.

3

Managerial Pathologies

WHEN THEY ARE not meeting, retreating, fund-raising, and planning, administrators claim to be managing the fiscal and other operational business of the university. And to bolster their claims of specialized managerial competence, an increasing number of university administrators have gone so far as to add MBA degrees to their dossiers. Some have actually attended business school, while others, as you may recall from chapter 1, simply added MBA degrees to their dossiers.

In point of fact, whether or not they hold MBAs, many deanlets' managerial savvy consists mainly of having the capacity to spout last year's management buzz words during meetings, retreats, and planning exercises.[1] I often ask for clarifications when I hear a deanlet using such acronyms as SWOT, ECM, TQM, or MBO, the term "benchmarking," or the ubiquitous "best practices." Of course, ambitious administrators hope that by demonstrating their familiarity with the latest managerial fads and buzz words they will persuade recruiters and search committees from other universities that they are just the sort of "visionary" academic leaders those schools need.[2] Since the corporate headhunters that control the recruitment of senior administrators generally know next to nothing about academic life and little about the universities they nominally represent, this strategy is often successful. And, why not? In the all-administrative university it is entirely appropriate that mastery of managerial psychobabble should pass for academic vision.

There are many reasons why the affairs of the university should not be controlled by members of the administrative stratum. Some of these reasons are academic, that is, related to the substance of the university's core teaching and research missions. We shall turn to these in the next chapter. The other reasons to be concerned about the growing power of administrators and managers within the university are essentially managerial. The university's organizational and institutional interests are not well served by the expanded role of its management cadre. Indeed, the growing power of management and the decline of the faculty's role in governance has exposed the university to such classic bureaucratic pathologies as shirking, squandering, and stealing. When all is said and done, in the spirit of best practices we might paraphrase Clemenceau by observing that university administration should not be left to administrators.

Every large organization suffers from collective action problems. Managers and administrators often find it expedient to pursue their own purposes rather than, or at the expense of, those of the larger organization or their supposed superiors.[3] Anthony Downs claimed that these "administrative biases," as he called them, were especially prevalent in the public sector.[4] Managers in private sector firms are mainly evaluated in terms of their contribution to the enterprise's income and find it difficult to avoid censure if their pursuit of self-defined objectives undermines the firm's profitability. In the public sector, however, goals and objectives tend to be more diffuse, and the criteria on which managers are judged are less certain.[5] Hence, public sector managers, as a group, may possess a greater opportunity than their private sector counterparts to put their own interests and perspectives ahead of the organization's nominal goals.

Whether in the public or private sectors, the problem of self-serving managers can be mitigated by staff professionalism. A profession is sometimes defined as an occupational group whose membership is limited to those who have undergone years of specialized training as well as considerable indoctrination designed to promote acceptance of the group's code of conduct.[6] Many public and not-for-profit institutions, and some for-profit institutions as well, are built around an elite profession—engineers, physicians, economists, and the like—whose members actually carry out the institution's core tasks. Typically, the members of this professional stratum believe that their norms should determine institutional conduct and will resist efforts by managers to deviate from professionally defined standards.[7] In hospitals, for example, physicians frequently oppose efforts by administrators and insurers to base patient-care decisions on ability to pay, staff convenience, bed utilization policies, and other factors inconsistent with medically accepted criteria.[8]

Professionalism is not an organizational panacea, and some organizations may lack a reliable professional backbone. Students of bureaucracy, however, have often observed that organizations that delegate power to professionals actually trained to implement the entity's mission generally perform more effectively than those in which decision-making authority is centralized in the hands of managers and administrators.[9] Critics of American military policy, for example, have noted that autocratic civilian defense secretaries like Robert McNamara and Donald Rumsfeld threatened the effectiveness of American forces when they reduced the discretionary authority allowed military professionals in the field.[10] In a similar vein, the ongoing shift in decision-making power from physicians to administrators within hospitals and other health care entities, very likely diminishes the quality of the care ultimately received by patients.[11] The shift in power within the university from academic professionals to administrators raises similar issues.

Administrative Sabotage

One major problem that can be traced to this power shift is administrative sabotage of university goals. The main goals of the university are usually thought to be teaching and research. These are certainly the commitments of the faculty, though individuals and schools have always varied in the relative importance they attach to each of these functions. At liberal arts colleges teaching has usually been assigned the highest priority, while the emphasis at research universities is laboratory work and writing. Leaving aside the recruited athletes, students attend colleges and universities to work with faculty members in seminar rooms, lecture halls, and laboratories, where they hope to strengthen their intellectual skills and prepare for meaningful careers. The interests of the students generally dovetail with the goals of the faculty. Students may not always receive the attention they want, and professors vary in ability. Nevertheless, faculty are professionally committed to producing, disseminating, and discussing knowledge. Students attend college and graduate school hoping to become more knowledgeable. This is a match made in heaven, with the assistance of the admissions office.

Nominally, college administrators work to facilitate this core relationship between students and faculty. Administrators recruit the students, manage the school's facilities, organize the academic calendar, and even see to it that the faculty is paid. The difficulty, though, is that like their counterparts throughout the world's bureaucracies, college administrators work in offices where amorphous aims or diffuse responsibilities make individual performances difficult to gauge. Hence, like other bureaucrats in similar situations, academic administrators often see little or no direct benefit to themselves from carrying out their assignments. Over the years, for example, I have encountered many admissions and registration officials who seemed to regard students as nuisances who interfered with the smooth operation of their offices. Of course, without students, there would be no need for admissions or registration officials. Nevertheless, in a classic illustration of the pitfalls of collective action, many individual officials feel little personal stake in catering to students' needs.

Within most university bureaucracies, at least some administrators can be found ignoring their nominal responsibilities in favor of shirking, squandering, and stealing, three of the classic ways in which managers sabotage the organizations they serve.

Administrative Shirking

Shirking refers to the propensity of employees to make less than a whole-hearted effort to complete their organization's assignments and achieve its goals. As anyone who has dealt with the phone company, the cable company, or any federal or municipal agency knows, shirking is a problem in all bureaucracies.[12] In a famous paper, the Nobel Prize–winning economist George Stigler once suggested that under certain circumstances corruption could actually enhance the efficiency of bureaucratic organizations by providing employees with a direct incentive to do their jobs.[13]

I was reminded of the Stigler article when I encountered an extremely annoying and damaging bit of employee shirking within a graduate program that I direct on my school's Washington, DC, campus. For several years, this program had been experiencing rather substantial growth, which had allowed me to add more faculty and a greater variety of courses. To my surprise and dismay, however, the program's growth came to a sudden end in 2007. In fact, the number of new applications began to drop sharply, threatening to force a halt not only to new academic initiatives but, possibly, to compel the cancellation of several of the offerings that had been added during the previous years of steady growth.

When I expressed my concern to a senior and very able college administrator, her response was to advise me to expect periods of stagnant or even declining enrollments. My program had grown steadily for several years but constant growth was simply not possible, she said. Of course, I knew she was correct in principle, but we had recently launched a major campaign to contact prospective students. Many individuals had attended our events, which included a very successful reception for Capitol Hill staffers. I thought we were receiving a promising stream of inquiries from individuals interested in applying for admission. Something was clearly wrong, and I sent two staffers to snoop around the admissions office to see what they might discover.

What they found was quite appalling but not completely surprising. Apparently one or more (now former) employees had decided it was too much trouble to answer inquiries from prospective students. Responding to these inquiries, after all, meant more work without any direct reward. My staffers found stacks of unanswered inquiries in file cabinets and desk drawers. Many more had probably been discarded. All our efforts to build programs and attract new students were being undermined by employee shirking. After new management systems were put into place, applications immediately increased by more than 30 percent and have continued to climb. Hundreds of opportunities, however, were permanently lost as students whose inquiries were never acknowledged found places at other universities.

When, as in the foregoing example, shirking involves low-level employees, it can be harmful but can be brought under control by better supervision. Often enough, however, it is mid- and upper-level managers, themselves, who are the shirkers, seeing no reason to expend time and energy on activities that might serve the organization's interests but from which they derive no direct or personal benefit.[14] This form of shirking is usually more costly and more difficult to curb. In the university, managerial shirking is so common that almost every senior faculty member can name several top-level administrators who appear to make little effort to advance the school's interests. For a number of years, for example, a major east coast university maintained an office in a centrally located European capital. The nominal purpose of this office, directed by a senior vice provost, was to build connections to

European universities and research institutions and to enhance the school's prominence and visibility in the European Union. Perhaps a diligent and energetic university official might have seen the open-ended character of his or her assignment as an opportunity to engage in creative program building for the school's benefit. Unfortunately, however, this particular vice provost seemed to see his assignment as a form of exile from his position in the university hierarchy and probably assumed he was too close to retirement to be placed in charge of any new programs that might result from his efforts. Accordingly, he took advantage of the amorphous character of his task, along with his distance from day-to-day campus oversight to perform his duties in a less enterprising manner than might have been possible.

The vice provost spent his time traveling around Europe and holding dinner and luncheon meetings with miscellaneous European scholars, academic administrators, and minor government officials. Several times a year, he flew back to the United States to report on his activities and to remind the campus of the importance of his office. The vice provost's report always consisted of a long list of prominent individuals whom he had met and the possible significance to the university of these newfound connections. He generally brushed off concrete programmatic proposals, averring that these might later be integrated into the university's overall European plan when this blueprint was more fully developed.

After several years of networking, the vice provost retired and his European office was closed. His activities had produced no discernable results and were quickly forgotten, but had been undertaken at a substantial cost to the university. The vice provost drew a hefty salary. He employed an assistant and other staffers. His office was in a fashionable part of the city where rents were high. And, of course, he required an adequate travel, dining, and entertainment budget. All in all, one might estimate that more than ten students paid tuition every year to support the vice provost's extended European stay. Moreover, because this vice provost failed to build new programs or develop new collaborations, years of opportunities to enrich the university's intellectual life were wasted.

Unfortunately, the wandering vice provost does not represent an isolated case. Colleagues at a variety of universities to whom I have mentioned this story have invariably replied by offering ever more egregious examples of administrative shirking at their own schools in a seemingly endless "Can you top this?" contest, which would be amusing if it did not reveal such an enormous waste of resources and opportunities.

Administrative Squandering

Closely related to the issue of managerial shirking is the problem of administrative squandering. The former refers to the often costly failure by officials to perform needed services for which they have been paid. The latter connotes their often even more costly tendency to pay for goods and services that are not actually needed—not, at least, by the university. Shirking might be viewed as a democratic practice that can be found at every level of an organization's hierarchy. The opportunity to squander, on the other hand, is usually greatest within the upper ranks of an organization where financial decisions are actually made. Hence, wasteful spending is a problem typically associated with high-level functionaries, from senior government officials through corporate purchasing officers and college presidents. Squandering, of course, is always a concern when people are spending other peoples' money. Most of us are quite capable of squandering our own resources, but the tendency to engage in profligate spending is greatest when individuals are making use of funds that are not drawn from their own purses or wallets.

In some instances, administrators seem to squander school funds as a simple result of ignorance, carelessness, or poor decision making. My university, for example, spent nearly $250 million between 2006 and 2010 to implement a new software system designed by SAP, a major international supplier of software to corporations and governments. The new system, an "enterprise resource planning system," initially dubbed "HopkinsOne," was designed to replace and integrate the university's existing finance, human resources, payroll, purchasing, accounts payable, materials management, and research administration systems. One university manager said, "This system should significantly reduce the amount of paperwork and effort to complete everyday tasks. It will improve our overall productivity with business and administrative functions that are modern, up-to-date, and more in line with our competitors."[15]

The faculty was dubious that the enormous cost of the system, initially estimated at as much as $150 million, could ever be recovered by the anticipated administrative savings projected by the university's senior managers. Indeed, some engineering and computer science professors who examined parts of the proposed system predicted flatly that it would never work and pointed to the expensive collapse of similar efforts at other universities and federal agencies. The university's administrative leaders, however, were determined to move forward and exhibited no interest in the faculty's views.

As HopkinsOne was gradually implemented in 2006 and 2007, it became clear that the system would be an enormously expensive disaster. Elements of the system did not work at all, and midlevel managers continually reported that previously simple tasks had now become extremely complex. Even as the cost of the system began to exceed initial estimates by tens of millions of dollars, the university's senior administrators claimed that training and start-up issues would soon be resolved.

By 2008, most of the technical staff members originally associated with the HopkinsOne project had left the university or been dismissed. And, while continuing to claim success, university leaders took the rather Orwellian step of expunging the name HopkinsOne from all university publications and communications. Midlevel administrators were told to stop using the term HopkinsOne, even in conversation and always to refer to the system as SAP. Indeed, as of mid-2008, even the school's previously ubiquitous and self-congratulatory online references to HopkinsOne had almost all been removed. University administrators appeared to believe that by erasing the system's name from the official record, they would also succeed in erasing all memory of the fact that they had squandered tens of millions of dollars. In 2010, a university administrative bulletin informed users that SAP was being renamed ECC even though, "no new functionality has been added."[16] With this new name change, the original and discredited name of the system would forever be lost.

The case of HopkinsOne may be nothing more than a story about lack of judgment and a stubborn refusal to face unpleasant realities, probably exacerbated by the fact that the school's administrators were spending other peoples' money. Administrative squandering, however, goes beyond simple errors and misjudgments. There are several basic reasons why academic administrators are often inclined to squander the university's money. One is status.

Many college and university administrators seem anxious to make certain that those with whom they come into contact recognize their rank and prominence on the campus and in the larger community. Of course, a desire for status is hardly limited to university bigwigs. Psychologist Steven Pinker has observed, "People everywhere strive for a ghostly substance called authority, cachet, dignity, dominance, eminence, esteem, face, position, preeminence, prestige, rank, regard, repute, respect, standing, stature or status."[17] Some university officials seem content simply to allow their rank to speak for itself. The presidency, say, of a well-known university or college is a prestigious position that confers considerable status on the individual holding the office. The president of Harvard, for example, derives enormous status from her job and would seem to have little reason to be concerned that she will not be treated with considerable respect by almost everyone she happens to meet.

Many university officials, though, seem to suffer from status anxiety. In some instances, the reason is obvious. Administrators responsible for student affairs, registration, facilities management, finance, scheduling, and the like may be well paid and might exercise considerable influence. These individuals, however, hold jobs from which they derive little status on campus. Some are notoriously sensitive to slights from members of the faculty.

But even many top university officials seem unsatisfied with the standing conferred by their positions, and constantly endeavor to surround themselves with highly visible symbols of rank. More than a few university presidents insist on being provided with luxurious offices and official residences in addition to princely salaries. Some enjoy the services of a chauffeur when they commute to work and a household staff when they entertain or even relax at home. These and many other perquisites are usually defended by administrators as needed to carry out their social duties and, particularly, to impress their schools' wealthy benefactors. Yet, no study has ever proven that presidents who arrive at fund-raising events in chauffeur-driven limousines are more likely to succeed than their counterparts who drive their own cars or come by taxi or, for that matter, by subway. I have personally known university presidents who were outstanding fund-raisers but, nevertheless, lived frugally and always traveled as cheaply as possible. Indeed, I still have vivid memories of accompanying a former Cornell president to out-of-town events when he would insist on chartering the cheapest aircraft available for our small group. Two of these flights ended in near disasters when in-the-air equipment failures helped explain why the charters had been available at such bargain prices. This perhaps excessively tight-fisted president was a far more effective fund-raiser than his predecessor, who had ordered the university to purchase a well-appointed airplane for his out-of-town travel.

The spendthrifts, though, seem to outnumber the penny pinchers among college officials. College presidents are usually the most guilty parties since they are in the best position to authorize expenditures and many are more than happy to use school funds to burnish their own images. One recent case in point is that of

Benjamin Ladner, the former president of American University (AU) in Washington, DC. Ladner, who began his academic career as a professor of philosophy and religion at the University of North Carolina, Greensboro, came to AU in 1994. In the years preceding Ladner's appointment, the university had experienced considerable executive turmoil, including the ouster of a president who had been making obscene telephone calls to female staffers. Ladner seemed to restore some stability to the campus and appeared to be putting the rather impecunious school on a firmer financial footing.

Unfortunately, Ladner and his wife, who dubbed herself AU's "First Lady," also seemed unable to resist the temptation to squander millions of dollars in university funds for image polishing, that is, to impress the Ladners' associates and to allow them to socialize with the wealthy and powerful individuals—multimillionaires, ambassadors, important lobbyists—with whom Ladner's position brought them into contact. Soon after arriving on the campus, the Ladners declared that the president's official residence was inadequate and had the university build an expensive new house, which included a waterfall and pond behind the patio, a few blocks from the campus. They outfitted the house with expensive furnishings, china, and stemware.[18] At university expense, the Ladners employed a chauffeur, a cook, a social secretary, and numerous other personal staff members. They hosted gala events to which they invited prominent Washington figures. They traveled abroad frequently, generally charging their first-class tickets to the university. Matters came to a head in March 2005, when an anonymous whistle blower wrote to the board of trustees accusing the Ladners of "severe expense account violations." The letter claimed that the Ladners had charged the university for, "their son's engagement party, lavish presents for their children, a personal French chef . . . long weekends in Europe for pleasure . . . daily wine for lunch and dinner at $50 to $100 per bottle, etc. . . ." The letter writer went on to say, "This needs to be made public because he may get away with taking hundreds of thousands of dollars from American University . . . Please investigate."[19]

An extensive audit revealed hundreds of thousands of dollars in questionable spending, some personal but most associated with Ladner's frenetic image polishing efforts. Over the past several years, the Ladners had charged the university for $6,000 in club dues, $54,000 in drivers' costs, $220,000 in chef services, $44,000 for alcohol, and $100,000 in services from their social secretary.[20] Ladner averred that these and other expenditures for travel and entertainment were justified by his official fund-raising and entertainment duties, but many expenditures appeared to indicate that the Ladners had opted to transact university business in the most lavish manner. Several board members demanded Ladner's immediate resignation, while others defended the president and sought to identify and punish the whistle blower who had prompted the investigation. After months of bruising battles within the AU board, though, Ladner's contract was terminated—though he and the First Lady received a generous severance package. While Ladner mingled with the rich and famous at the school's expense, faculty members had to settle for miserly annual salary increases and students saw their tuitions rise markedly every year.

Though egregious, the Ladner case is hardly unique. In recent years, the presidents of a number of schools have been accused of squandering college funds to polish their own images. One of the most amusing examples involves former Chicago State University (CSU) president, Elnora Daniel. After being forced to resign for her questionable spending practices, but before actually leaving the campus, Daniel authorized the expenditure of $18,000 in university funds to pay for the publication of a "tribute book" extolling her accomplishments as president. The glossy volume entitled, "A Retrospective: Ten Years of Vision and Leadership," featured photos of Daniel posing with political leaders, university staff members, and her own family. One photo showed Daniel and five family members dressed in formal dinner attire standing near an ornate staircase. This scene was especially ironic because Daniel's ouster had been precipitated by a state auditor's report that found she had spent thousands of dollars in school funds to take her family on a Caribbean cruise when she attended a "leadership conference" in 2006.[21] No doubt, Daniel met other university presidents—and their family members—on the same cruise.

A second reason administrators are inclined to squander school funds is their continuous need to build political support. Some support-enhancing activities, to be sure, are institutional rather than personal. Constituencies inside and outside the university are more likely to support the school and its programs if they see some benefit to themselves from so doing. At my university, for example, a dean sought to establish several part-time programs that he hoped might strengthen the shaky base of the College of Arts and Science. Immediately, several major academic departments opposed the idea, which they saw as a potential diversion of resources from their own efforts. The dean responded by offering each of these departments a share of the income from the proposed endeavor if each would agree to "sponsor" a program and identify a faculty member to provide academic supervision for it. After lengthy negotiations over their income shares, the departments dropped their opposition and happily accepted this new income stream. The money diverted to the departments could be seen as the political cost of the program much as public works projects slated for the districts of key members of Congress represent the political cost of programs at the national level.

Not all politically important university constituencies are primarily interested in pecuniary rewards. For example, some university presidents find it necessary to invest enormous resources in athletic programs, particularly football and basketball, to retain the support of wealthy alumni "boosters" who seem obsessed with their schools' athletic teams. Collegiate athletic programs are almost never profitable. Usually, whatever revenues are produced by sports programs flow back into the athletic department rather than the school's general coffers.[22] Nevertheless, the presidents of schools with histories of athletic prominence and well-organized booster groups usually find it expedient to devote millions of dollars—to say nothing of significantly lowering their schools' academic standards—in a constant effort to field winning sports teams.

There is a thin but important line between expenditures designed to bolster the university's constituent base and a second type of support-building outlay—one intended mainly to protect the perquisites and positions of presidents and other top administrators. In a number of cases, college leaders presided over business deals with companies owned or controlled by members of their boards of trustees, or at least looked the other way as such deals were fashioned. The parties to such insider arrangements invariably aver that the school is receiving goods and services at a fair or even discounted price from its friends and deny that school funds are being squandered. Indeed, federal law prohibits insiders from selling goods and services for more than their fair market value. Yet, in all such arrangements there is at least an implicit understanding that the school's administration will not scrutinize the cost and quality or even the need for its purchases too carefully and, in turn, the board will heap praises on the president and his staff. In effect, the school's officials are spending the institution's money to safeguard their own jobs.

In addition to the examples to be discussed below, cases of insider dealing have arisen in recent years at Adelphi University, Auburn, the University of Idaho, the University of Hawaii, the University of Georgia, and a number of other schools. At Adelphi, the state board of regents ousted the school's president and eighteen of its nineteen trustees. Several of the trustees had been profiting from business deals with the university that had not been publicly disclosed.[23] Auburn was placed on probation by the Southern Association of Colleges and Schools because of concerns that the board lacked "sufficient safeguards" to ensure that its members did not have personal financial interests in the institution.[24] At the University of Georgia, firms associated with a number of trustees did more than $30 million in business with the school.[25] At the University of Hawaii–Manoa, the administration failed to inform the board that it awarded a major housing contract to a firm owned by the vice chairman of the UH Foundation.[26] And, at the University of Idaho, the school's president retained a law firm headed by a board member to represent the school's interests in the development of a $136 million satellite campus. The same law firm also represented the developer hired by the university to spearhead the project. The potential conflicts of interest came to light only when the collapse of the project prompted the state's attorney general to begin a criminal inquiry.[27]

The presidents and top administrators of state universities may also find it useful to do favors for important legislators whose support can be critical not only to the school's budget but also to the careers of its top officials. Often, this involves hiring the friends and associates of key politicians or making certain that the school purchases goods and services from firms associated with such individuals. For example, the University of Medicine and Dentistry of New Jersey (UMDNJ) was for many years known as a "political patronage pit," whose officials routinely provided jobs for the relatives of trustees and New Jersey's political leaders.[28] A former university president allegedly went so far as to institute a ranking system for political referrals, assigning candidates scores from "1" to "3" based on their connections. Particularly important politicians were wont to call the school's president directly to demand jobs for constituents and family members.[29] In a similar vein, Alabama newspapers recently reported that the state's community college system had awarded contracts and jobs to forty-three members of the state legislature or their close relatives. The chancellor of the community college system, Roy W. Johnson, himself a former Alabama state legislator, viewed his position as an opportunity to build a "power pyramid," according to U.S. Attorney Alice Martin.[30] Johnson allegedly directed tens of millions of dollars in contracts, campaign assistance, and jobs to state legislators whom he regarded as political allies.

In a similar vein, in 2007, Mike Garrison, president of the University of West Virginia, had the school award an MBA degree to Heather Bresch, a drug company executive, even though Bresch had never completed the course work required for the degree when she attended the school a decade earlier.[31] Bresch is the daughter of West Virginia governor, Joe Manchin, and also serves as chief operating officer at Mylan, a drug company chaired by Milan Puskar, one of the university's most important benefactors. Garrison is a long-time friend of the Manchin family and apparently viewed the unearned and retroactive degree for Bresch as a favor that would strengthen his ties to both Manchin and Puskar. When news of the phony degree leaked, however, Garrison and several other university officials implicated in falsifying Bresch's records were forced to resign. Similarly, in 2009, the chancellor of the University of Illinois and a number of other school officials were forced to resign when it was revealed that they had arranged admission to the school for unqualified but politically well-connected applicants. Two university trustees involved in the scandal left the board.[32]

Still another reason that administrators sometimes squander their schools' funds has to do with *turf*. Many college administrators, like bureaucrats in other realms, stand ready to use the school's money to defend or expand their own bureaucratic domains. Take the case of Harvard Medical International (HMI), established by Harvard Medical School in 1994. The former Harvard Medical School dean Daniel Tosteson conceived HMI as an organization that would undertake medical education and research activities in nations where health care expertise was badly needed. Not coincidentally, HMI was expected to produce a profit for the medical school, which was then seeking additional sources of income. Tosteson declared that HMI's mission was "to do good by doing well."[33]

Over the next several years, HMI was quite successful, bringing its services to more than thirty countries and generating several million dollars in annual profits for the medical school. The medical school's administration was very well pleased with HMI and worked to expand its efforts from education and research to consulting, management, and the actual delivery of medical services.

In 2003, HMI contracted with Phyathai Hospitals in Bangkok, Thailand, for a long-term partnership in which Harvard would provide clinical services, education, and management for the entire hospital network. In the same year, HMI contracted with the emirate of Dubai to build the nation's health care infrastructure from the ground up.[34]

HMI's efforts were applauded not only by the medical school, but also by the university's then president, Lawrence Summers, who strongly supported the enlargement of HMI's mission and personally approved HMI's contracts in Thailand, Dubai, and elsewhere. Summers saw HMI as a model for the expansion of Harvard's international presence. Summers's views, however, were not shared by others within the university. At Harvard as elsewhere, the university's several schools and divisions compete for money and influence. The success of HMI and the special presidential favor it seemed to enjoy were resented by schools whose own international programs had not been so successful or profitable. The continued growth of HMI threatened to upset the balance of power within the university by providing the medical school with a substantial new source of revenue and a claim of leadership in the realm of international programming—a realm that was certain to become increasingly important in the years to come.

In 2006, Summers was forced to resign as Harvard's president after his ill-considered comments about women and science produced an uproar on the campus. In the wake of the departure of its strongest supporter outside the medical school, HMI became vulnerable and soon found itself under fire from other university divisions. Even before Summers's departure, criticism of HMI from other schools, most notably the Faculty of Arts and Sciences (FAS), had led the university's administration to ask the medical school to conduct a review of HMI's programs and activities. Though the medical school's dean, now Joseph Martin, resented the demand, so long as the review was to be conducted by the medical school, itself, and presented to HMI's ally, President Summers for approval, it was not expected to pose serious problems for HMI.

By the time the review was completed, however, the political situation at Harvard had changed. President Summers was on his way out and no longer in a position to defend HMI. Instead of the president's office, where the report, "might have sat on a shelf," the review was now to be submitted to the University Committee on International Projects and Sites (UCIPS), chaired by a vice provost who had been recruited from the FAS and controlled by administrators and faculty who were not friendly to the medical school and its growing dominance of international programming. UCIPS and its chair seized the opportunity to launch a fierce attack against HMI. According to the vice provost and his committee, the medical school's own report provided unambiguous proof that HMI had deviated significantly from its teaching and research mission into the fields of consulting and management, where it threatened to undermine Harvard's reputation and "brand name."[35]

Like most prestigious universities, Harvard undertakes a number of for-profit activities that might seem inconsistent with the school's reputation for scholarship and quality. Harvard, for example, has for years operated a very profitable extension division that awards undergraduate degrees to individuals who would never even come close to meeting the standards for admission to Harvard College. In this context, it is somewhat difficult to take seriously the notion that HMI, which associated Harvard's name with improvements in the quality of health care throughout the world, should be seen as a threat to the university's reputation. Nevertheless, UCIPS called on the university to end its relationship with HMI. Unfortunately for HMI, at this critical moment not only was its ally, President Summers, out of office, but the medical school was, itself, temporarily without a leader. Joseph Martin had stepped down and a new dean had not yet been named when Harvard's central administration accepted UCIPS's recommendation and moved to jettison HMI. The new medical school dean was informed of the decision, after the fact, when he took office.

In the wake of HMI's demise, other university divisions have moved quickly to take lead roles in international programming. UCIPS has supported funding for a program in South Asia, and Harvard's new president has helped foster science, social science. and engineering programs abroad. All these new programs, to be sure, have cost money—so far more than $50 million— while HMI actually generated revenue. In the world of administrative politics, though, this minor balance-sheet issue is irrelevant. What is important is that an effort by the medical school dean to expand that school's influence in the increasingly important area of international programming was beaten back. Bureaucratic turf was protected, albeit at a substantial cost to the university.

Of course, administrators are not the university's only turf warriors. Turf battles among groups and factions within the faculty are common features of academic life. I often tell graduate students that the university resembles a World War I battlefield. Competing factions have fortified bits of territory with barbed wire and machine gun emplacements and are prepared to unleash artillery barrages and even poison gas against hostile forces. At the very least, administrators add new fronts to the existing battles among faculty groups.

But, beyond increasing the number of struggles afflicting the campus, the ascendance of administrators has changed the character of academic warfare. Even when their underlying motivations may be questionable, professors are obligated, at least in public, to present strong intellectual justifications for their positions. In turf wars among faculty members, victory is most often secured by those who succeed in framing the issue and offering the most compelling philosophical or scientific arguments on behalf of their cause. The best faculty debates have an educational value. Like a campaign debate among skilled political candidates, or a courtroom clash between learned advocates, faculty battles can elevate the issue at hand from its, perhaps, mundane roots to its most interesting philosophical expression.

I can recall, as a student at the University of Chicago in the 1960s, listening to faculty members debate the content of the school's "core curriculum"—the package of courses required of all Chicago undergraduates. The underlying motives of the debaters might have been prosaic or even self-serving. Some professors certainly knew that inclusion of their field within the core would likely entitle their own department or program to more professorial positions as well as to the services of additional staff and graduate assistants to support their teaching responsibilities. Yet, whatever the underlying motives of the antagonists, the debate itself was edifying. Philosophers, scientists, social scientists, and others carried on lengthy discussions, at least nominally designed to determine what knowledge was most worth having and imparting to undergraduates. So what if selfish considerations sometimes lay beneath the rhetorical surface. Knowing that their interests could only be served if their principles triumphed in the battle of ideas, faculty antagonists transformed the discussion into a struggle that was enlightening, edifying, and an excellent educational experience. In faculty turf wars, the World War I battlefield can resemble the Athenian marketplace. War becomes an educational experience—the mother of ideas if not invention.

Alas, few of our deanlets are comfortable on the battlefield of ideas. Turf wars involving administrators resemble Hobbes's state of nature more than ancient Athens—they are nasty and brutish, albeit of indeterminate length. Faculty turf wars can elevate mundane interests into matters of high principle that inform and educate the community. Administrators, on the other hand, are more likely to ignore or fail to see the larger principles that may be at stake in a dispute and to focus entirely on the questions of who is in charge, how many people will report to them, and who will be invited to go on the next administrative retreat.

The difference between the manner in which faculty members and administrators comport themselves in turf battles was brought home to me during a recent controversy on my campus regarding the issue of civility. I mentioned in chapter 1 that in

2008 the Hopkins administration sought to impose "civility train-ing" and a new civility code on the campus in order to expand its power over the faculty. At an open meeting called by the adminis-tration to allow members of the university community to express their views on the matter, a number of faculty members spoke in opposition. Professors spoke on the history of such codes, experi-ences on other campuses, and even the various meanings of the term civility. Faculty, of course, understood that they had much to lose and little to gain from an administration-imposed civility regime, so their comments were certainly not without a firm basis in self-interest. Nevertheless, as the faculty made its case, listeners could learn much about academic history, modes of social control, and the hidden meanings of civility. Whatever the pur-poses of the war, the battle, as fought by the faculty, was a good learning experience.

The administrators who spoke, on the other hand, did not seem to see, or were perhaps unable to articulate, any principles at stake in the discussion. One deanlet declared that she had some-times been treated rudely by faculty members and believed, there-fore, that it was essential to subject everyone to civility training. A medical school administrator was difficult to understand but seemed to think that a campuswide civility code was needed because the medical school had already taken steps in that direc-tion. Indeed, he declared, medical school administrators had recently organized a retreat to study the issue. The vice president for human resources, a champion of mandatory civility training (which she would organize and direct) and chair of the committee presenting the proposal, was asked to offer facts or examples that might justify the need for action. She replied that her committee had been a "policy-making" and not a "fact-finding" body. Hence, she saw no reason to provide examples or even arguments on behalf of her position. The faculty was incredulous that she seemed to see no relationship between policies and facts, but this vice president seemed satisfied that the administration's desire to introduce the proposed program was, in and of itself, a sufficient reason to move forward. Neither she nor the other administrators in the room saw any reason to elevate the discussion to the realm of ideas and principles.

Corruption

The expansion of college and university administration has not been coupled with the development of adequate mechanisms of oversight and supervision, particularly for senior managers. University boards, which technically oversee the administrations, are generally not well prepared for the task. One recent study found that 40 percent of university trustees said they were not prepared for the job and 42 percent indicated that they spent less than five hours a month on board business.[36] Many trustees serve because of loyalty to their school and say they have "faith" in its administration. They do not go out of their way to look for problems, and administrators are generally able to satisfy trustees with the rosy pictures of college life presented at weekend board meetings. University boards do not have the same legal responsibilities borne by corporate boards. Most federal regulations establishing management standards for private sector firms, such as the 2002 Sarbanes-Oxley Act, do not apply to nonprofit entities, and state regulation of university administration is spotty. At the same time, while schools have developed many internal rules and standards applying to the conduct of faculty members and students, few if any have established standards governing administrative conduct or established oversight mechanisms. For the most part, senior administrators police themselves.

The result of this lack of supervision is that a number of college and university administrators in recent years, have succumbed to the temptation to engage in corrupt practices. Administrative corruption takes three general forms. These are theft, insider dealing, and academic fraud and plagiarism. Let us examine each in turn.

Administrative Theft

Lax financial controls combined with weak external oversight allow dishonest administrators to hide behind the institution's carefully cultivated reputation for virtue and probity while they accept kickbacks from contractors or embezzle funds from the organization's treasury. In 2008, for example, the director of Tufts University's Office of Student Activities, Josephine Nealley, was indicted on three counts of larceny for embezzling more than $300,000 in student activities funds. She allegedly transferred the money to her personal bank accounts and used it for purchases and trips. While acting on an anonymous tip regarding Nealley's activities, university auditors uncovered a second, apparently unrelated case of embezzlement. Raymond Rodriguez, a budget officer, allegedly stole more than $600,000 from the university which he spent on trips and luxury goods. Rodriguez was indicted on two counts of larceny for his alleged thefts.[37] Both Nealley and Rodriguez entered guilty pleas and were sentenced to prison terms.

At Wesleyan University, the chief investment officer Thomas Kannam was forced to resign in 2009 amid charges of theft, fraud, forgery, and breach of contract. The university charges that Kannam enriched himself through the use of his position to bolster his outside entrepreneurial activities while ignoring his university job. Kannam denies the charge.[38]

Another notable example of administrative corruption is the recent scandal involving student loan officers. At a number of schools, loan officers accepted gifts and kickbacks from private lenders, most notably Student Loan Xpress, to direct students and their parents to these firms.[39] The practice was pervasive, and its revelation led to forced resignations by loan officers at a number of schools including such prominent institutions as Columbia, the University of Southern California, and Johns Hopkins.[40] In recent years, similar scandals have affected managers responsible for contracting, construction, and even study abroad programs.[41] Who can forget the Stanford president who allowed money generated by federal research grants to be used for entertainment, flower arrangements, and furnishings at his official residence?[42] One of the most bizarre recent cases of administrative fraud involved Cecilia Chang, a former dean and vice president at St. John's University in Queens, New York. Chang was accused by prosecutors in 2010 of embezzling about $1 million from the college and forcing a number of foreign students to work as her personal servants to keep their scholarships. In her capacity as dean of the Institute of Asian Studies at St. John's, Chang granted 15 scholarships every year, mainly to foreign students. Chang allegedly told a number of the recipients that they would lose their scholarships if they did not clean, cook, and perform other duties in her home.[43]

In a similar vein, the president of the University of Tennessee was forced to resign when an audit revealed that he had spent hundreds of thousands of dollars in university funds for personal trips, entertainment, and purchases. The president's travel at university expense allegedly included trips to Birmingham, Alabama, where he was said to have a "personal involvement," with the president of another school.[44]

In a particularly egregious fraud case, the president and chief financial officer of Texas Southern University (TSU) were both charged with defrauding the school of hundreds of thousands of dollars in separate schemes. The school's former CFO is currently serving a ten-year prison term while the former president, Patricia Slade, avoided possible prison time by reaching a plea agreement with federal prosecutors to repay approximately $100, 000 of the more than $600,000 she is alleged to have misappropriated. An unusual feature of this case involves three TSU students who helped authorities expose Slade's misdeeds. The students, members of the TSU student government, came across suspicious payroll records in 2005 and brought them to the attention of law enforcement officials. When they became aware of the students' actions, university authorities responded by charging the students with harassment and violations of the school's speech code. The students were arrested by the university police and expelled from the school. In 2008, after Slade had been fired, a federal jury awarded the students more than $200,000 in damages to be assessed against the school and its administrators.[45]

In addition to fraud and embezzlement, a number of bribery and kickback schemes involving university administrators have been uncovered in recent years. For example, in 2007, two administrators at New York's Touro College were indicted for conspiring to create and sell fraudulent student transcripts. The indictment charged that Andrique Baron, the school's former director of admissions and Michael Cherner, the former director of the computer center had conspired with a number of others to alter, create, and delete transcripts for a fee. Among those allegedly purchasing false transcripts were several New York City schoolteachers who needed masters' degrees to obtain teaching certificates. A number of other individuals allegedly paid Baron and Cherner to have their grades improved or to have failing grades expunged from their records.[46] Both Baron and Cherner were convicted and sentenced to prison in 2009.

While the Touro case is not unique, most of the bribery schemes that come to light involve kickbacks from service providers and contractors to university administrators in a position to decide which companies will be asked to do business with the school. In a typical example, Theodore Chiu, a former administrator at the University of California, Riverside, recently pled guilty to soliciting a $50,000 bribe from a construction company for his help in dealing with problems that had arisen regarding the company's contract to construct a new psychology building on the campus.[47]

Some bribery and kickback schemes involve millions of dollars in payments to university administrators. In January 2008, for example, Roy Johnson, chancellor of Alabama's community college system, pled guilty to accepting millions of dollars in bribes from companies doing business with the state's twenty-seven two-year colleges and technical schools. Johnson, the same individual whose efforts to build a base of political support by providing jobs and other favors to state legislators were discussed above, also became a multimillionaire at the college system's expense. Federal prosecutors charged Johnson with accepting more than $250,000 in kickbacks from Access Software Co. in exchange for helping the firm win $14 million in state contracts. Johnson received more than $50,000 in services from Alabama Contract Sales in exchange for helping the company secure $9 million in business. Johnson received more than $70,000 in services and goods in exchange for helping an architectural firm win more than $5 million in state contracts. The list goes on and on. As part of his guilty plea, Johnson was required to forfeit the astonishing sum of $18 million he admitted receiving in direct and indirect benefits from his various schemes and conspiracies. As the U.S. attorney who prosecuted the case observed, "Taxpayers must wonder how many more Alabama students could have been educated had money not been wasted on fraud."[48]

Fraud is a pervasive problem throughout the not-for-profit sector. One study estimated that theft and embezzlement in the not-for-profit world totaled more than $40 billion per year.[49] Often, frauds go unnoticed for years because the perpetrators are the accountants and financial officers responsible for financial oversight. There is no way to know what portion of this $40 billion in fraud is attributable to crimes at America's colleges and universities, but numerous cases come to light every year. In even more instances, when fraudulent conduct is discovered, university officials prefer to allow the perpetrators to resign or retire quietly rather than risk a public brouhaha that might upset donors and lead to questions about the quality of the school's leadership. Most professors can point to cases at their own school when crooked administrators were allowed to leave quietly, sometimes even without being compelled to make restitution for their offenses. The question posed by the U.S. Attorney in Alabama about the Johnson case could be asked more generally. How many more students could be educated if administrators were not lining their own pockets?

Insider Deals

A second form of administrative corruption affecting universities is one that is common throughout the nonprofit world. Quite often, senior administrators and members of the institution's board of directors make insider deals in which the institution purchases goods, services, or property from companies linked to their board members. Faculty members, of course, have always noticed that the construction cranes and service trucks on their campuses tend to bear logos associated with companies controlled by prominent board members. This pattern is widespread and pervasive. One major study conducted in 2007 indicated that administrators and directors were involved in insider arrangements at nearly half of large nonprofit organizations, including universities.[50] The participants in such deals deny that any financial improprieties are involved and assert that the organization is receiving goods and services from board members at market or even below-market rates. The validity of such claims is difficult to judge, and the potential for conflicts of interest is very high even where insider deals do not involve kickbacks, shoddy goods, or price gouging—as apparently occurred at the University of Idaho.[51]

The existence of an insider deal between board members and top university administrators, even when financial impropriety is not involved, means that at least some trustees will have a financial stake in supporting the continuation in office of a school's administration even if it is ineffective and incompetent. Knowing that trustees will protect their own business interests, unscrupulous administrators will encourage business dealings between board members and the university, thereby ensuring a firm base of support for themselves among the trustees. One notable example is the case of Boston University whose long-time president John Silber was supported by important trustees even when it was clear that Silber had reached an advanced stage of senescence. When Silber finally stepped down in 2003 after more than thirty years in office, the incoming president, Daniel Goldin, announced that he planned to reexamine the university's business relationships with its trustees.[52] The board responded by rescinding its offer to Goldin and paying him $1.8 million to give up the job one day before he was scheduled to take office.[53]

In a similar vein, for many years a number of individuals with close ties to WellMark Blue Cross and Blue Shield, the state's leading health insurer, served as regents of the University of Iowa. The insurance company did a great deal of business involving the university's hospitals and clinics and had a strong stake in making certain that university policies remained congenial to the company's financial interests. A number of faculty members expressed concern about what they saw as a troubling appearance of conflicts of interest arising from the relationship.[54] In recent years, collusion between presidents and board members have come to light at several other schools including Auburn and the University of Georgia. There is every reason to believe that these represent the proverbial tip of the iceberg. Faculty who wonder why their school's board continues, year after year, to support an utterly incompetent president, or why the board has opted to summarily fire a competent one, might do well to follow the money.

Plagiarism and Academic Fraud

Thievery can be found among managers of all large organizations, and collusive arrangements between administrators and board members are common in the nonprofit realm. Neither form of corruption is unique to university administrators. A third form of administrative turpitude, though, is probably more widespread among university administrators than managers in most other professions. This is the problem of plagiarism and academic fraud. Colleges and universities are institutions that assign unique importance to ideas and to the written word. Many administrators have neither the ability nor the inclination to develop their own ideas or write their own words. As a result, they appropriate the thoughts and publications of others or claim to have authored books and articles that do not actually exist.

In some instances that have come to light in recent years, administrators have secured the academic credentials needed for their university positions through fraudulent practices. For example, in 2007 Southern Illinois University's student newspaper examined the 1984 doctoral dissertation ostensibly written by the school's president and discovered that substantial portions were lifted from other works without attribution.[55] This same president had previously fired a campus chancellor who had submitted a plagiarized strategic plan. In other instances, administrators have not bothered even to plagiarize to establish their credentials. They have simply claimed works that were never published or even degrees they never earned. I referred above to the case of the Albright College president whose resume claimed that he had authored books that turned out not to exist. Another college president resigned when it was revealed that his claims of holding an MBA and PhD were false.[56] Other recent cases include the long-time MIT dean of admissions who was discovered to have falsified virtually her entire resume.[57] One enterprising college administrator was accused of using his access to his school's computer system to award himself two degrees, which he added to his resume.[58]

Some equally enterprising administrators have apparently sold false credentials to others. For example, Robert Felner, the former education dean at the University of Louisville, allegedly awarded a PhD to an individual who had only attended classes for one semester after that individual awarded a $375,000 grant to a university center run by Felner.[59] Felner was also indicted for mail fraud, money laundering, and tax evasion for siphoning federal grant funds into his personal bank accounts.[60] Prior to his 2010 conviction on these charges, Felner had been named chancellor of the University of Wisconsin's Parkside campus but, alas, was forced to step down when news of his misdeeds at Louisville became public.[61] Felner was eventually sentenced to sixty-three months in federal prison.

More common, or at least more frequently brought to light than outright falsification of credentials, is administrative plagiarism in speeches, reports, papers, and even publications. In 2006, for example, the president of Delaware's Wesley College was found to have claimed as his own a speech, an article, and a position statement apparently copied from work published by others.[62] Proving that plagiarism no longer disqualifies anyone from becoming a college president, this individual was later named president of Bethany College in West Virginia.[63] Earlier, the former dean of Boston University's School of Communication admitted to having used plagiarized material in a commencement speech.[64] In a similar vein, the former dean of Arts and Sciences at the University of Missouri, Kansas City, plagiarized material for his 2003 commencement speech.[65] The president of Central Connecticut State University was found to have plagiarized from no fewer than three sources in an opinion piece published in a Hartford newspaper.[66] And, setting a rather questionable example, the former president of Hamilton College delivered a 2003 welcome address to freshmen in which he used numerous phrases and passages without citation from book reviews posted on the Amazon.com Web site. Before resigning, the president acknowledged that he had tended to keep poor records of references and citations when undertaking research for speeches.[67] In 2004, the president of Central Connecticut State University was found to have plagiarized portions of an article that he published. The same individual had previously been accused of impersonating a police officer.[68]

These examples of plagiarism on the part of college administrators are the exception, not the rule. What makes them exceptional, though, is not that most administrators would never claim credit for the work of others. Rather, they are exceptional because they are individual acts of plagiarism. Senior administrators today, especially college and university presidents, like their counterparts in business and politics, typically engage in what might be called institutionalized plagiarism.[69] They employ ghost writers to craft their speeches, commencement addresses, and columns in campus publications.[70] Some have published books and articles written by staffers. One president, the head of Alabama's Jacksonville State University, seemed to write a weekly column for the *Jacksonville News*, a daily city newspaper. It turned out that the columns published under the president's byline were actually being written by university staffers. These staffers, moreover, apparently plagiarized many of the columns from material they found on the Internet. Ironically, when the story broke in August 2007, the university president was not available for comment because—what else?—he was away at a retreat.[71] Perhaps he was working on the strategic plan. All this seems not only unethical but unfair as well. After all, with an occasional exception like John F. Kennedy, students are not allowed to employ ghostwriters. And, faculty members who plagiarize must generally do so at their own expense.

4

The Realpolitik of Race and Gender

IT IS CERTAINLY no secret that professors tend to have liberal political orientations.[1] Most academics, especially but not exclusively those in the humanities and social sciences, strongly support racial and gender equality, social justice, protection of the environment, constraints on the use of force in international affairs, and other elements of America's liberal Democratic agenda.[2] Faculty generally explain the academy's ideological imbalance, especially marked at elite universities, as a natural consequence of the fact that liberals are smarter than conservatives.

In recent years, unfortunately, on many campuses the political commitments of the faculty have been hijacked and perverted by administrators. Issues that to many professors represent moral imperatives have been transformed into powerful instruments of administrative aggrandizement. Ironically, administrators have brought about this transformation by forging what amount to tactical alliances with representatives of minority groups as well as activist groups on their campuses. Indeed, since it was not so long ago that campus administrators responded to the legitimate grievances of minority groups and liberal activists by calling the police, it is fascinating to observe the apparent sympathy shown for these same groups by university administrators today.

At my university, for example, the administration strongly supported liberal activists' protests in response to what some termed a fraternity's racial insensitivity. The fraternity had called its 2006 All Hallow's Eve party, "Halloween in the Hood," invited guests to wear their "bling," and decorated its chapter house with a plastic skeleton in pirate garb dangling from a rope noose. The precise meaning of this display was far from clear. A noose might have a racist connotation, but skeletons and pirates would seem, at first blush, to be devoid of racial antecedents. Campus and community activists, however, chose to interpret the unfortunate skeleton as a symbolic affirmation of the idea of lynching black people. This understanding was vigorously contested by the fraternity, which boasted a multiethnic membership. The university administration, nevertheless, supported the activists' interpretation and agreed with them that investigations, punishments, and policy changes would be required to prevent such events from occurring in the future.[3]

In a similar vein, during the spring of 2008, Brandeis University administrators overrode a finding by the faculty's Committee on Faculty Rights and Responsibilities (CFRR) regarding the case of Donald Hindley, a long-time and somewhat cantankerous political science professor who had been accused of racial harassment by an anonymous student in his Latin American politics class.[4] The accuser averred that Hindley had used the term "wetback," to refer to illegal immigrants from Mexico. Hindley asserted, in response, that he had employed the term during a historical discussion as an example of the racist invective to which Mexican immigrants had been subjected. While the facts continue to be a matter of dispute, university officials seemed to have little or no interest in determining exactly what was said in Hindley's class. Instead, they sided with campus activists and treated the episode as an opportunity to take a strong public stand against racism and discriminatory conduct. The university's provost assigned human resources staffers to conduct a brief investigation, sent a deanlet to monitor Hindley's classes, and threatened the professor with termination if he failed to modify his classroom conduct. CFRR and the faculty senate vehemently protested these actions as violations of due process and the university regulations, but these institutions were ignored by the president and provost, who asserted that they alone possessed legal authority and responsibility in these matters.

At Yale in 2009, university administrators provided funds for the establishment of the Office of LGBTQ (Lesbian, Gay, Bisexual, Transgender, and Queer) Resources, which, according to its director, was designed to make the university "feel like a friendly place as opposed to an alien and hostile place" to its constituents.[5] Shortly before announcing the creation of this new office, the university had announced a series of budget cuts in response to a sharp drop in the value of its endowment and a projected $100 million deficit. While many of Yale's established academic programs were affected by the school's financial crisis, Yale administrators seemed eager to make an exception for a program supported by a tiny group of activists.

What accounts for the solicitude shown by university administrators for campus activists and minorities? In some instances perhaps, administrators themselves possess deep and abiding commitments to social justice and change and support the same causes espoused by the minority and activist communities. Yale's Kingman Brewster was a leading example. For many university administrators, though, two other factors are more important in leading them to cooperate with liberal activists and minorities on their campuses.

The first of these factors is, of course, a desire to protect themselves from criticism from the often vocal and vehement campus left.[6] Since the 1960s, the campus left has been well organized and vocal, especially at major colleges and universities. Administrators have learned, through the application of repeated electric shocks, as it were, that a failure to placate the liberal left could result in demonstrations, disturbances, and the potential destruction of administrative careers. During the 1960s and 1970s, university presidents who sought to battle campus protests, like Columbia's Grayson Kirk, saw their careers ruined, while those who learned to work with and placate militant forces, like a subsequent Columbia president, Michael Sovern, had relatively uneventful presidencies.[7]

Administrators who come into conflict with campus radicals or, for that matter, minority groups are, at the very least, likely to be labeled "controversial," and shunned by the search firms that hold the keys to new positions and promotions in the administrative world. Corporate headhunters will never touch a "controversial" individual, though of course such traits as indolence, ineptitude, and out-and-out stupidity are rarely disqualifications for career advancement in the field of higher education administration. The demands of the campus left, moreover, are seldom counterbalanced by conservative or moderate opinion. There are virtually no conservatives on leading campuses, while the moderate liberal majority generally takes little or no part in university politics. Only on the issue of Israel, where campus Jews are usually well organized and prepared to engage in vigorous political struggle, is significant opposition likely to be voiced to the views of the strident campus left.

Take, for example, the now-infamous 2006 case of the three Duke lacrosse players falsely accused of raping an African American exotic dancer. Radical activists, though constituting only a small fraction of the Duke faculty, were extremely vocal in their demands for summary punishment of the accused athletes even before the facts of the case were examined. The campus's more mainstream liberals were dubious about the allegations but generally remained aloof from the fray, reluctant to be seen as taking the side of privileged white students against a poor black woman. The university's president and other administrators, with the notable exception of the school's provost, shamelessly backed the outrageous claims of campus and community activists even after the case began to publicly unravel.[8] In two recent, but unrelated, cases at the University of Iowa, professors accused of sexual harassment killed themselves before their cases were adjudicated and the facts fully established. Among the factors that drove both to suicide was the despair they felt when they saw how eager university administrators seemed to be to throw them to the wolves.[9]

A desire to avoid clashes with vocal and well-organized college groups is only one reason that administrators often find it expedient to maintain good relations with liberal activists and minority groups on their campuses. A second, and even more important reason is that this alliance can, in several ways, help administrators to bolster their own power vis-à-vis the faculty. Because most professors are progressive in their political commitments they are, as in the Duke case, unwilling to be seen as siding with putative oppressors against the oppressed and, hence, are generally reluctant to oppose programs and proposals that are presented as efforts to foster campus equality, diversity, multiculturalism, and the like. At some point during the past several decades, some college administrators became aware of the political possibilities inherent in this situation and developed a model that the others could imitate.

Put simply, university administrators will often package proposals designed mainly to enhance their own power on campus as altruistic and public-spirited efforts to promote social and political goals, such as equality and diversity, that the faculty cannot oppose. This tactic can succeed if and only if administrative proposals are endorsed by the school's political activists, as well as spokespersons for the women's groups and various racial and ethnic groups that, together, constitute a self-appointed but effective political *Vaad Ha'ir* on many campuses. For this reason, administrators view these coalitions of minorities and activists as important allies and frequently work to retain their support with symbolic and material rewards including positions for spouses, funding for scholarly initiatives, released time for research, and higher salaries than are received by other professors.

The political alliance between administrators, minorities, and liberal activists, an alliance born in the turmoil of the 1960s, serves the interests of both parties and has become an important force at a number of colleges and universities. The most obvious and best documented expression of this alliance is the strong support shown in recent years by so many university presidents for affirmative action and other racial preferences in both graduate and professional school admissions.[10] But four other institutional expressions of this alliance are even more important with respect to the power of university administrators, especially vis-à-vis the faculty. These are the proliferation of multicultural programs and centers, the expansion of administrative influence in faculty hiring and promotion nominally designed to promote racial and gender diversity, the emergence of a punitive regime of speech and "civility" codes on a number of university campuses, and the development of often ideologically freighted "student life" or "residence life" curricula at many schools.

Diversity and civility are valued by virtually all members of the university community. But unfortunately, as we shall see below, for university administrators, diversity and civility are instruments of managerial power rather than philosophical principles.

Multicultural Programs

During the 1960s, liberal activists on a number of campuses demanded that their schools establish academic units dedicated to scholarship and teaching about and by women and people of color. Advocates of these programs pointed out correctly that women, along with African Americans and other ethnic minorities had little presence on university faculties and, moreover, that their scholarly work was given little attention in college classes. Initially, college and university administrators resisted such demands, arguing that the numbers of women, African Americans, and others could and would be increased within established university departments. Indeed, a small number of black intellectuals opposed the idea of setting up "sealed-up black studies centers," where black academics and students would be kept isolated from the mainstream of academic discourse.[11] These views, though, were generally dismissed on the campus left, and as they learned the benefits of deflecting criticism from the left, administrators quickly accepted the idea of establishing programs and departments in such fields as women's studies and Africana studies, followed later by programs focusing on other varieties of ethnic and gender issues. During the 1970s, hundreds of women's and black studies programs sprang up on America's campuses, and today virtually every significant college and university boasts at least one and usually several departments, programs, or centers dedicated to these matters.

Conservative critics of race and gender studies have, of course, long charged that these programs lack academic validity and rigor. In truth, however, black studies, women's studies, and the like, vary in quality from school to school and, in terms of methodology and epistemology, do not seem terribly different from their cognate fields in the humanities and social sciences. But whatever the intellectual validity of race and gender studies, a quarter of a century of attacks from the political right have succeeded in convincing many prospective students that a degree in, say, Africana studies or women's studies would not constitute an appropriate credential from the perspective of future employers and might, instead, suggest college years devoted to a search for cultural affirmation rather than the acquisition of useful skills or analytic abilities.

Hence, at most schools, few students choose programs in race and gender studies as their major field and, even if interested in the area, few take more than one or two courses offered by race and gender studies faculty. At my university, for example, though several Africana studies professors have excellent scholarly reputations, in 2007–2008, of some 3,200 arts and sciences undergraduates, only four chose to major in Africana studies. During the same year, by comparison, 145 students majored in psychology, 148 majored in economics, and 222 selected international studies as their principal field of study.

The narrow student base for race and gender studies programs has important ramifications. At most colleges and universities, budgets and faculty "lines," that is, the number of professors that a department or other unit is authorized to employ, are tied, albeit loosely, to student majors and enrollments. An academic department whose offerings are not attractive to students will often be threatened with a loss of lines and ancillary budgetary allocations, while a department whose enrollments grow will generally be able to demand additional faculty lines and other resources to serve the needs of the students whose tuition or tax dollars represent the school's lifeblood. The relationship between enrollments and budgets is by no means absolute, but over time, university administrators are usually compelled to shift faculty, staff, and budgetary resources to match changes in student interests and demands.

Race and gender studies are frequently an exception to this rule. At Hopkins, for example, the four undergraduate students majoring in Africana studies in 2007–08 were served by a program director, an eleven-person executive board, ten affiliated faculty, two visiting faculty, an associate research scholar, and a program administrator. The program also boasts ample office space and staff support. As is the case at some schools, Africana studies at Hopkins is not a fully fledged department, and most of its faculty are jointly appointed with other, more established, academic units. But be that as it may, the resources devoted to Africana studies are far out of proportion to its enrollment base. Any other program with only four undergraduate majors might very well be closed by the university's administration unless, like Jewish studies on most campuses, it is able to secure external funding. Precisely this fate has befallen a number of academically well regarded sociology programs around the nation in recent years as student interest in the field has all but disappeared.

Administrators have political reasons to provide Africana studies with a much larger share of the school's budget pie than it merits strictly on the basis of student enrollments. Their actions are fiscally imprudent but politically correct. At the same time, constantly having to defend its share of the school's budget against rival claimants with demonstrably more student need, gives Africana studies and similar programs a stake in supporting the college presidents, provosts, or deans from whom it has received its largesse and on whose sufferance it depends. The upshot, on many, though not all campuses, is a symbiotic relationship between the leaders of ethnic and gender studies programs and top university administrators. The former receive extra resources while the latter are assured of important political support.

Take the recent imbroglio at Harvard leading to the ouster of President Larry Summers. Somewhat arrogant and high-handed, Summers had managed to offend large numbers of faculty members. And, though he was a Democrat and former treasury secretary in the Clinton administration, Summers was seen by many of Harvard's more progressive faculty as too conservative for the school's presidency. Summers had, for example, publicly praised young Americans who had volunteered for military service and been rather dismissive of left-liberal causes including the campaign to divest university holdings in companies deemed unfriendly to the environment or too friendly with Israel.

Two events, in particular, however, gave Summers's foes the ammunition with which to force Harvard's board to demand his resignation. The first of these involved a prominent Afro-American Studies professor, Cornel West. In a face-to-face meeting, Summers allegedly urged West to repair the quality of his scholarly work, to put a halt to grade inflation in his classes, and to limit his absences from campus during the school term. West, a public intellectual with numerous off-campus and nonacademic commitments including a career as a "Rap" music artist, took umbrage at Summers' comments and announced that he was leaving Harvard for a position at Princeton. Another prominent black professor, Anthony Appiah, also accepted an offer from Princeton, though it was not clear that his departure was tied to West's. Two other black scholars, a husband and wife, left for Stanford when Summers refused to allow the wife's promotion to a tenured professorship. In the wake of these resignations, Summers was excoriated by many members of the faculty for his administrative clumsiness and worse. Interestingly, however, Summers was seldom if ever publicly criticized by Professor Henry Louis "Skip" Gates, Harvard's W. E. B. Du Bois Professor of the Humanities, director of the Du Bois Institute, and chair of the Afro-American Studies Department.

Though Summers had been clumsy in his dealings with Cornel West, he had been careful to provide the Afro-American Studies department with substantial resources and faculty positions. When Gates threatened to follow West and Appiah to Princeton, Summers moved to reassure him that he could continue to rely on the university's largesse—in the immediate form of a donation to one of Gates's projects—and that he would be able to recruit a bevy of new faculty members to more than replenish his department's ranks.[12] "I look forward to working with Skip and his colleagues and with those who will join the department and the Du Bois Institute in the months and years ahead," Summers said.[13] Gates replied, "Because of my devotion to the department and the Du Bois Institute, I felt it crucial that I remain here and join my colleagues in this exciting process of rebuilding. In the last few months we have attracted significant talent to the department . . . and we have the opportunity to bring more people here."[14] In other words, despite Summers's alleged mistreatment of an important black faculty member, the university's president and the chair of Afro-American studies had negotiated a mutually satisfactory renewal of their previous accommodation. Later, seeking to maintain the support of another important constituency, Summers pledged $50 million to improve opportunities for women at Harvard.

In 2005, a storm of protest erupted when Summers appeared to question the ability of women to undertake significant research in the sciences. Gates continued to support Summers during this period, though the opposition of Afro-American studies, added to Summers's other foes, would almost certainly have ended his presidency. Instead, Gates gave President Summers a vote of confidence. "I am on excellent terms with President Summers," Gates said, "and expect to work with him for a very long time."[15] After Summers's eventual resignation, though, Gates warmly greeted the appointment of a new president, Drew Gilpin Faust. Gates seemed particularly to welcome her after Faust pledged to greatly increase the number of black faculty at Harvard.[16] Apparently a new president did not mean the end of the now-traditional quid pro quo.

The relationship between the administration and ethnic studies faculty also has been important at Columbia University in recent years. Soon after assuming Columbia's presidency in 2002, Lee Bollinger announced an ambitious plan to enlarge Columbia's campus by clearing and redeveloping a 17-acre plot of land in the southernmost portion of West Harlem, just north of the school's current campus. In an effort to avoid the negative symbolism that might be associated with the idea that the university was planning further encroachments into Harlem, Columbia's publicists dubbed the tract, "Manhattanville," and declared that its economic redevelopment would provide jobs and many other benefits to all the residents of Harlem.

Opposition to the plan developed quickly. A number of commercial landowners who would be displaced by Columbia announced plans for a court fight, particularly if the university sought to induce state agencies to use their powers of eminent domain to seize land on the school's behalf. Community leaders claiming to speak for the area's black and Latino residents denounced the plan as an effort by the university to pursue its interests at the expense of people of color. And, on the Columbia campus, a number of students, staff, and faculty declared their solidarity with the people of the neighborhood.[17] Over the next several years, the university's administration moved forward with its planning processes, buying additional land within the tract and securing municipal zoning and planning approvals for its proposed redevelopment of the area. Opponents, for their part, sought to block the university in the municipal political arena through unfavorable publicity, and via student and community activism—the latter culminating in a well-publicized 2007 hunger strike by a number of student militants.

During this period, Columbia's administration was eager to discourage faculty—particularly minority faculty—from adding their voices to the chorus of opposition to the Manhattanville project. Unfortunately, from the administration's perspective, Columbia's black faculty had an activist tradition, and did not always enjoy a good relationship with President Bollinger despite his history of civil rights advocacy. African American professors, at any rate, could not allow themselves to be seen as helping to drive black residents of Harlem from their homes to make way for Columbia's expansion. Without the *quid* there was no *pro quo*, and the programs controlled by black professors, namely the African American studies program and the Institute for Research in African American Studies (IRAAS), did not enjoy the privileged budgetary position of their Harvard counterparts.

Rather than seek to repair his relations with African American studies and IRAAS, Bollinger chose to focus primarily on Latino faculty in an attempt to create a campus environment more favorable to the Manhattanville project. To begin with, though many different groups and entities claimed to represent the citizens of Manhattanville, the university chose to emphasize the Latino character of the area's population by working mainly with Jordi Reyes-Montblanc, a Cuban-born shipping consultant who headed a local community board. The school negotiated what was called a "community benefits agreement" with Reyes-Montblanc that promised jobs and other forms of compensation for area residents who would be displaced by the proposed project.[18] At the same time, the university ignored the mainly black leadership of the Harlem Tenant's Council, which had put forward a competing proposal.

On the campus, itself, student activists opposed to the Manhattanville project, calling themselves the Coalition to Preserve Community, had composed a lengthy and heterogeneous set of demands more or less related to the issue at hand and eventually launched a hunger strike to garner publicity for their cause. The coalition called for an end to university programs that would result in the displacement of West Harlem residents. At the same time, though, the coalition demanded changes in Columbia's curriculum to emphasize issues of race, ethnicity, and gender, expansion of the school's Office of Multicultural Affairs, diversity training for security staff and new faculty, and the appointment of more faculty in black, Latino, and other ethnic studies programs. A number of campus groups expressed solidarity with the students. Among the most important of these was the faculty of the Center for the Study of Ethnicity and Race (CSER). Though CSER oversaw programs in comparative ethnic studies, Asian American studies, and Native American studies, its main focus was Latino and Latina studies, and the faculty representing this academic specialty were the dominant force within CSER. Opposition from CSER would certainly not derail the Mahattanville project, but CSER's support coupled with the endorsement of Reyes-Montblanc's community board could go a long way toward creating the impression that the university's development plan was sensitive to the needs of poor community residents rather than a callous land grab by a wealthy and powerful institution.

Accordingly, from among the hodgepodge of demands put forward by Coalition students, university administrators chose those they found to be most useful to Columbia. After discussions with CSER director, Claudio Lomnitz, the university agreed to invest $20 million in CSER programs and activities, which would include the creation of three new professorships in CSER and a new slot in Native American studies also to be housed in CSER.[19] Student protestors were initially unsure what to make of these nominal concessions. They were, however, encouraged by their faculty mentors and their allies on the community board to regard this outcome as a victory for the oppressed and downtrodden people of West Harlem.

Over the next few months, student protestors ended their hunger strike and moved on to other issues. The CSER faculty celebrated its new relationship with the university administration, inviting President Bollinger to its offices for a VIP briefing on CSER's programs and activities. The Manhattanville project was temporarily slowed in 2009, when a state appeals court said that the state could not use eminent domain on behalf of the university.[20] By this time, however, Columbia had already acquired most of the land it needed, and in 2010 the state's highest court overturned the lower court ruling and allowed the project to move forward.[21] As to the residents of Manhattanville, it probably goes without saying that they have all been removed to make way for university expansion. Perhaps the new CSER faculty members could be housed in one of the new buildings on the Manhattanville campus. After all, their appointments were part of the price the university paid for access to the land.

Faculty Diversity

Most colleges and universities in the United States appear to be campaigning vigorously to promote faculty diversity, that is, the hiring and retention of women and people of color as full-time professors. Usually led by the president and provost and other high-ranking officials, university administrators throughout the nation have declared diversity to rank among their institutions' very highest priorities. University of Rochester president Joel Seligman, for example, recently declared that faculty diversity was an institutional priority and a "fundamental value" of his university.[22] The school adopted a thirty-one-point program to enhance the diversity of its tenured and tenure-track faculty. Like many other college leaders, Rochester's president has appointed diversity officials, instituted procedures to ensure that diversity goals will figure prominently in faculty searches, and encouraged members of search committees to undergo "diversity training." The officials of some schools have gone even further than their Rochester counterparts, mandating diversity training for those involved in searches and requiring that diversity officers be included in all faculty search committees. Hundreds of schools have appointed "Chief Diversity Officers," with the authority to implement diversity plans.[23] And still others have employed the services of one or another of the now-ubiquitous diversity consulting firms, which will, for a hefty fee, help ensure that they do not overlook any possibilities that might help to speed them along the road to greater and greater diversity.[24]

While diversity is an important goal, at first blush the current administrative full-speed-ahead drive to add underrepresented minorities and women to college faculties seems a bit off the mark. The simple, if unfortunate, fact of the matter is that in many fields there are few women and virtually no minority faculty available to be hired. In a recent year, only ten African Americans earned PhD degrees in mathematics and only thirteen in physics.[25] Given these numbers, it might appear that the only way to bolster the presence of minority faculty in such fields would involve a long-term effort to identify and nurture math and science skills among talented minority secondary-school students. A crash program to hire minority scientists when none are being produced seems misguided, to say the least.

In the humanities and social sciences, to be sure, women and members of racial and ethnic minorities constitute a larger fraction of the graduate school population and, hence, the pool of individuals from which professors can be recruited. In these fields, though, the academic departments have been actively hiring minority faculty for a number of years. My department of eighteen full-time political science professors was, until 2010, chaired by a woman. The full-time faculty include two African Americans, one African, six women, and one Arab American. Two of the six women are Asian American. By some counts, we might be considered a majority/minority department. Most of the university's other humanities and social science departments became similarly diverse long before our president and provost learned that the term did not merely refer to the mix of securities in the school's investment portfolio.

Thus, in some fields, professorial diversity cannot be achieved simply though university hiring processes, while in those fields where women and minority professors are actually available to be recruited, efforts to do so have been under way for a number of years and have been fairly successful. Why then have university presidents, provosts, and other high-ranking officials suddenly, and somewhat belatedly, become outspoken diversity advocates, seemingly on a collective quest to drastically change the gender and racial balance of their faculties? As in the case of their support for multicultural programs, the answer to this question has more to do with administrative interests than long-standing moral commitments.

To begin with, the diversity plan has become as important an assertion of administrative leadership as the strategic plan. When they announce a bold new diversity plan, presidents and other top administrators are, in effect, averring that only they, and not department chairs or other campus luminaries, are capable of providing leadership in this important realm. An ambitious new diversity plan is likely to be endorsed by the school's liberal activists and minority faculty and staff, particularly if the administration involves these groups in the planning process. Once liberal activists and minority representatives endorse the plan, faculty members who might have doubts about the administration's ideas and intentions generally remain silent for fear of being seen as lacking proper enthusiasm for racial and gender equality. Indeed, clever administrators will make increased diversity and an imaginative diversity plan the centerpiece of their vision for the school— a fundamental value, as Rochester's president put it. By wrapping themselves and their programs in the mantle of diversity, university presidents hope to broaden their base of support on the campus and to intimidate potential critics. Administrators who are insufficiently clever to think of this tactic on their own, often benefit nonetheless, from the usual administrative propensity to do what everyone else is doing.

Not surprisingly, newly appointed university presidents and provosts are today as likely to promulgate new diversity plans as they are to develop new strategic plans. Both are useful leadership tools. And, as in the case of the strategic plan, the fact that the diversity plan seldom produces concrete results is almost never held against it. It's the process that counts. Speaking of process, administrative plagiarism seems as common in diversity planning as in strategic planning. My own university's 2008 "Commission on Equity, Civility, and Respect," seemed to produce ideas remarkably similar in character to those published by the University of Virginia's 2005 "Commission on Diversity and Equity." The overlaps must represent more examples of that ever popular administrative principle—best practices.

Diversity plans often have more than a symbolic significance. On many campuses, the quest for diversity has allowed administrators to intrude into and gain a greater measure of control over the faculty hiring process. Since the emergence of the tenure system, faculties, particularly at research universities, have strongly resisted even the slightest encroachments by administrators into faculty autonomy in the realm of hiring. Typically, university departments have defined their own academic needs and, subject to budgetary approval, identified, interviewed, and hired professors deemed to fill those needs. Efforts by administrators to intervene in the process were almost always firmly rebuffed. When I was a government professor at Cornell, for example, an individual with political connections wrote to the school's president offering his services as an instructor in my department. The president, thinking to politely brush the fellow off, met with him for a few minutes and indicated he would forward his credentials to the department. I believe the credentials were promptly forwarded to the president's waste basket. Nevertheless, when the department learned of this meeting, a delegation consisting of our three most senior professors called on the president to berate him for his interference in departmental affairs. The president properly apologized and said it would never happen again.

Today, under the rubric of diversity, university administrators have been able to arrogate to themselves an ever-growing role in the faculty hiring process. The rationale for this administrative encroachment into what had been a faculty domain is the idea that university departments are not well suited in terms of their own interests and sense of purpose to work diligently on behalf of diversity. According to one scholar, university departments assign too much weight to "their notion of quality, appropriate credentials, and scholarly research/productivity expectations."[26] The only solution to this departmental myopia is "leadership intervention" to set appropriate hiring standards and recruitment policies.

Such intervention has become the norm at a growing number of colleges and universities. At many schools, staffers from human resources or the diversity office play an active role in faculty searches. One modest form of intervention is diversity training—sometimes mandatory—for members of search committees. The University of Virginia, for example, recently adopted such a requirement.[27] At Hopkins, I once served on a campuswide search committee for a senior college staffer. The deanlet who chaired the committee insisted that we undergo diversity training before we began the search and invited a well-known diversity consultant to help us understand such issues as biases in labor markets and racial stereotyping. My recollection of the training session is that the consultant seemed decidedly less conversant than the faculty members on the committee with the major issues in these fields. The consultant also seemed altogether too eager to share with us various religious and ethnic stereotypes, as he warned us against them. Perhaps ours was an unusually poorly prepared consultant, but there was something odd about compelling a group of professors who included some of the nation's leading authorities on race relations to listen to the rather uninformed views and banal opinions of a consultant whose credentials were markedly inferior to our own.

Some schools have moved beyond diversity training to require that all search plans be approved by diversity officials and that all search committees include human resources or diversity staffers as voting members. At one large community college in the South, for example, human resources and diversity staff screen all potential candidates for faculty positions before they can be interviewed by the search committee. At a midwestern state college, human resources personnel organize all faculty search committees. At one southern college, a human resources, equal opportunity staffer serves as a member of every search committee, and at a midwestern state college an "Inclusion Advocate" is assigned to every search committee by the human resources department. At the University of California, Berkeley, where the faculty resisted the idea of including human resources staffers on search committees, the Faculty Equity Office moved to train students, who often had a role in faculty hiring, to serve as the office's de facto agents on search committees.[28]

All this effort might have some value if it demonstrably resulted in enhanced faculty diversity. But, "inclusion advocates" and the like cannot make up for the absence of minority PhDs in some fields and offer little or no improvement over the faculty's own efforts in others.[29] Diversity campaigns do produce an increase in the number of diversity officials, which by administrative logic might in and of itself be seen as evidence of a more diverse campus. Such campaigns, however, cannot produce minority physicists and mathematicians. Administrators and diversity consultants, groups with short time horizons, sometimes appear to have little interest in the longer term efforts that might actually produce minority physicists and mathematicians. Some dismiss the idea that such programs might be effective as "an insidious myth."[30]

But, while they do not produce much actual diversity, administrative diversity campaigns have given university officials a tool with which to attack the autonomy of the faculty recruitment and promotion process and, perhaps, the tenure system itself. My own school's Commission on Civility Equity and Respect, created by the president to promote diversity, among its other goals, recently recommended mandatory diversity education for search committees, recommended that faculty performance evaluations include an assessment of professors' "contribution to diversity," and, to promote diversity, encouraged university administrators to review, "current policies on promotion and time related assessment of employment," i.e., the tenure system.[31] Clearly, under the rubric of diversity, administrators are seeking and finding ways to enhance their power vis-à-vis the faculty.

Speech and Civility Codes

Since the 1980s, hundreds of colleges and universities have enacted codes proscribing forms of speech and conduct that might be seen as offensive or hostile by particular groups or designed to intimidate or harass individuals based on their racial, religious, social, gender, or other characteristics. Administrators sometimes justify these codes by asserting that they are required by federal law or that failure to promulgate a speech or conduct code might leave a school open to suit, under federal employment or equal opportunity laws, by individuals alleging that the institution had failed in its duty to prevent the development of a hostile or harassing environment. In point of fact, however, far from requiring colleges to adopt codes, the U.S. Department of Education has actually warned schools against adopting antiharassment codes that might infringe on First Amendment rights.[32] And, as to the problem of litigation, one prominent attorney has pointed out that efforts by schools to enforce their codes have generated more litigation than the lack of such codes.[33]

As in the cases of both multicultural programs and the quest for faculty diversity, speech and civility codes actually reflect the tacit alliance that has emerged between university administrators and activist and minority groups on the campus. The latter have sought speech, diversity, and civility codes to block racist, sexist, or homophobic expression and, mainly in the case of Muslim students, criticisms of Islam. In 2009, for example, Yale's president ordered the university's press to remove cartoons critical of Muhammad from a forthcoming book, *The Cartoons That Shook the World*, which discussed Muslim reactions to twelve cartoons published by a Danish newspaper in 2005 that led to deadly protests in the Muslim world. Those perusing the book could read about the cartoons, but Yale administrators concluded that they might be seen as insensitive if the university was associated with an actual display of the cartoons.[34]

Campus administrators are anxious to avoid trouble from vocal and sometimes militant forces. Increasingly, too, administrators have come to see speech and civility codes as management tools that might help them intimidate or silence their own critics. One cadre of campus functionaries likely to be particularly outspoken in its support for restrictions on speech consists of the bureaucrats who administer diversity, multicultural, and similar campus offices. These officials tend to regard any criticism of their programs as attacks on the validity and legitimacy of their own positions in the university and will respond aggressively to even the mildest questions. One example of this phenomenon took place on my own campus in June 2008. That month, university administrators organized a series of open meetings to present the report of a presidentially appointed commission on "equity and civility," which, among other things, supported strengthening our campus civility code. A number of faculty members spoke against the commission's report, which, as was noted earlier, seemed calculated to promote administrative intrusion into the faculty hiring and promotion process. When faculty members completed their comments, they were castigated, in the most uncivil terms, by administrators from the campus multicultural office, who essentially accused the faculty-as-a-whole of fostering a racist and abusive climate on the campus—as now evidenced by faculty expressions of opposition to the proposed new civility code.

Thus, hoping to intimidate critics and protect their own jobs, campus bureaucrats have reason to agree with campus activists that speech or civility codes can be useful devices. Of course, as Jon Gould has observed, some college administrators adopted speech codes without giving the matter much thought just because everyone else seemed to have them.[35] As in so many other realms, one should never underestimate the prevalence of mindless administrative mimicry, enshrined under the rubric of best practices. Should we be surprised or upset to learn, for example, that the University of Florida's Internet use code, outlawing behavior that "would include but not be limited to the use of abusive or otherwise objectionable language and/or materials in either public or private messages," is echoed by Alvernia College's policy banning behavior that, "would include but not be limited to the use of obscene, abusive or otherwise objectionable language and/or materials in either public or private messages?"[36] Perhaps college administrators believe that if they are going to violate student and faculty First Amendment rights, their conduct is justified if they are merely copying some other school's violation of the Constitution.

The codes adopted by many schools during the 1980s and 1990s sought to prohibit forms of speech or expression deemed to be offensive by campus administrators and faculty or student activists. For example, the 1989 "policy against racism" adopted by the University of Massachusetts board of regents outlawed speech that was racist "in any form, expressed or implied, intentional or inadvertent."[37] In a similar vein, the Syracuse University code forbade "offensive remarks," including "sexually suggestive staring, leering, sounds or gestures" and "sexual, sexist, or heterosexist remarks or jokes."[38] The University of Wisconsin outlawed "racist or discriminatory comments, epithets or other expressive behavior."[39] The University of Pennsylvania's speech code prohibited "any verbal or symbolic behavior that . . . insults or demeans the person or persons to whom the behavior is directed . . . on the basis of his or her race, color, ethnicity or national origin, such as (but not limited to) by the use of slurs, epithets, hate words, demeaning jokes, or derogatory stereotypes."[40]

This code figured in Penn's well-known "water buffalo" case. In 1993, Penn charged a freshman, Eden Jacobowitz, with violating its speech code by allegedly shouting a racial slur at a group of fifteen black sorority members who had been loudly singing and stomping outside the window of his dorm room one night while he was trying to write a paper. Jacobowitz had yelled, "Shut up, you water buffalo!" Though Jacobowitz certainly meant to express his annoyance with the women, it was not clear why the term water buffalo—a notoriously unruly gray ox native to Southeast Asia— constituted a racial epithet or hate word and Jacobowitz denied that this was his intent. Nevertheless, the freshman was charged with racial harassment and ordered to acknowledge his racial offense, placed on "residential probation," and directed to perform a number of tasks designed to promote his understanding of the meaning of diversity.[41] Though Jacobowitz continued to assert his innocence, university administrators—including those specifically assigned to assist with his defense—apparently united against him. One faculty member, though, Professor Alan Kors, worked vigorously to defend the freshman and, eventually the *Wall Street Journal* columnist Dorothy Rabinowitz brought the case to the attention of the national media, which for several weeks savaged the university and its then president, Sheldon Hackney. Coincidentally, Hackney had been nominated to head the National Endowment for the Humanities and was facing Senate confirmation hearings, which were now likely to focus on his understanding of Asian oxen. Like their counterparts at Duke a decade later, university officials and spokespersons lied repeatedly to the media, only making matters worse, until the deluge of negative publicity finally forced Penn to drop the case against Jacobowitz.[42] As in so many other speech cases, only outside intervention saved the accused individual from being steamrollered by university bureaucrats.

Obviously, all of the speech codes promulgated by public universities seemed, on their face, to violate the First Amendment's guarantee of free speech. If challenged on free speech grounds, however, university administrators generally sought to justify their codes on the basis of the U.S. Supreme Court's decision in the 1942 case of *Chaplinsky v. New Hampshire*, which held that "fighting words," defined as words meant to incite an immediate breach of the peace, were not protected by the First Amendment.[43] College and university administrators contended that the racist or sexist speech their codes outlawed represented precisely the sorts of utterances likely to provoke a violent reaction and, as a result, were not constitutionally protected. This argument, though, ignored legal precedent regarding the meaning of incitement as well as the fact that the federal courts had construed the fighting words doctrine very narrowly, seldom finding mere words to be so violence-provoking as to have no constitutional protection. As a result, the early college speech codes could not survive judicial scrutiny, and codes at Wisconsin, Michigan, and several other public universities were invalidated by the courts.

In recent years, colleges and universities have generally turned from speech codes to harassment or civility codes covering students, faculty, and other members of the university community. These codes purport to be based on federal employment and education law. Title VII of the U.S. code prohibits employment discrimination, while Title IX outlaws discrimination by educational institutions receiving public funds. As interpreted by the Equal Employment Opportunity Commission, the Department of Education's Office of Civil Rights, and the courts, these laws have been held to hold both employers and schools liable when their actions or failure to take action helped to bring about an environment that was hostile or harassing to women, members of minority groups, or other persons.[44]

Contemporary civility and harassment codes claim to ban speech and behavior that might be deemed hostile or harassing, possibly in violation of federal law. Thus, for example, the University of

Miami prohibits, "any words or acts . . . which cause or result in physical or emotional harm to others, or which intimidate, degrade, demean, threaten, haze or otherwise interfere with another person's rightful actions or comfort."[45] Similarly, the University of Pennsylvania's new code, prohibits, "any behavior, verbal or physical that stigmatizes or victimizes individual on the basis of race, ethnic or national origin . . . and that has the purpose or effect of interfering with an individual's academic or work performance, and/or creates an intimidating or offensive academic, living or work environment."[46] The University of Iowa's harassment code declares that sexual harassment, "occurs when somebody says or does something sexually related that you don't want them to say or do."[47] My own school's civility code declares that, "rude, disrespectful behavior is unwelcome and will not be tolerated."[48]

Though nominally grounded in employment and education law, civility and harassment codes enacted by public universities have not fared well in the courts when schools have attempted to apply them in disciplinary settings rather than merely trumpet them as aspirations. In the educational context, true harassment was defined by the Supreme Court in the case of *Davis v. Monroe County Board of Education* as conduct, "so severe, pervasive, and objectively offensive that it effectively bars the victim's access to an educational opportunity or benefit."[49] The expression of words, symbols, or views that someone finds offensive is not harassment. Rather, it is constitutionally protected speech. Accordingly, judges have tended to see civility and harassment codes as efforts to circumvent the First Amendment and have found them to be unconstitutional when their application has been challenged. For example, a federal judge in Pennsylvania recently ordered Shippensburg University to stop enforcing a provision of its code that declared, "the expression of one's beliefs should be communicated in a manner that does not provoke, harass, intimidate or harm another."[50]

Despite their poor record in the courts, many public universities continue to promulgate civility and harassment codes and endeavor to punish students who violate them. When students or faculty members are disciplined under even the most patently unconstitutional code they, of course, bear the burden of time, money, effort, and anguish associated with vindicating their rights in court. For example, a group of San Francisco State students recently was threatened with disciplinary action under the school's harassment code when they held an antiterrorism protest that included stepping on images of the flags used by Hamas and Hezbollah, two organizations officially classified as terrorist groups by the United States government. After a complaint from Muslim students, the antiterrorism protestors were charged with "attempting to create a hostile environment" and "incivility" in violation of the Student Code of Conduct. Political protest and flag desecration—even of the American flag—are certainly First Amendment rights, but the students were subjected to five months of hearings until threatened action by a civil libertarian group led the school to drop its charges. Without external intervention, the students would very likely have been punished for their constitutionally sanctioned protest.

An even more egregious violation of a student's rights by university bureaucrats enforcing the school's racial harassment code took place at Indiana University-Purdue University, Indianapolis (IUPUI) in 2008. Keith Sampson, a student working part-time as a school janitor to help finance his education, was observed reading a book entitled *Notre Dame vs the Klan: How the Fighting Irish Defeated the Ku Klux Klan*, a history of events in the 1920s when Notre Dame students confronted klansmen in South Bend, Indiana. Sampson had obtained the book from IUPUI's library. After a coworker complained that Sampson was reading a book on an "inflammatory topic," he was charged by the school's chief affirmative action officer with, "openly reading the book related to a historically and racially abhorrent subject in the presence of your Black co-workers." Such conduct, according to this university functionary, constituted racial harassment.[51] After a number of civil libertarian groups, including FIRE and the Indiana chapter of the ACLU intervened, and the case began to receive negative publicity, the university dropped all charges, issuing a number of evasive explanations of the events in question.

Private colleges and universities are generally not bound by the First Amendment and have broad leeway to discipline students and faculty under their civility and harassment codes.[52] Thus, as mentioned above, in 2006 a Johns Hopkins student was disciplined for publishing invitations and displaying a plastic skeleton announcing his fraternity's "Halloween in the Hood" party. In 2007 a group of Tufts writers were disciplined for a satiric essay on minority admission. In 2008 a Colorado College student was punished for posting a flyer parodying a flyer posted by the school's feminist and gender studies program. If these events had taken place at public institutions, the students and faculty involved might have been able to vindicate their rights in court, but this option is probably not available to them in the private setting.

As I noted earlier, university administrators have a number of reasons to seek to regulate campus speech through civility and harassment codes. Such codes can placate campus activists and minority groups. Indeed, when they charge a student or faculty member with sexual or racial harassment, administrators are signaling to groups capable of making trouble that the school's administration is on their side. At the same time, administrators have their own agendas. The growing stratum of administrators of multicultural and diversity programs regard speech restrictions as useful and proper instruments through which to silence those who might question the legitimacy and validity of their own positions on the campus. For the more general cadre of campus functionaries, civility and harassment codes seem to be attractive means of intimidating critics of every stripe.

A recent case from Georgia is a telling example. In 2007, T. Hayden Barnes, a student at Valdosta State University in Georgia posted flyers and sent letters and e-mails to newspapers raising environmental and fiscal objections to his university's plan to build two large parking garages adjacent to the campus. The school's president, Ronald Zaccari, apparently regarded the proposed garages as an important part of his administrative legacy and took offense at the student's criticisms. In a letter slipped under Barnes's door during the night, Zaccari informed him that he had been "administratively withdrawn" from the school for his alleged violation of harassment regulations and because he presented a "clear and present danger" to the campus.[53] Only after the Foundation for Individual Rights in Education (FIRE) provided Barnes with a pro bono attorney who filed suit on his behalf in federal court was Barnes allowed to return to school.

When employed by public universities, virtually no civility or harassment code has been able to withstand judicial scrutiny. They all violate the First Amendment if actually employed for disciplinary purposes rather than merely to trumpet a school's values. But, despite defeats in the courts, more and more codes are written every year.[54] From the perspective of college administrators, the very fact that use of a code almost certainly will violate the constitutional rights of the student or faculty member against whom charges are brought is actually an advantage rather than a problem. Unconstitutionality is an advantage because it facilitates selective enforcement. If administrators find it politically useful to bring charges they do so, in effect telling the defendant, "so, sue me" if you don't like it. Where, on the other hand, administrators believe that bringing charges would not serve their political interests, they piously cite their own First Amendment concerns.

Recent events at the University of California, Irvine, exemplify this phenomenon. While campus administrators were quick to investigate charges made by African Americans and women of harassment and hate speech, similar allegations made by Jewish students against Muslim and Palestinian groups were ignored. When challenged, administrators cited First Amendment concerns as their reason for not taking action.[55] This form of selective enforcement of civility and diversity codes is an example of what Frederick Schauer has called "First Amendment opportunism."[56]

The Shadow Curriculum

A fourth institutional expression of the tacit alliance between university administrators, on the one hand, and minority groups and campus activists on the other, is the development of a shadow curriculum consisting of a mix of "life skills" or "student life" courses and a set of classes and seminars that come perilously close to political indoctrination. Many schools have long offered special curricula designed for students who were not prepared to do college-level work, such as many Division I varsity football and basketball players. In recent years, however, the concept of an alternative curriculum has expanded in response to the needs of campus deanlets and the wishes of campus activists as well as multicultural and diversity administrators. Working together, these forces have brought about the development of an ever-expanding nonacademic curriculum largely outside the faculty's purview at many colleges and universities.

The deanlets, for their part, have created a for-credit life skills curriculum, available and sometimes required at three-fourths of the nation's colleges. This curriculum consists of classes ostensibly designed to help students adjust to life away from home and to the subsequent rigors of "real life" off the campus. Classes in the life skills curriculum typically include lessons in budgeting and personal finance, good eating habits, and getting along with roommates. At the University of Connecticut, a special class, "Life Skills for Athletes," emphasizes the importance of attending class while in college—a concept that may have been unfamiliar to many of the student athletes seen dozing during one of the class's meetings.[57] Even at Harvard, students may choose from among a variety of Life Skills courses including real estate, auto repair, cooking, and plumbing repair.[58] These courses, to be sure, seem innocuous enough, but parents paying nearly $40,000 in tuition and fees plus probably another $20,000 in living expenses to send their children to Harvard might wonder why their mechanically challenged offspring could not take such classes for $75 at the local community college.

The deanlets and staffers who organize and often teach life skills courses view the growth of this curriculum as an affirmation and expansion of their own role on the campus. As we saw in chapter 1, as part of their effort to marginalize the faculty, administrators are fond of asserting that much education occurs "outside the classroom." The life skills curriculum expands this outside-the-classroom portion of college and, ironically, validates it with inside-the-classroom academic credit. Deanlets and staffers also believe that teaching life skills classes strengthens their resumes and will help them win promotions or to find better positions at other schools. For this reason, most deanlets are willing to give up valuable time which they might have devoted to meetings, conferences, retreats, or even strategic planning, to participate in life skills education.

While run-of-the-mill deanlets organize life skills courses, college diversity and multicultural staffers contribute to the shadow curriculum in another way. These functionaries organize courses whose goal seems to be the transformation of students' values and beliefs regarding matters of race, gender, public morality, the environment, and a variety of other political topics. The University of Delaware, for example, adopted a mandatory residence life education program in which students were taught that only white people were capable of true racism, as defined by the curriculum. Students also were taught that the oppression suffered by people of African descent, along with perhaps the genocide suffered by Native Americans and the colonialism experienced by Chicanos, Puerto Ricans, and Filipinos was much more onerous than any forms of persecution that might have been experienced by whites. Presumably, this comparison was designed to validate the victimhood avowed by blacks, Native Americans, and Chicanos while questioning the historical legitimacy of the grievances sometimes asserted by white groups such as the Jews, Armenians, and Irish.

The curriculum went on to explain that militarism, economic inequality, environmental degradation and unspecified problems surrounding America's health care system were all manifestations of racial oppression.[59] During the course of the program, students were required to demonstrate that they had achieved certain basic competencies such as recognizing the existence of systematic oppression in American society and were pressured to take actions such as advocating for an oppressed social group or advocating for a "sustainable world." Delaware's curriculum was developed by Dr. Shakti Butler, a diversity consultant and self-styled "creative and visionary bridge builder," who holds her PhD from the School of Transformative Learning and Change of the California Institute of Integral Studies.

Delaware's program seems to be an extreme example of indoctrination, but many schools have developed courses and seminars, led by staffers rather than faculty, designed to mold students' values and views. At my university, in response to a racially charged campus incident that infuriated campus and community activists, incoming freshmen were advised by the administration to read a book entitled *Why Are All the Black Kids Sitting Together in the Cafeteria* by Beverly Tatum, and required to attend discussions and seminars on the book when they arrived for fall classes.[60] The book, a discussion of the development of racial perspectives in America, was chosen by a group of deanlets and diversity staffers. To be sure, *Why Are All the Black Kids* is well written and interesting, and as a result is often used in secondary schools. It does not, however, represent the most sophisticated scholarship in this realm. At any rate, the seminars in which the book was discussed were led almost exclusively by staffers who, no doubt, found the book's accessibility attractive. I have asked many faculty members whose areas of academic specialization included race relations, if they were approached by administrators for advice on reading material or even to lead a seminar on issues of race. I could find none who had been invited. Presumably, this topic was simply too important to be left to the faculty.

Not surprisingly, the same deanlets who work to expand the university's student life curriculum also defend mandatory diversity training. Deanlets and diversity staffers can happily work together to promote the onward march of the shadow curriculum, a course of study that seems to create an incongruous pairing of auto mechanics with political indoctrination. The only losers from this curricular innovation are the tuition-paying parents who might properly wonder why they are paying tens of thousands of dollars for lessons in plumbing and hours of political indoctrination led by staffers and developed by consultants with rather dubious credentials. As to the students compelled to take these classes, as far as I can tell, neither life skills nor diversity classes have much effect on college students, a group that ends to dismiss—I believe the term they use is "blow off"—nonsensical requirements imposed on them by foolish administrators.

Administrative Harassment and Incivility

Disarmed by its own progressive commitments, the faculty has been largely silent as administrators have used the language of diversity and civility to trample on faculty prerogatives and to advance administrative agendas. Administrative abuse of multicultural programs, diversity planning, civility rules, and the like should be a punishable offense. I would call it *administrative harassment* and would recommend that the mere charge, brought by any faculty member or student, should result in the administrator's removal from campus without a trial or appeal. This suggested procedure, echoing their own methods, should seem only fair to college and university deanlets.

Occasionally, of course, faculty have dug in their heels to resist some new administrative intrusion. The recent case of the Brandeis professor Donald Hindley, mentioned above, is an example. Hindley was disciplined for racial harassment after he sought to explain the history of the term "wetback" in a class discussion of anti-immigrant racism. Friends with ties to Brandeis tell me that Hindley was a competent teacher, but difficult to get along with and, after 50 years on the faculty, well past his prime in terms of the scholarly productivity wanted by a research university. Apparently, Hindley had long resisted strong suggestions that he retire. Administrators may have seen the dubious racial harassment charge as a tool that could be used to push Hindley into finally leaving the university and were quite surprised when the elderly professor chose to publicize his case and to make a fight of it.

If this interpretation of events is correct, the Hindley case is another example of administrators' readiness to cynically use speech and harassment codes as managerial instruments when it suits their purposes. Hindley was probably not guilty of racial harassment but had, instead, committed the ultimate sin from an administrator's perspective—he was insubordinate.

Though, again, Hindley is not a popular figure on the campus, the Brandeis faculty senate felt compelled to come to his defense, especially after administrators expressed their utter indifference to university rules and established principles of shared governance. The fact that Hindley, himself, is known to have left-liberal leanings probably made it easier to defend him without running the risk of being branded some sort of dangerous reactionary. By the end of the 2007–08 academic year, the faculty senate was in the process of breaking off relations with the administration and seemed likely to call for a vote of no confidence in the provost and other university officials. In 2008, administrators formally declared Hindley guilty of racial harassment, though the Brandeis administration never fully clarified the precise character of his misconduct. The faculty senate continues to protest the administration's actions though its energies have been diverted by other administrative outrages including the effort to close the school's art museum and sell its irreplaceable collection. Administrators were driven to this dire expedient by the school's fiscal distress which was caused, in part, by years of administrative mismanagement.

Perhaps, the faculty will prevail in the Hindley case, as it does from time to time in similar matters. Indeed, negative publicity plus a faculty revolt recently forced the University of Delaware to modify its shadow-curriculum program of ideological indoctrination. Despite the occasional victory, the faculty, and the students, are losing the war. Most Hindleys retire quietly; most Keith Sampsons stop reading their banned books; most Haydon Barnes withdraw their objections to the president's construction projects. Most of the time, the deanlets march inexorably forward having succeeded in hijacking and distorting the faculty's moral and political principles.

5

There Is No Such Thing as Academic Freedom (For Professors): The Rise and Fall of the Tenure System

MANY ACADEMICS WHO are troubled by the growing power of administrators on their campuses believe that their jobs are protected by tenure and their campus activities by academic freedom. Hence, they believe that they, personally, have little to fear from the advent of the all-administrative university. Yet, these unworried professors might do well to fret just a bit. Tenure does not provide absolute protection, and at any rate only about 30 percent of the current professorate is tenured or even on the tenure track. The remaining 70 percent are hired on a contingent basis and can be dismissed at any time.

The question of academic freedom is more complex and more dispiriting. In recent years, the federal courts have decided that deanlets, not professors, are entitled to academic freedom. This proposition may be surprising to academics, who, usually without giving the matter much thought, believe they possess a special freedom derived from the German concept of *Lehrfreiheit*, which they think protects their freedom to teach, to express opinions, and to engage in scholarly inquiry without interference from university administrators or government officials.[1]

It certainly seems reasonable to think that professors should possess *Lehrfreiheit*. Academics play an important part in the production, dissemination, and evaluation of ideas, and a free and dynamic society depends on a steady flow of new ideas in the sciences, politics, and the arts. The late Chief Justice Earl Warren once opined that American society would "stagnate and die" if scholars were not free to inquire, study, and evaluate. Accordingly, he said, academic freedom "is of transcendent value to all of us and not merely to the teachers concerned."[2]

Despite Chief Justice Warren's endorsement, professors' ideas and utterances do not have any special constitutional status. Like other Americans, professors have free speech rights under the First Amendment. In a number of cases decided during the 1950s and 1960s, the Supreme Court made it clear that the First Amendment offered professors considerable protection from the efforts of federal, state, and local governments to intrude on their freedom of speech and association. For example, in the 1957 case of *Sweezy v. New Hampshire*, the Court reversed a contempt judgment against a professor who had refused to answer the state attorney general's questions about a lecture delivered at the university. Similarly, in the 1960 case of *Shelton v. Tucker*, the Supreme Court struck down a state statute requiring professors to reveal the names of all organizations to which they had belonged or contributed for the previous five years.[3] And, in *Keyishian v. Board of Regents*, decided in 1967, the Court invalidated New York's "Feinberg Law," which required professors at public colleges to affirm that they were not Communists and authorized colleges to dismiss faculty members who belonged to subversive organizations or who advocated actions deemed to be treasonable or seditious.[4]

Two points should be made about these rulings. First, though the cases involved professors, the Court did not extend special constitutional protection to college faculty members. The Court might have applied the same principles to journalists, architects, or, for that matter, plumbers. The freedoms affirmed by the Court were asseverated for all Americans. Second, in these cases, the effort to interfere with professors' constitutional freedoms came from outside the university. *Sweezy*, *Shelton*, and *Keyishian* all involved efforts by state legislatures to stifle professorial speech. Most academic freedom cases, however, arise inside the university, itself, and involve attempts by university administrators or governing boards—not state legislatures—to interfere with professorial freedom.[5] In these "internal" cases, the federal courts have been far less sympathetic to professorial claims than in the "external" cases cited above.

To begin with, constitutional protection for professors applies only to state action. It is important to remember that the First Amendment does not protect faculty members employed by private colleges from the actions of their administrations. Scholars who work for private universities may enjoy contractual rights or, like other Americans, rights under federal and state employment laws. Federal law, for example, prohibits private employers from discriminating on the basis of race and gender or against people with disabilities. There are, however, no special First Amendment protections for professors employed by private institutions who believe that administrators are seeking to stifle their speech or interfere with their freedom of association.

Faculty employed by public institutions, on the other hand, would seem to enjoy constitutional protection. Since their employer is a state agency, in principle, public school faculty should be able to assert First Amendment claims if administrators attempt to interfere with their speech or writing or research activities. In practice, though, the federal courts are usually reluctant to intervene in disputes between professors and administrators at state schools, and prefer to grant these institutions a measure of autonomy in decision making.

Professors at state colleges and universities have been reprimanded, disciplined, and fired for opinions they voiced inside and outside the classroom. Professors have even lost their jobs for refusing to assign grades demanded by campus administrators. In recent years, federal courts have begun to apply the Supreme Court's 2006 decision in the case of *Garcetti v. Ceballos*, to public university faculty. In that case, involving a deputy district attorney who was demoted for raising objections about a local sheriff's conduct to his supervisors, the Supreme Court ruled that the First Amendment did not protect public employees who criticized their supervisors in the context of their official duties.[6] Justice Kennedy who wrote the decision specifically indicated that it should probably not apply to the realm of higher education where traditions of shared governance called for professors to question administrators. Nevertheless, recent federal court decisions have applied the *Garcetti* precedent to universities. In a 2008 case, for example, a U.S. district court in California held that a UC Irvine chemical engineering professor was not entitled to First Amendment protection when he was disciplined for asserting at a faculty meeting that his department relied too heavily on part-time instructors.[7] The court cited the *Garcetti* decision as stipulating that such objections to official policy were not protected speech. Other courts have reached similar conclusions in cases involving such public universities as Delaware State and the University of Wisconsin, Milwaukee.[8] The same conclusion was reached quite recently by a federal court in Idaho in a case involving the firing of a tenured professor, Habib Sadid, who was a frequent critic of the Idaho State University administration.[9]

In most instances when professors have sued their schools for violating academic freedom, faculty have found the courts unsympathetic to their assertions.[10] Indeed, through a curious process of constitutional construction, the federal courts have developed a concept sometimes known as "institutional academic freedom," holding that the First Amendment limits state interference with the decisions made by college administrators.[11] This conception has effectively transferred the special constitutional protection recommended by Justice Warren from the scholar to the school.[12] Indeed, in a recent decision, the Fourth Circuit Court of Appeals said, "To the extent the Constitution recognizes any right of 'academic freedom,' . . . the right inheres in the university, not in individual professors."[13]

Some commentators have welcomed this development. Law Professor J. Peter Byrne, for example, asserts that academic speech is "distinctively collective in character." Hence, for Byrne, the essence of academic freedom is institutional autonomy "over certain core educational and scholarly policies."[14] But this position is questionable. In reality, the university's "collective" speech is generally that of the administration, not the faculty, and it is difficult to see why university administrators' communications and decision-making processes would be entitled to any more deference than those of any other private entity or state agency.[15] For the most part, administrative communications consist of advertising and self-puffery that should be seen as commercial speech, while administrative decision-making processes are no more refined or elevated then those of any other run-of-the-mill bureaucracy. As Amy Gutman observed, the collective notion of academic freedom might have been appropriate when applied to, say, a German university, which functioned historically as a self-governing body of scholars. In the American context, though, universities are governed by boards and administrators, which may themselves pose a threat to academic freedom.[16]

The academic freedom with which Justice Warren was concerned, protection for the expression and dissemination of new and perhaps unpopular political, social, or scientific ideas, is a privilege needed by the faculty, not the administration. It is professors, not administrators, who introduce and promulgate ideas. Professors, particularly at research universities, seek to advance their careers by advancing ideas different from and superior to those of their professional colleagues. The same is most definitely not true of administrators. In my four decades in the academy I have seldom heard an administrator voice an idea that diverged much from those concurrently being articulated by virtually every other administrator. Imitation seems to be the norm in the world of higher education administration.[17] Indeed, under the rubric of "best practices," college deanlets have elevated mindless mimicry to a matter of high principle. Nevertheless, through the doctrine of institutional academic freedom, the courts have declared that administrative decision making deserves special constitutional protection. The irony of this position is that it is often the administration that seeks to stifle the ideas and speech of the faculty. Hence, institutional academic freedom can stand in the way of real academic freedom.

To the extent that academic freedom has any reality for professors, it derives from contractual rather than juridical principles. In particular, the tenure system, which developed in the early decades of the twentieth century, promotes academic freedom by making it difficult, albeit not impossible, to dismiss faculty members—once they have completed a lengthy probationary period—for the ideas they aver in or out of the classroom. Since the 1930s tenure and academic freedom have been synonymous. Professors are free to write and speak only when administrators lack the means with which to stop them.

During the past three decades, unfortunately, the concept of academic tenure has come under attack from a variety of quarters. The percentage of college and university professors who hold tenured appointments or are even eligible to earn tenure—so-called tenure track appointees—has dropped to about 30 percent of the professoriate from 67 percent in the 1970s.[18] Nearly two-thirds of the nation's faculty consists of "adjuncts," individuals hired to teach on a year-to-year, semester-to-semester, or even course-to-course basis. Since adjuncts are much cheaper than tenure-track or tenured faculty, as well as more fully subject to administrative supervision, there is every reason to believe that adjuncts will continue to replace full-time faculty at most of America's colleges and universities. Within a few decades, it is likely that only a very small percentage of faculty members, mainly at elite schools, will hold tenured or tenure-track appointments. And, even tenured faculty seem less secure than they once were. During the 2009–10 economic recession, as we shall see below, a number of colleges seized the opportunity to dismiss tenured professors and chip away at the tenure system. With the collapse of the tenure system, academic freedom is likely to become little more than an empty slogan or, worse, a form of protection for administrative mediocrity.

Academic Life Before Tenure

For much of America's history, academic freedom was hardly even a slogan. College faculty generally held one-year contracts and assumed that they could and would be penalized or terminated for utterances that offended the religious or political sensitivities of the day. Even college presidents knew that their school's trustees would not hesitate to demand their resignation if they were so much as suspected of harboring nonconformist views on major issues. As a result, if they entertained heretical thoughts, most college personnel kept these to themselves. Those who did not, usually suffered the consequences.

Early in the nineteenth century professors, and sometimes presidents, were frequently shown the door because of matters of religious doctrine. For example, in 1812, Samuel S. Smith, president of Princeton University was compelled to resign when Presbyterian clerics on the Princeton board questioned Smith's religious orthodoxy. Smith was accused of endorsing polygamy and expressing doubt about the need for baptism, as well as a number of other heresies.[19] Even as late as the 1870s, professors who taught Darwin's theory of evolution could come under fire from religious zealots. In 1878, for instance, Professor Alexander Winchell was dismissed by the Vanderbilt Board of Supervisors, which was then composed of a group of Methodist bishops. Winchell's crime was to write a tract attempting to prove the inferiority of the black race by examining the pre-Adamite origin of man. Vanderbilt's board did not object to the racist character of Winchell's writings. Rather, it objected strongly to Winchell's apparent assumption that humans existed before God's creation of Adam and Eve.[20]

During the partisan struggles of the Jacksonian era, college faculty could lose their posts for harboring or seeming to harbor the wrong political loyalties. In 1851, for example, the well-known historian Francis Bowen lost his chair at Harvard when the board of overseers questioned his political views. In that period, the Harvard board was appointed by the Massachusetts legislature, which had recently come under the control of a coalition of Democrats and Free Soilers. Democrats thought Bowen's politics too conservative and pointed to his opposition to Hungarian independence as evidence of his "aristocratic" leanings. Free Soilers, for their part, were angered by Bowen's support for the Compromise of 1850.[21] A reconstituted board restored Bowen to his position two years later.

Of course, during the 1850s many academic careers were interrupted or even destroyed over the issue of slavery. In the South, faculty members did not have to attack slavery to lose their positions. Merely displaying insufficient zeal in defense of the region's peculiar institution was usually sufficient grounds for termination. In 1856, the University of North Carolina dismissed a talented chemistry professor, Benjamin Hedrick, for expressing sympathy for John Fremont's presidential bid. Though Hedrick was not a vocal supporter of the abolition of slavery, he did question the propriety of slavery's expansion into the western territories. This subversive view led students to burn him in effigy and generated hundreds of newspaper editorials demanding his dismissal. The university's regents were only too happy to fire the unfortunate chemist.[22]

After the Civil War, a number of college professors became victims of the economic conflicts of the period. College boards were generally controlled by leading members of the business community, and these individuals usually took quite seriously their duty to protect America's youth from radical ideas.[23] Professors or administrators who dared to express views, inside or outside the classroom, that deviated from the prevailing business orthodoxy, could almost always expect to be handed their walking papers.

Writing in 1901, Thomas Will, then-president of Kansas State Agricultural College, a bastion of populism, reviewed some of the major cases of the period in which corporate interests on college boards had forced the resignations of faculty members who dared to question business's power in American society.[24] According to Will, these included George Steele, president of Lawrence College, fired in 1892 for supporting free trade and "greenback" dollars; Docent Hourwich of the University of Chicago, dismissed in 1894 for participating in a Populist convention; the economist Edward Bemis, fired by the University of Chicago in 1895 for asserting antimonopoly views; James Smith, dismissed from Marietta College in 1897 for attacking monopolies; President E. Benjamin Andrews of Brown, forced to resign in 1897 for his alleged support of the free coinage of silver; the economist John R. Commons dismissed from Indiana in 1896 and Syracuse in 1899 for his economic views; President Henry Rogers from Northwestern, forced to resign in 1900 because of his criticism of imperialism; and, in the same year, the economist Edward Ross, dismissed from his post at Stanford for his antibusiness speeches and papers.

This list does not include a number of prominent academics— such as Richard Ely, director of the University of Wisconsin School of Economics, Politics, and History—who came under attack but were able to retain their positions. Ely was tried by a committee of the University of Wisconsin Board of Regents for allegedly supporting strikes and labor boycotts. Fortunately for Ely, the university's president was a personal friend, and his chief antagonist was unpopular among the other board members. Ely was exonerated and continued teaching at Wisconsin.

The popular press of the period devoted considerable attention to the Ely case but even more to the Ross case. Not only was Ross a nationally visible academic, but his chief accuser was none other than Jane Lathrop Stanford, prominent socialite and self-styled, "mother of the university." In 1900 Mrs. Stanford, widow of the university's founder was the sole member of the school's board of trustees. Mrs. Stanford basically believed herself to be the school's owner. The corporation's bylaws supported this notion by giving the board, in the person of Mrs. Stanford, absolute power to hire and fire the university's president. This being the case, Stanford's chief executive, David Starr Jordan, generally made haste to obey Mrs. Stanford's dictates.

The unfortunate Professor Ross had incurred Mrs. Stanford's displeasure with a number of his public lectures and writings. Ross advocated municipal ownership of utilities and an end to the Chinese immigration on which railroads—especially the Stanfords' Southern Pacific—depended for cheap labor. Ross had also written a tract favoring free silver that had been used by the Democratic Party during the 1896 presidential campaign. All this was too much for Mrs. Stanford to bear. "All that I have to say regarding Professor Ross, however brilliant and talented he may be, is that a man cannot entertain such rabid ideas without inculcating them in the minds of the students under his charge. There is a very deep and bitter feeling of indignation throughout the community . . . that Stanford University is lending itself to partisanship and even to dangerous socialism . . . Professor Ross cannot be trusted and he should go."[25]

In the wake of Ross's departure, a number of other Stanford professors tendered their resignations in support of their former colleague. To lessen the damage to the university's reputation, President Jordan required remaining faculty members to sign a statement averring that they had seen confidential correspondence and unpublished documents proving conclusively that Mrs. Stanford and the president had been correct in forcing Professor Ross's resignation. Those who refused to sign the statement were, themselves, asked to resign.[26]

At a small number of schools, mainly western state colleges, Democrats and Populists controlled the boards of regents. At these schools, conservative or probusiness members of the faculty were likely to find their jobs imperiled. For example, in 1896 after

Democrats and Populists took total control of the state of Kansas, the faculty of the Kansas State Agricultural College was purged of its conservative professors, and a group of Populists and reformers was brought in to replace them. Similarly, academic posts at Missouri and the University of Washington seem to have been reserved for professors with Populist leanings.[27] For the most part, however, institutions of higher education were controlled by boards composed of conservative members of the business community. These boards expected professors to express orthodox economic and social views and to avoid utterances that might be deemed to be critical of the established order. As Alton B. Parker, a conservative judge, one-time presidential candidate, and prominent defender of business interests put it, "When in opposition to the wishes or without the consent of the supporters of the institution [a professor] persists in a course that must tend to impress upon the tender minds of the young under his charge theories deemed to be false by a vast majority of the most intelligent minds of the age, it seems to me that he has abused his privilege of expression of opinion to such an extent as to justify the governing board in terminating his engagement."[28]

Emergence of the Tenure System

In the early years of the twentieth century, professors began to organize to defend their academic freedom and job security. The chief vehicle for this effort was the American Association of University Professors (AAUP), founded in 1915. The AAUP grew out of a series of discussions and planning sessions conducted by three already-established scholarly bodies, the American Economic Association (AEA), the American Sociological Society, and the American Political Science Association. These societies had been formed to advance scholarship in their respective fields. Increasingly, however, they had been drawn into turn-of-the-century academic freedom disputes. In 1900, for example, the AEA launched an investigation of the Ross case. Not surprisingly, neither Mrs. Stanford nor President Jordan was willing to speak to the investigative committee, and those members of the Stanford faculty who had not resigned in protest of Ross's dismissal now closed ranks behind the president.[29] Nevertheless, the AEI committee made national headlines when it reported that there was evidence to indicate that Ross had been fired for his political statements and, moreover, that official explanations to the contrary were false.

The three scholarly associations began collaborating in 1913, hoping to formulate general principles of academic freedom and job security for college professors. These meetings led to a series of conferences and, in 1915, to the formation of a national organization open to all faculty members—though not administrators—regardless of their school or field. No less prominent an academic personage than John Dewey was elected the new organization's president. Within a few months, 1,362 scholars, representing 75 institutions had joined. Over the next seven years, membership more than tripled.[30] Newly formed, the AAUP continued its investigations of cases in which professors alleged that they had been fired for their political beliefs.

At the same time, the AAUP worked to codify a set of general principles governing academic freedom and job security for college and university faculty. Within a few months of the AAUP's founding, a committee chaired by the economist Edwin Seligman of Columbia issued a declaration of principles, focusing on questions of academic freedom.[31] The report asserted that the professor's "independence of thought and utterance" whether in the laboratory, the classroom, or in a public setting, must be protected from the actions of trustees and administrators. To this end, the committee proposed the creation of what eventually became today's tenure system.

As outlined by the committee, after a period of academic apprenticeship—which might be as long as ten years, a faculty member would be entitled to permanent tenure at his school. Once tenured, a faculty member might only be dismissed for cause. The judge of the propriety of the cause would be not the school's administration nor the board of trustees but rather the professor's academic colleagues. If a school's president or board sought to dismiss a tenured professor, they would be required to bring formal charges, which would be heard by a faculty committee. College presidents would retain the power to dismiss untenured professors but would be required to give them one year's notice. The committee saw this proposal as a means of guaranteeing academic freedom. If colleges and universities adopted the AAUP standard, the Jane Stanfords and their ilk would no longer have the power to terminate professors simply because they did not care for their views. This, in turn, would mean that professors would be free to conduct research, write books and papers, and give speeches without fear of losing their jobs. Tenure, as the committee saw it, would serve as the guarantor of academic freedom. And, for this reason, tenure would serve not only the professor but the entire society, since a free faculty would more effectively advance human knowledge, provide better instruction to students, and promote public service.

It goes without saying that most professors supported the idea of the tenure system. Few outside the academic world however saw tenure, or even academic freedom, as particularly desirable. The *New York Times* railed against "organized dons," and defined academic freedom as, "the unalienable right of every college instructor to make a fool of himself and the college by . . . intemperate, sensational prattle about every subject under the sun, to his classes and the public, and still be kept on the payroll or be reft therefrom only by elaborate process."[32] Opposition to the AAUP's proposal was also voiced by college and university presidents. These presidents had formed an organization calling itself the Association of American Colleges (AAC) not long after professors established the AAUP. The AAC was the forerunner of today's Association of American Colleges and Universities (AAC&U). In response to the AAUP's 1915 report, the AAC issued a document of its own criticizing the AAUP's proposal.

According to the AAC, a professor whose views were inconsistent with those held by a school's board and president could undermine the "harmony" of the institution and should be expected to resign. As the AAC report put it, "The man called to the average college which believes in monogamy as essential to the upbuilding of student character can scarcely expect the college to submit to a long judicial process in tardily effecting his release if he openly states and on inquiry admits that he believes in free love."[33] And, as to the question of tenure, the AAC asked rhetorically, "Shall any association of university professors compel a corporation to retain in office for an indefinite time one who is manifestly unfit for that particular place . . .?"[34] The answer was an unequivocal no.

In truth, the idea of general tenure was somewhat uncommon in the American context. Tenure to be sure, was not an entirely new concept in 1915. Indeed, the idea of academic tenure dates to the twelfth century in Europe, where it was widely recognized.[35] During the Middle Ages, academic tenure sometimes included exemption from military service and from tax obligations. In the United States, during the eighteenth and nineteenth centuries, professors were typically appointed for indefinite periods with some presumption that they would keep their positions so long as they satisfied their employers. Schools, however, were under no legal obligation to continue a professor's employment. Professors were considered "at will" employees who could be fired for any reason, whatsoever.

During the late eighteenth and early nineteenth centuries, several professors actually brought suit in court challenging their terminations on the grounds that they possessed a "freehold" or property right in their positions and could not be deprived of this right without due process. These claims were almost always dismissed. In a 1790 case, for example, *The Reverend John Bracken v. The Visitors of William and Mary College*, the Virginia Court of Appeals supported the right of the college's board to terminate the contract of a professor who had argued that his job constituted a freehold.[36] The trustees were ably represented by a well-known attorney and future chief justice of the United States, John Marshall. Over the ensuing years, the courts of virtually all the states and most federal courts continually asserted the principle that professors were employees who could be terminated at the will of the board of trustees or regents.[37] The 8th Federal Circuit Court of Appeals even went so far as to say that the regents could remove any state college professor "whenever the interests of the college required," even if this might violate some provision of the professor's contract.[38] Hence, the idea of tenure, though not entirely novel, ran counter to long-established practice in American higher education.

For a number of years, the AAUP's statement of principle had little practical effect. Few, if any, schools were prepared to accept the notion of permanent tenure for their faculty members. Most college presidents and administrators viewed the AAUP report as an unwelcome intrusion by the professors on their own powers and prerogatives. Perhaps some of the AAUP's leaders thought the organization could function like a labor union, putting pressure on college administrations through protests and job actions. Few professors, though, were willing to countenance tactics they associated with the working class. Hence, the AAUP was compelled to rely chiefly on investigations, moral suasion, and philosophical argument. And, like Machiavelli's unarmed prophet, the organization made little headway in its efforts.

In 1922, though, the AAUP received help from an unexpected quarter. After having summarily rejected the AAUP's call for a system of professorial tenure in 1915, the AAC now declared that the work of the AAUP had been "significant and highly important," and endorsed virtually the entire AAUP report. In particular, the AAC accepted the idea that professors should be awarded indefinite tenure following a probationary period.[39]

What accounts for this rather drastic shift in position on the part of the organization representing college presidents? One part of the explanation has to do with growing demand for professorial services. Before the Civil War, a college degree was not viewed as being at all necessary for a successful career or for admission to polite society. Even physicians and attorneys learned their crafts by apprenticing themselves to established practitioners, while individuals aspiring to a career in business often saw four years of college as representing time when they might have been making money.[40] By the end of the nineteenth century, though, a college degree had come to be considered a necessary mark of social distinction and an essential entry ticket to the learned professions. Going to college became fashionable and prestigious, and the demand for places in America's colleges expanded exponentially.[41] Between 1870 and 1920, the number of students enrolled in degree-granting institutions increased by an astonishing 1043 percent! And, during the same period, nearly five hundred new colleges were established to take advantage of this incredible growth in student demand.[42]

Increases in enrollments and in the sheer number of colleges meant, in turn, increased demand for faculty. At the turn of the century, competitive bidding for professorial services became a common phenomenon as established schools sought to expand their faculties to meet student demand while new schools endeavored to lure professors away from existing institutions. The most accomplished or promising professors were often courted by many schools. Universities hoped that star faculty would attract students and impress donors. When, for example, the promising young physicist Ernest O. Lawrence felt unappreciated at Yale, he welcomed an offer from the University of California at Berkeley, which happily provided Lawrence with additional titles and resources. The physicist lived up to Berkeley's hopes by establishing his famous radiation laboratory and bringing a Nobel Prize to the California campus. University presidents were especially interested in professors whose research and publication would be attractive to potential students. Cornell's A.D. White wrote, "The numbers of Cornell's students will be determined largely by its reputation for research as well as for instruction."[43] To promote faculty research, White reduced professors' teaching hours and improved the school's laboratory and library facilities.

When it came to recruiting faculty, the most aggressive institution was the University of Chicago. Led by the ambitious president William Rainey Harper and backed by John D. Rockefeller's resources, Chicago worked diligently to lure faculty from other schools. In 1893, in what came to be called, "Harper's raid," Chicago lured away several Clark faculty members. These included three of Clark's leading professors, whom Harper enticed to move to Chicago by doubling their salaries and appointing them to chair new Chicago departments in biology, chemistry, and physics. Harper even offered Clark's president, G. Stanley Hall, a position in Chicago's psychology department. Hall refused the offer, telling Harper that his raid was, "an act of wreckage comparable to anything that the worst trust had ever attempted against its competitors."[44]

Against this backdrop, college presidents had every reason to treat faculty with new courtesy. Given the growth in demand for professorial services, an able professor would have little difficulty finding a position elsewhere. Hence, schools that treated their faculties with respect and assured them of continuing employment would have a competitive advantage over institutions that did not offer fair treatment and job security. One reason that Harvard enhanced its prominence during the early 1900s was President Charles Eliot's policy of respecting and protecting professors' right to assert their views. Often, this policy led to battles with the board, but Eliot believed that protecting academic freedom served the interests of the university by enhancing its ability to attract and retain top-notch faculty. According to one biographer, Eliot once encountered a young assistant professor who had opposed him at a faculty meeting but was then considering an offer from another university. "I suppose you understand that your opposition to my policy will not in the slightest degree interfere with your promotion here," Eliot is reported to have said.[45]

As they were forced to compete to recruit and retain faculty, college leaders began to see tenure as a mechanism through which faculty loyalty could be bolstered without the necessity of having to pay Chicago-level salaries. Tenure, moreover, would prevent trustees with political agendas from angering or even seeking the termination of valuable, if sometimes abrasive, faculty members like an Edward Ross or a Richard Ely, who might then move to a competing school. What had once seemed an unacceptable idea, now became a sound business practice.

Captains of Erudition

A growing demand for professorial services is only part of the reason that college presidents began to embrace the idea of professorial tenure. A second element of the explanation is a change in the composition of the AAC's leadership and in the character of college presidents, more generally. Between 1915 and 1922 the AAC and particularly its academic freedom committee saw substantial leadership turnover, bringing to the fore individuals whom the historian Lawrence Veysey has labeled the "new administrators" of the early twentieth century.[46] The "old administrators" had been recruited for their social connections, religious backgrounds, and willingness to do the bidding of the trustees or regents. Also, in the nineteenth century colleges and universities were small, and their business affairs could easily be directed by the trustees. College presidents were expected to look after the educational affairs of the institution and to leave matters of administration and governance to the board.

By the end of the nineteenth century, colleges and universities had grown substantially in size. The surge in student enrollments after the Civil War was, as we saw, accompanied by the establishment of a number of new schools. For the most part, however, new student numbers were accommodated by the expansion of established institutions. Between 1900 and 1919, college enrollments increased by more than 260,000 students, but only 64 new schools were established. Many established colleges grew from small schools enrolling a few hundred students to major enterprises.

Before the Civil War, no college in America enrolled more than a few hundred students and many only a few dozen. By 1910, seven schools boasted between four and five thousand students, and Columbia, the nation's largest college, enrolled 6,232 students in its various programs.[47] Since every school was highly dependent on tuition revenue, most were eager to continually increase their enrollments.

Increases in school size necessitated a change in the character of college leadership. Larger schools could not be administered effectively by a part-time board of trustees or regents and a president recruited for his piety or social standing. Such enterprises required presidents and other administrators with some managerial ability and the entrepreneurial aptitude needed to generate growth in enrollments and revenues. Writing in 1916, Thorstein Veblen likened the new generation of college presidents to business entrepreneurs and dubbed them "captains of erudition," to underscore their similarity to corporate chieftains.[48]

Among the most prominent of these educational captains were Cornell's Andrew Dickson White, Harvard's Charles W. Eliot, Michigan's James B. Angell, Columbia's Nicholas Murray Butler, and Chicago's William Rainey Harper. These educational leaders were concerned with organization, fund-raising, public relations, and institutional growth. Captains of erudition were ambitious, sometimes ruthless, and believed themselves to be in competition with other schools for academic prestige, student numbers, and revenues. To advance their institutions' interests, they recruited eminent professors, emphasized research, designed beautiful campuses, sought to build successful athletic teams, and turned to corporate public relations techniques to polish their schools' images. By the 1880s Harvard and Cornell were advertising for students in newspapers and through direct mail solicitations After its founding in 1892, the University of Chicago became notorious for its advertising and public relations efforts. One Chicago official said, "We must obey the first and last law of advertising—keep everlastingly at it."[49] Other schools followed suit. Penn established

a bureau of publicity with its own director and staff, and Columbia, borrowing a page from corporate public relations, sought to
plant its press releases, disguised as genuine news stories, in the
New York papers.[50]

The captains of erudition were also not eager to share power
with their boards. Like their corporate counterparts, educational
captains saw their boards as sources of advice, money, contacts,
and so forth, but they worked to keep to a minimum the trustees'
and—where they were still alive—the founders' involvement in
the actual operations of their schools. Like their corporate counterparts, university presidents sought to bring about what the
economic historian Adolf Berle characterized as a separation of
ownership from control.[51] The board might, in some sense, own
the university but, if the captain of erudition had his way, trustees
and even founders would have only minimal involvement in the
actual operations of the university.

Thus, at Vanderbilt, President Holland McTyeire discouraged
Cornelius Vanderbilt from even setting foot on the campus of the
school he founded. At Cornell, one trustee complained that President Andrew Dickson White "plans new professorships and costly
buildings and neither consults the faculty nor the trustees and
expects [the trustees] to pass his measures."[52] A similar lament
was voiced by a Harvard board member who said, "We hear [sec-
ond hand] President Eliot has decided to do this; or has determined to do that."[53] And, at Chicago, William Rainey Harper
sought constantly to maneuver John D. Rockefeller into providing
more money while generally relegating Rockefeller and the other
board members to the position of interested onlookers.

For captains of erudition, faculty could be useful allies in their
efforts to marginalize the trustees. To begin with, the faculty could
be mobilized in support of presidential plans and initiatives. So
long as the president and faculty presented a united front, the trustees were hard pressed to oppose them. Cornell's A. D. White, for
example, discovered early in his administration that proposals
seeming to emanate from the deliberations of faculty committees

tended to be more acceptable to the trustees than ideas deemed to belong exclusively to the president.[54] Accordingly, White convened many meetings of the faculty, where he had little trouble persuading the assembled professors to adopt his plans as their own. "It may seem that by this system [of faculty consultation] that the president is stripped of power," White wrote, "but I have always found myself easily able to retain all desirable influence under it."[55]

Second, an alliance with the faculty could enhance the president's reach and power within the university by providing an administrative infrastructure that made it possible for a school to grow in size. In the absence of the bureaucratic apparatus that has become all too common today, presidents depended on members of the faculty for administrative support. Faculty managed every aspect of college and university life. Such matters as student recruitment, admissions, curricular planning, registration, and counseling were mainly faculty responsibilities. Without faculty support, the president could rule but not govern. On almost every campus, a small number of senior faculty members served as the president's right arms. At Chicago, for example, most senior faculty members, including such luminaries as John Dewey, Albion Small, and James H. Breasted, served as part-time administrators.[56] Small, a well-known sociology professor was President Harper's second-in-command, often traveling on the president's behalf to meet with donors, prospective students, and other university constituencies. In a similar vein, William C. Russel served as A. D. White's lieutenant and often took his place during White's frequent absences from the Cornell campus.

Larger universities, at the end of the nineteenth century, began to organize themselves into academic departments. Gradually, the department chairs became important figures in the management of school affairs. Presidents began to look to the chairs to play lead roles in the realm of appointments and promotions as well as curriculum and research priorities.[57] Initially, department chairs were appointed by university presidents. Appointed chairs, however, seemed to produce considerable faculty grumbling.

Gradually, after 1900, chairs came to be selected or at least nominated by the members of their departments and to see themselves as representatives of the faculty in its dealings with the president and trustees. For decades to come, the departments would be universities' most important academic units, and their chairs and senior faculty would function as de facto university administrators, developing considerable influence over academic decision making, including curriculum planning and faculty appointments. Presidents who wanted their schools to grow were willing to cede or at least share these powers with the professors.

To the captains of erudition, and to their lieutenants, the idea of a tenure system for faculty made sense. The promise of tenure facilitated the recruitment and retention of star faculty. Tenure, moreover, could protect valuable professors and the university's administrative structure from the whims of trustees, regents, state legislators, and others who might seek to intervene in a school's affairs. In addition, the university's new administrative cadre itself consisted of professors who had every reason to seek the protection of tenure for themselves. A. D. White and other Cornell administrators, for example, began to see the potential merits of tenure when the board, while White was in Europe, forced the resignation of White's lieutenant, William Russel, thereby threatening to undermine the administrative mechanisms White had created.[58] The tenure system gradually came to be viewed by the captains and lieutenants of erudition as an instrument for shielding their universities—and themselves—from external intervention. And, as the new generation of university presidents rose to power, support for the AAUP's tenure proposals grew.

The experience of World War I underlined the danger that colleges could face if their boards were in a position to dismiss faculty members whose ideas they found inappropriate. An upsurge in jingoism, fanned by the Wilson administration, prompted boards at many universities to seek the dismissal of professors deemed to be insufficiently patriotic. During the course of the war, professors were attacked by trustees, state legislatures, and newspaper editorial writers for allegedly expressing pro-German or antiwar views. Three professors at the University of Nebraska were dismissed when an investigation revealed that one believed in internationalism, one had failed to cooperate with the sale of liberty bonds, and the third had criticized the chauvinism of some of his colleagues.[59] A professor at the University of Virginia was fired for expressing good will toward the German people, and a professor at the University of Minnesota lost his job for asserting that the Hohenzollern monarchy should be kept in place after Germany's defeat.

To some university administrators, these attacks on academic freedom represented object lessons in the need to protect the university from external assault by the forces of ignorance. At Harvard, for example, the administration refused to dismiss Hugo Munsterberg, an openly pro-German professor, despite pressure from the press and from alumni.[60] Other administrators, however, used the patriotic frenzy sweeping the country as an opportunity to settle scores and rid themselves of troublesome faculty members. One of the most egregious cases of this sort took place at Columbia. Columbia's trustees dismissed Professor J. McKeen Cattell, one of the nation's leading psychologists, after he sent a letter to several members of Congress urging them to oppose a pending bill authorizing the use of American conscripts on European battlefields.[61] One of the recipients of the letter publicly accused Cattell of "sowing the seeds of sedition and treason," and the board of trustees promptly fired Cattell on the basis of his alleged disloyalty. Rather than defend Cattell, Columbia's president, Nicholas Murray Butler joined his accusers. Butler detested Cattell, who had often clashed with the president, and was happy to see him ousted from the university. Following Cattell's dismissal, Columbia's board fired several other professors. Charles Beard, one of America's best-known historians, resigned in protest. Butler's conduct sullied Columbia's reputation and, for a time, hurt the university's ability to compete with other leading schools for star faculty.

After the war, the AAC accepted the AAUP statement of principles, agreeing in particular that member schools should work toward the creation of tenure systems. The AAC's Academic Freedom Commission called the work of the AAUP "significant and highly important" and recommended that, with some slight modifications, it be adopted by member schools. By 1940, the AAC and AAUP had reached full agreement on a set of principles governing academic freedom and tenure. The joint declaration of principles stated that after the expiration of a probationary period of not more than seven years, professors should have permanent tenure. Once tenured, a professor might be dismissed only for cause or because of extraordinary financial exigency. "Cause" was to be judged not by the university administration, but by the faculty itself. University administrators would no longer have the power to terminate faculty members with whom they disagreed. In a joint statement, the AAC and AAUP declared that the mission of the university depended on "the free search for truth and its free exposition."[62] Tenure was declared to be the necessary means to this end, protecting freedom in research and publication, freedom in the classroom and free from institutional censorship or discipline when speaking or writing outside the university as a citizen.

This 1940 statement of principles—in effect a contract between professors and administrators to extrude trustees and legislators from university decision making—is the basis for most academic tenure systems today. The 1940 principles were not adopted instantly by America's colleges and universities. Most boards of trustees were not eager to accept the idea of faculty tenure. Indeed, in 1940, the same year that the AAC and AAUP were promulgating their joint statement, boards at a number of schools were endeavoring to dismiss faculty members suspected of having leftist sympathies.[63] Interrupted by the war, the anti-Communist crusade on campus continued into the 1950s as the House Un-American Activities Committee, the McCarthy committee, and their various state counterparts sought to sniff out subversives hiding in college libraries and laboratories.

During the 1950s, though, economic pressures compelled most college and university boards to set aside their concerns and offer tenure as a perquisite of professorial employment.[64] The pressure came in the form of a postwar upsurge in student registrations. The GI Bill made higher education funding available to millions of World War II and Korean War veterans, and many sought to take advantage of the opportunity by enrolling in postsecondary programs. Between 1939 and 1959, college enrollments in the United States increased approximately 257 percent. This surge in enrollments created enormous demand for faculty in every field. In fact, many professors of that era found themselves teaching subjects with which they had little familiarity because their college needed someone—anyone—with a PhD to meet student demand. I recall one distinguished professor of constitutional law at Princeton who, for a time, taught freshman economics because no one else was available. When he told the dean that he really did not know much about economics, that worthy official replied, "That's why we have a library." Facing an enormous shortage of faculty, colleges were willing to pay more and to offer the promise of tenure to attract and retain professors. By the 1970s, about 80 percent of full-time faculty at America's colleges and universities held tenured or tenure-track positions.[65]

Tenure does not guarantee absolute job security, and its protection seems to be diminishing. Tenured faculty may be dismissed if a university can document financial exigency or if their department or academic unit is dissolved. During the 2009–10 recession, a number of schools moved to eliminate programs and dismiss tenured faculty. Several schools declared "financial exigency," usually defined as a state so dire that it threatens the survival of the institution, which gives administrators the contractual right to close departments and terminate tenured professors. This is what happened at Southern Mississippi in 2009, when the economics and technical education programs were closed and professors fired.[66] A number of other schools summarily cut programs and dismissed tenured faculty citing financial pressures but refraining from formally declaring a state of financial exigency. Administrators averred that a formal declaration of financial exigency would hurt their schools' bond and credit ratings and frighten potential applicants. In the perilous financial climate of the times, administrators claimed they must have the flexibility to terminate tenured faculty without declaring exigency. Thus, Florida State University terminated twenty-one tenured faculty without declaring financial exigency, Clark Atlanta University similarly eliminated the positions of twenty tenured professors, and the university systems of Idaho and Georgia changed their rules to allow tenured faculty members to be fired without a declaration of financial exigency.[67] Though these cases have led to litigation and few other schools have thus far followed suit, any weakening of the financial exigency rule represents a threat to the very idea of tenure. A spokesperson for the Idaho Board of Education declared that in tough financial times, "You've got to give the presidents all the tools possible to manage."[68] One of these essential tools seems to be the summary elimination of tenure.

Tenured faculty may also be dismissed for cause if appropriate procedures are followed. About 50 to 75 tenured faculty are fired every year for such offenses as moral turpitude, embezzlement of research funds, refusing to meet classes, plagiarism, and falsification of academic credentials. In some instances, the formal charges mask what is, at bottom, an effort to fire a professor with politically unpopular views. For example, in 2005, Ward Churchill was nominally terminated by the University of Colorado because he was found guilty of plagiarism and falsifying his academic credentials. The investigation documenting these charges, however, was launched only when Churchill's controversial statements about the 9-11 terrorist attacks against the United States generated a firestorm of negative publicity. In 2009, a jury awarded Churchill $1 in damages, apparently agreeing that his termination violated Churchill's constitutional rights but, at the same time, wishing to avoid any expression of sympathy for the radical professor.

Tenure and Academic Freedom

The concept of academic tenure is often criticized. Tenure is some-times said to provide job security for indolent and incompetent professors who spend their afternoons sipping sherry at the faculty club. College administrators frequently claim that faculty tenure prevents them from more effectively adapting the curriculum to changes in the economy and patterns of student demand.[69] No doubt, there is some truth to these criticisms. There are lazy and incompetent tenured professors who drone through the same lectures year after year after year. Yet, tenure, especially at research universities, is difficult to achieve. Promotion to tenure requires a substantial record of research and publication as well as evidence of an ongoing commitment to research. Tenure also requires evidence of teaching ability and a willingness to devote time to graduate and undergraduate students. Often, tenure cases involve heated struggles among various faculty factions over the quality of a professor's work. Mistakes are made in the process. Generally, however, those who achieve tenure are excellent, or at least promising, scholars and teachers whose commitment to their work does not end when they acquire job security.

Indeed, in virtually every field of inquiry, it is members of the tenured faculty at research universities who produce the books, papers, reports, inventions, and studies that drive the American economy and make higher education one of the nation's leading export industries. I do not believe that millions of foreign students come to America for the opportunity to work with our nation's famous deanlets and deanlings, but I could be wrong. For most professors, tenure is not a license to retire. It is, instead, an opportunity to work on intellectually exciting projects without the pressure to abandon important lines of inquiry simply because no immediate conclusion or pecuniary return is in sight. And, the charge that tenured faculty are hidebound and unwilling to adapt their teaching and research to the emergence of new areas of pedagogy and inquiry seems to miss a very important point. New fields "emerge" precisely because tenured or tenure-track professors create them. As far as I know, university administrators have pioneered very few new academic fields—unless event planning counts.

In point of fact, tenure is the chief guarantor of the intellectual freedom that makes it possible for faculty members to pursue new ideas and to teach concepts in the sciences and humanities that fly in the face of conventionally accepted wisdom. Put simply, without tenure there is no academic freedom. Where the faculty lacks the protection of tenure it is the administrators who are free to interfere in the classroom and in the laboratory—and they do so with alacrity. Where they can, administrators will interfere with even the most meritorious academic research, publication, and communication if their results challenge the interests of important donors and constituencies or threaten administrators' own interests. Two cases arising in recent years at the University of Toronto, a distinguished research university, generated a great deal of commentary and are well worth noting as examples. In one case, Dr. Nancy Olivieri, a well-known academic physician was fired from her post at the Toronto-affiliated Hospital for Sick Children after she raised questions, based on her clinical research, about the safety of a drug marketed by the Apotex Pharmaceutical Co., a major source of funding for the university and the hospital. To justify the dismissal, university administrators apparently spread rumors that Olivieri was incompetent, stole research funds, and slept with colleagues.[70] After several years, an independent inquiry found that Olivieri's actions had been completely warranted by her ethical duties as a physician.

A second case involving administrators at the University of Toronto concerned Dr. David Healy, an academic psychiatrist who had been hired to head the university's Centre for Addiction and Mental Health (CAMH). Shortly before Healy arrived on the campus from his university appointment in Wales, university administrators learned that Healy had published research critical of the drug Prozac, marketed by Eli Lilly & Co., one of the school's important corporate funders. Healy was one of the first researchers to suggest that Prozac might be associated with an increased risk of patient suicide, a finding that subsequent research has supported. University administrators, however, were not concerned with whether Healy's scholarship was good or bad. Their concern was the reaction of Eli Lilly & Co. In an e-mail to Healy "unhiring" him, the university said, "While you are held in high regard as a scholar . . . we do not feel your approach is compatible with the goals for development of the academic and clinical resource that we have."[71] In other words, the drug company might cut off funding for the school. As in the Olivieri case, administrators subsequently spread rumors about Healy, claiming he was a bad clinician, a racist, and a Scientologist.

Administrative interference is, of course, not limited to research. Where they can, administrators will interfere in the classroom, as well. A typical case is that of Steven Aird, a biology professor at Norfolk State University in Virginia. Aird was denied tenure and dismissed despite outstanding performance evaluations and support from many students because campus administrators thought he had embarrassed them and the college by failing too many students. Contrary to college policy, which apparently called for passing students regardless of performance, Aird had the temerity to fail students who did not attend classes. The dean who dismissed Aird wrote that students' failure to succeed was the fault of the professor.[72] In other words, with a better grade, these students would have "succeeded." Indeed, they would have overcome the obstacle of never having attended class. As we have noted before, in the administrative realm, words and actions are often confused.

Administrators are especially likely to interfere in the classroom if they are concerned that the views of donors and important college constituencies are not being treated with proper respect. In some instances, administrators will even organize classes or alter the content of existing courses to please important interests. One recent case involved Hunter College, part of the City University of New York. Faculty there discovered that the school's

administrators had worked with the International Anticounter-
feiting Coalition (IACC), a consortium of companies concerned
with the spread of low-cost knockoffs of their products, to create a
course that would function as part of the IACC's ongoing publicity
campaign. The mission of the "course" was the creation of an
IACC-sponsored Web site and the development of an advertising
campaign aimed at college-age students. The administration
"drafted" an untenured faculty member to lead the class. Why
were Hunter administrators so interested in helping the IACC? It
seems that the CEO of one of the IACC member companies was a
Hunter alumnus and major donor.[73]

And, where they can, administrators will work diligently to sup-
press faculty criticism. One particularly amusing example recently
came to light at the State University of New York at Fredonia.
Stephen Kershnar, a philosophy professor, had been turned down
for promotion by the college's president, Dennis Hefner. President
Hefner conceded that Kershnar's teaching and publication record
were adequate for promotion. However, Hefner objected to Kershnar's public criticisms of college policies in ways that he said
"impugned" the school's reputation. Subsequently, Hefner offered
to promote Kershnar if he refrained from criticizing the college for
one year. A spokesperson for the school said it was "absolutely"
incorrect to characterize the president's offer as an attempt to
limit dissent.[74] Or, take the experience of the "Phantom Professor," the name used by a blogger who wrote about students' use of
illegal drugs, crime on campus, student stress, the campus social
hierarchy, and administrative shortcomings at Southern Methodist University. University officials decided that the anonymous
blogger was Elaine Liner, a well-regarded adjunct writing instructor on the Dallas campus. What did campus administrators do
when faced with a bit of criticism? It almost goes without saying
that they fired the suspected phantom.[75]

Perhaps we should be relieved that the Phantom only lost her
job. At the Autonomous University of Sinaloa in Mexico, a professor, Florencio Posadas Segura, who recently criticized his rector in

a campus radio broadcast, was told that university authorities had ordered him banned from the station. Segura was also told, "Be careful what you say because a car could run you over."[76]

The End of Tenure

It is because there is no academic freedom without tenure that ongoing trends in higher education are so disturbing. As we noted above, nearly 70 percent of those currently teaching in America's colleges and universities are neither tenured nor in the tenure track. Some of these are full-time faculty on year-to-year contracts. The majority are so-called adjunct or "contingent" faculty. These are individuals hired and paid on a course-by-course basis.[77] At some schools, adjuncts far outnumber regular faculty. If present trends continue, tenure will either disappear or continue to exist only at a small number of elite schools. Indeed, even at the nation's top research universities tenure is under attack.

The tenure system arose out of an alliance between top administrators and faculty. Both saw advantages in protecting the faculty and the administrative structure of the university from interference on the part of trustees and, in some instances, college founders. Faculty tenure worked well for both groups, providing job security for faculty and helping university presidents to recruit faculty, to create a reliable administrative apparatus, and to marginalize their trustees, regents, and intrusive benefactors. In recent years, though, university administrators have seen less reason to maintain their alliance with the faculty. Three developments have undermined the administrator-faculty alliance of the early twentieth century.

First, the alliance between administrators and faculty members was too successful in relegating boards to a marginal position in the university governance structure. At most universities, boards choose the president. Once they have accomplished this task, though, few boards have any expectation of direct involvement in university governance.[78] Boards lack expertise and lack time and, over a period of years, presidents will generally secure the appointment of board members with whom they can work, i.e., who will not challenge them. Occasionally, an activist board chair may exert some influence in campus affairs. For the most part, though, contemporary trustees are content to attend regular meetings at which university officials make well-orchestrated presentations designed to demonstrate the wisdom, diligence, and dedication of the school's leaders. Few trustees seem inclined to peer behind the curtain. As a result, administrators no longer have much need of the faculty as a counterweight to the trustees.

Second, the alliance between administrators and faculty once helped provide college presidents with an administrative structure through which to govern their institutions. As we saw above, presidents relied on faculty to organize and staff every university function from the academic departments through admissions and public relations. Today, of course, administrative tasks have been turned over to an enormous and growing army of deans, deanlets, and staffers. These functionaries, whose numbers have shown a triple digit increase in recent years are much more pliable than faculty administrators. They cheerfully undertake whatever tasks are assigned to them by senior administrators and, often, invent new tasks whose main function seems to be to bolster administrative employment. The "Director of Student Liasons" we encountered in chapter 1 might be an example. With more than 750,000 administrators and other professionals hard at work meeting and retreating on the nation's campuses, senior managers have no need of the faculty's administrative services and push them out of the way whenever possible.

Finally, except at the most elite academic levels, the promise of tenure is hardly needed these days to recruit professors. Though the oversupply varies from field to field, in virtually every academic field, graduate programs have, for years, produced many more PhDs than could be absorbed by the nation's colleges and universities. At the present time, about 45,000 PhD degrees are awarded every year, and about 15 percent of each year's degree recipients can expect to be unable to find jobs in their field. The situation is worst in the humanities and social sciences, but even in the sciences too many new PhDs are applying for too few positions.[79]

The reasons for this overproduction are complex. They include myopic behavior on the part of the professoriate, the end of mandatory retirement, and the effects of well-intentioned but misguided government financial aid policies. Whatever the causes, though, the consequence is the existence of a large and ever-growing "reserve army" of unemployed or marginally employed PhDs who are available to staff courses in almost every conceivable field for far less than the minimum wage. Bright, energetic, and well-trained young PhDs often have no choice but to teach courses for salaries that can range from a top of perhaps $6,500 per course to as little as $1,800 per course with no health insurance or pension benefits. Some adjuncts, known as "freeway flyers," simultaneously teach courses at several different schools, hoping to make ends meet. Universities have, so far, successfully resisted efforts by contingent faculty to improve their salaries and working conditions.[80]

University administrators, more and more, turn to this growing pool of adjuncts to staff courses. Adjuncts are inexpensive, can be hired as needed—often at the last minute—and can be discarded at the end of the term if their courses no longer comport with administrative plans. Adjuncts do not require laboratories, offices, telephones, computers, or support services. Unlike the annoying tenured faculty, adjuncts do not endeavor to play any role, whatsoever, in university governance. And, adjuncts possess no claims to academic freedom. If administrators are even the least bit annoyed by the views expressed by an adjunct, whether inside or outside the classroom, they simply refrain from hiring that individual again. Like the "Phantom Professor," adjuncts who are not rehired disappear from the university without a trace.

This shift to contingent faculty, by the way, has not led to lower tuition costs for students and parents. Instead, the use of less expensive faculty has allowed universities to employ more administrators and to pay them more. The same schools that pay adjuncts $2500 per course with no benefits, pay six-figure salaries—even as much as $1 million or more—to their presidents and six-figure salaries to many administrators as well. I would submit to financially hard-pressed parents that they receive far more value from the impoverished adjuncts who teach their children than from the well-heeled presidents who nominally manage the schools their children attend. The $2500 adjunct prepares lectures, demonstrations, and discussions. She meets with students and corrects papers and exams. She may offer advice and counseling to students. As to the million-dollar presidents, when not meeting, retreating, looking for better jobs, or perfecting their strategic plans, some of these worthies actually do very little. One president whom I know found time to earn a commercial pilot's license and to become quite proficient at Mandarin Chinese. These are very impressive accomplishments, indeed, but also reveal that he had far too much spare time. Generally speaking, a million-dollar president could be kidnapped by space aliens and it would be weeks or even months before his or her absence from campus was noticed. Indeed, if the same space aliens also took all the well-paid deanlets and deanlings, their absence would also have little effect on the university. It would simply be assumed that they were all away on retreat. The disappearance of the contingent faculty, on the other hand, would have a real impact on students' lives.

Many community colleges already rely almost exclusively on adjuncts with a very small core of full-time faculty. Since adjuncts are hardly in a position to become involved in research and publication, research universities will never be able to fully rely on contingent faculty to staff their courses. But, even research universities are searching for ways to delimit or eliminate tenure in favor of employment contracts that would make full-time faculty more fully subject to administrative control. In one well-known case, a new provost at the University of Minnesota, William Brody, persuaded the board of regents to "reengineer" the school along a

corporate model that would allow administrators to dismiss tenured faculty without peer review.[81] After a year-long battle, Brody
and the chairman of the board both resigned and the tenure system remained intact.

No one would argue that tenure systems produce perfect results.
Professors who do not merit tenure are sometimes promoted.
Promising professors receive tenure and fail to live up to the potential they seemed to manifest. Nevertheless, without tenure there
is no academic freedom. And, without academic freedom, as Chief
Justice Warren intimated, universities would be managed by their
deanlets and the intellectual life of the nation would suffer. This
is, unfortunately, the direction in which American academic life
seems to be moving. The faculty, as Stanley Aronowitz has noted,
is experiencing a "long winter of retreat."[82] The event planners
and their ilk are gradually gaining control over the physicists.

6

Research and Teaching at the All-Administrative University

THE ONGOING TRANSFER of power from professors to administrators has important implications for the curricula and research agendas of America's colleges and universities. On the surface, faculty members and administrators seem to share a general understanding of the university and its place in American society. If asked to characterize the "mission" of the university, members of both groups will usually agree with the broad idea that the university is an institution that produces and disseminates knowledge through its teaching, research, public outreach, and other programs.

This surface similarity of professorial and administrative perspectives, however, is deceptive. To members of the faculty, the university exists mainly to promote their own research and teaching endeavors. While professors may be quite fond of their schools, for most, scholarship is the purpose of academic life, and the university primarily serves as a useful instrument to promote that purpose. Many professors are driven by love of teaching and the process of discovery. Others crave the adulation of students or the scholarly fame that can result from important discoveries and publications. But whatever their underlying motivations, most professors view scholarship and teaching as ends and the university as an institutional means or instrument through which to achieve those ends.

For administrators, on the other hand, it is the faculty's research and teaching enterprise that is the means and not the end. Some administrators, to be sure, mainly those who plan to return to scholarship and teaching, may put academic matters first. Most administrators, though, tend to manifest a perspective similar to that affected by business managers or owners. They view the university as the equivalent of a firm manufacturing goods and providing services whose main products happen to be various forms of knowledge rather than automobiles, computers, or widgets.[1] This perspective was famously articulated by the late president of the University of California, Clark Kerr, when he characterized higher education as the "knowledge industry," and suggested that universities should focus on producing forms of knowledge likely to be useful in the marketplace.[2] To the managers of a firm in the knowledge industry, or "knowledge factory," in Stanley Aronowitz's phrase, the manufacture of one or another product or service is not an end in and of itself but is, instead, evaluated on the basis of its contribution to the overall financial well-being of the enterprise.[3]

From an administrative perspective, generally speaking, forms of knowledge that cannot profitably be sold to customers—be they students, corporations, the government, or private donors— should be scrapped in favor of investments in more financially promising areas of inquiry. Kerr advocated shifting resources away from the humanities to forms of applied scientific research that would be of interest to federal agencies and private firms in the then-rapidly-expanding high technology sector. Many schools today chase biotechnology dollars and seek contracts with pharmaceutical companies.

Indeed, today's captains of erudition sometimes even find it expedient to move at least some of their investment funds away from the academic realm, altogether, toward potentially more lucrative uses of capital such as real estate, athletic facilities, luxurious dormitories, equities, expansion of the campus shopping mall, and even the construction of parking ramps. After all, if the university is simply another purveyor of goods and services why stop at intellectual products. And, of course, many schools *have* invested heavily in lovely dormitories, dining facilities, and garages while closing language and philosophy departments for budgetary reasons. It is a wonder that college administrators do not simply sell degrees without requiring the students to attend school. Think of the efficiencies. The university or college would save the cost of classrooms, laboratories, and professors. These savings could be turned into administrative salaries. Come to think of it, some of the new online proprietary universities approach this model, while administrators at traditional schools must be content with selling places to wealthy, albeit poorly prepared customers.[4]

Given a choice, some administrators actually prefer to invest in auditoriums and shopping malls rather than work to improve the quality of their university's academic endeavors. Construction projects can be very visible symbols of administrative achievement and can be completed within a relatively short time frame, allowing immediate credit-claiming at board meetings and job interviews. Investments in academic departments and programs, on the other hand, can take years to produce results—so many years that any resulting credit is likely to be claimed by some future group of managers.

The unfortunate fact of the matter is that with the exception of a dwindling group of faculty part-timers and a stalwart band of old hands who do much of the real managerial work of the university, today's senior administrators have no more institutional constancy or loyalty than the mercenary managers of other enterprises. They flit from school to school as they battle to climb the managerial ladder and, accordingly, have short time horizons at any given institution.

Knowing that their ability to move onward and upward will, in the short term, not be much affected by the work done in their current schools' libraries, classrooms, or even its laboratories, many administrators do little more than give lip service to the long-term investments usually needed to have a real impact on the quality of these academic undertakings. In view of their fanatical devotion to the strategic planning process, it seems ironic that administrators have little actual incentive to think in the long term. This is another reason why so many strategic plans, as we observed in chapter 2, are left to gather dust in file cabinets soon after the fanfare surrounding their introduction has subsided.

Teaching

The first dimension along which the all-administrative university differs from its faculty-directed counterpart is pedagogy. From the professorial perspective, the university exists to promote teaching by providing faculty members with classrooms, laboratories, libraries, computers, and other instructional resources. From the administrative perspective, however, the purpose of teaching is to bring fees-paying customers (sometimes known as students) into its dormitories and classrooms. Administrators think teaching serves the university, not the converse.

Their conception of teaching as a means rather than an end tends, in turn, to give administrators what might be called a demand-side view of the curriculum. To put it simply, administrators believe that a college curriculum should be heavily influenced, if not completely governed, by the interests and preferences of students, parents, and others who pay the bills. In the 1960s, radical students argued in favor of the elimination of many existing requirements, and administrators at such schools as Brown could find little reason not to accommodate them. In recent years, academic "customers" mainly have been concerned with the future economic benefits likely to accrue from their hefty investment of tuition dollars and time. Accordingly, the administration's demand-side perspective has gradually reoriented the curriculum toward the acquisition of what are currently thought to be economically relevant skills. For this reason, education in today's all-administrative university, consists mainly of employment or career preparation with a smattering of identity courses and, at the larger and better-established institutions, a hefty dollop of clubs, sports, and other activities deemed likely to attract more customers.

University administrators usually claim that sports and the like serve as a useful form of preparation for adult life. Most students, however, watch rather than participate in college sports, so this claim seems rather fatuous. It is difficult to understand why affording students an opportunity to observe gangs of large dummies (aka "scholar athletes") beat one another to a pulp on the football field, should be understood as anything more than an administrative effort to attract more current customers and alumni interest with the promise of spectacle and mayhem.

Viewing teaching as an end more than a means, on the other hand, usually leads the faculty to take what might be called a supply-side view of the curriculum. That is, professors are more concerned with teaching what they, themselves, deem to be important than simply complying with the preferences of students and other campus constituencies. This perspective is sometimes criticized as indicative of the faculty's self-indulgence. Yet, professors quite reasonably believe that they are better qualified than students to decide what the latter should learn. Most students come to college with immature and uninformed preferences, or unconsciously echoing some parental agenda, and require considerable experience, exposure to a variety of disciplines, and a good deal of faculty guidance before they are sufficiently aware of the intellectual and even economic possibilities open to them. Few students actually arrive on campus with preferences that should be taken seriously. I have, for example, spoken to many students who told me they wanted to attend law school, but clearly had no idea what a legal career entailed. And, I will never forget the student who said she hoped to become an options trader but then recoiled in dismay when she discovered that options traders were, for the most part, only interested in making money. She had found the mental math and frenetic activity of the trading floor interesting but had not quite discerned the underlying purpose of the enterprise.

One expression of the faculty's supply-side perspective is the support that many professors manifest for the concept of a liberal arts education for undergraduates. Every college and university, of course, has its own notion of the precise way in which the liberal arts should be taught. Generally speaking, though, these include writing requirements as well as exposure to introductory course work in mathematics, science, the humanities, the social sciences, and languages—sometimes organized as a general education or core curriculum—followed by some degree of specialization in "major" and "minor" fields. These major and minor subjects usually include "distribution requirements" that direct students to courses in cognate disciplines deemed likely to expand their intellectual horizons. Over the past two decades most schools, as we shall see below, have reduced or "watered down" their core liberal arts requirements.[5] Nevertheless, these remain important elements of the curriculum—where the faculty has anything to say about it.

Columbia University, for example, requires all students to complete its "Core Curriculum," which according to Columbia's catalog is designed to promote "examination of serious ideas in the context of small and intensive classes."[6] The centerpiece of the core is a two-semester course called Contemporary Civilization in the West, which examines the history of moral and political thought from the ancient Greeks to the present. Students must also take two semesters of Masterpieces of European Literature and Philosophy (known as Lit Hum), a term of art, a term of music, a term of writing, courses in science, a foreign language, and two terms of global studies for a total of sixteen required general education courses plus two terms of physical education. And, of course, every student must select a major field, which will mandate its own set of introductory and more advanced required classes, electives, and distribution requirements.

The University of Chicago, famous for its general education requirements, is equally insistent that students receive a broad liberal arts education, requiring fifteen courses plus demonstrated competence in a foreign language. During their first and second years, Chicago undergraduates complete a variety of general education courses chosen from a long list of approved classes. These include a three-class humanities sequence, a two-class civilization studies sequence, and one course in the dramatic, musical, or visual arts. Students must select six classes in the physical sciences, biological sciences, and mathematics. A three-course social science sequence must be chosen from among several possibilities. In addition to fulfilling these requirements, of course, students must select and complete the mandated classes in one of several major fields of study. And, last but not least, students are required to successfully complete a year of physical education by engaging in sports, exercise, or dance programs. It is worth contrasting Chicago's requirement that students actually take part in an athletic activity with the practice at many schools of encouraging students to watch sports. The University of Chicago is hardly noted for its intercollegiate sports prowess, but as part of their liberal education, nerdy Chicago undergraduates actually learn to play a sport while their counterparts at some of the nation's premier athletic powers merely learn to sit in the stands and eat junk food.

In a similar vein, Harvard's "core program" requires undergraduates to complete course work in foreign cultures, historical study, literature and arts, moral reasoning, quantitative reasoning, science, and social analysis. Students must devote about a year of their time at Harvard to completion of these core requirements. The Harvard catalog asserts that this effort is necessary to ensure that every student graduating with a Harvard degree will be broadly educated as well as trained in a particular academic specialty.

The nation's most comprehensive and uncompromising liberal arts curriculum is to be found at St. John's, a liberal arts college with campuses in Annapolis, Maryland, and Santa Fe, New

Mexico. Among other requirements, St. John's students must complete four years of seminars in which they read and discuss the works of the world's "great thinkers" from ancient times through the modern period; three years of classroom and laboratory work in the sciences; four years of mathematics tutorials; four years of language tutorials; and a year of music. The college catalog declares that St. John's students, "cultivate habits of mind that will last a lifetime: a deepened capacity for reflective thought, an appreciation of the persisting questions of human existence, an abiding love of serious conversation, and a lasting love of inquiry."[7]

Every school, of course, claims that its particular version of the core curriculum or general education requirements is superior to those offered by competing colleges. Chicago, for instance, in a bow to its "great books" tradition, extols the virtues of the humanities classes in which students learn "how to interpret literary, philosophical, and historical texts in depth; how to identify significant intellectual problems posed by those texts; and how to discuss and write about them perceptively and persuasively."[8] Harvard, on the other hand, in a not very veiled swipe at Chicago and Columbia, avers that its core most certainly does not define intellectual breadth as merely, "the mastery of a set of Great Books."[9] Instead, declares Harvard's catalog, its core "introduces students to the major approaches to knowledge" in fields the faculty deems "indispensable."

Each school is certainly entitled to prefer its own version of a liberal arts education but, in truth, the similarities among these programs are more obvious than the differences. Each school's particular formula reflects the results of conversations, disputes, and compromises on its own campus. Nevertheless, each attempts to introduce students to a variety of different disciplines, intellectual issues, and analytical perspectives. Columbia, Harvard, St. John's, and Chicago students, to use the examples cited above, will graduate with some basic understanding of the major issues in the sciences, social sciences, and humanities. While many will not be outstanding writers, all will have the capacity to express themselves with reasonable clarity. Many will have learned the rudiments of a foreign language and some will, as a result, have achieved a better understanding of another culture. Most students will have acquired the capacity to read a text or listen to an argument or presentation with a critical ear. As the Harvard catalog puts it, students will have been taught to think critically about moral and ethical problems and even to examine their own preconceptions and assumptions with a critical eye.

Some critics regard the goals of a liberal arts education as antiquated relics of an earlier time. As one prominent higher education accreditation official and former college administrator recently put it, though once seen as a route to "personal growth and development," higher education today should be understood more as, "a strategic investment of resources to produce benefits for business and industry by leveraging fiscal and human capital to produce a direct, immediate and positive financial return on those investments."[10] Presumably, the impact of a liberal arts education is not sufficiently direct or immediate to satisfy the criteria advanced by this worthy individual. This same criticism is sometimes echoed by students, parents, and employers. Liberal arts graduates, they say, are not prepared for the labor force or "job market." What good, they ask, is mastery of a core curriculum followed by a degree in philosophy, English literature, or political science? Some critics of liberal education aver that students from working-class backgrounds, in particular, need to be taught marketable skills rather than philosophical principles.[11]

The faculty's response is that liberal arts graduates are taught to think, to learn, to criticize, to imagine, to compare, and to discover. Not only is a liberal education the premier gateway to the learned professions, but a liberal education also encourages students to cultivate a sense of intellectual curiosity, to appreciate debate and diversity, and to make aesthetic choices and moral judgments. Students, the faculty avers, should be prepared to understand and challenge established perspectives, not merely to find a niche within the existing social and economic order. The

habits of mind taught in liberal arts classrooms may not be immediately or directly marketable but those who possess them have a
chance to become autonomous human beings and effective citizens. Some may even acquire the intellectual wherewithal to control their own economic destinies rather than be forced to serve
life sentences as corporate drudges or bureaucratic drones.

Indeed, the intellectual tools and analytical capabilities acquired
by the liberally educated help them continue learning long after
they graduate rather than simply equip them with some set of
currently accepted facts, techniques, and ideas. The ability to
engage in continuous learning, in turn, helps the liberally educated navigate and manage the social and economic changes that
inevitably render obsolete the more narrow forms of education to
which others, perhaps working-class students in particular, are
often directed.

I often tell students that "practical" courses have a short half life
while more theoretical or philosophical classes will leave them with
ideas on which they will draw forever. Lest anyone doubt the quality or objectivity of my advice, a recent study by the National
Association of Colleges and Employers (NACE) reached parallel
conclusions. The NACE study indicated that even in the work
world, many "practical" skills turned out to be less important in the
long term than ability to communicate, intellectual adaptability,
and the capacity to understand and solve complex problems, skills
that are consistent with a liberal arts background.[12] Other studies
have found that in the corporate world, liberal arts graduates were
more likely than others to rise to senior management positions.[13] It
seems that a bit of theory, history, and training in critical reasoning doesn't hurt even in the philistine business world.

Unfortunately, the sorts of general education and core curricula
required by Columbia and Chicago, to say nothing of St. John's,
are unusual in today's academic world. More common is the
stripped-down "core" offered by a middle-size midwestern state
university. At this school, students may complete their general
education requirement with six classes distributed across the

sciences, social sciences, and humanities. Some may also be required to study writing and math for a year if they are not able to demonstrate modest levels of proficiency in these topics. The liberal arts are given even less weight at a large western state university. At this school, which boasts beautiful facilities and an able faculty, undergraduates are required to take two terms of English composition, one term of math, one term of natural science, and one term in a social science or humanities class. Thus, at this school, a "general education" might consist of five classes after which students move on to study more specialized and, perhaps, more practical matters. In terms of their liberal arts requirements, these schools could hardly be distinguished from the for-profit and career-focused University of Phoenix, which should at least be commended for not pretending to be more than it is.

At most schools, the faculty supports preservation and expansion of liberal arts requirements. From their demand-side perspective, though, administrators are prone to favor a narrower and more vocational curriculum or, as they sometimes put it, one oriented toward "skills acquisition."[14] After all, many students, parents, and other stakeholders are concerned with the marketability of an undergraduate degree and seek a direct return on their financial investment. In their capacity as managers of knowledge factories, administrators have little reason to refuse to respond to customers' expressed or presumed preferences and generally work to develop what they see as a more practical course of study.

At one small private university in the South, for example, the faculty fought unsuccessfully to block an administrative effort to reduce the liberal arts core requirement by 25 percent. The administration was responding to demands from students in the school's vocational and professional programs to have more opportunity to take "relevant" classes. Administrators declared that "nothing would be lost" from cuts in the liberal arts.[15] At a number of schools, foreign language requirements have been eliminated and writing requirements reduced.[16] Even at elite schools with strong liberal arts traditions, administrators have sought to reduce liberal arts requirements in favor of a more vocationally oriented curriculum. While there is certainly a place for vocational training, it is rapidly becoming all that is offered at many schools.

Perhaps the most surprising example of such an effort occurred in the late 1990s at the University of Chicago, traditional home of the "Great Books" curriculum and a bastion of the liberal arts. The school's then new (and now former) president, Hugo Sonnenschein, proposed cutting the general education requirement from twenty-one to nine courses to allow students a better opportunity to choose electives they deemed relevant to their career goals. Sonnenschein averred that the university must accommodate itself to "commodification and marketing in higher education," and declared that the sort of curricular change he sought was part of a trend that was, "unmistakable today." "We can't jolly well dance along and not pay attention," Sonnenschein said.[17] Chicago's faculty vigorously resisted the administration's efforts, charging that the school's intellectual traditions were being ignored.[18] Nevertheless, after a prolonged battle, the general education requirement was cut to its present level of fifteen courses plus language proficiency—still a substantial requirement by contemporary standards but less than the Chicago faculty had thought appropriate.

The efforts of administrators to address what they deem to be customer demand may help to explain the results of a comprehensive study reported by the National Association of Scholars (NAS) in 1996. The NAS study confirmed that in the latter years of the twentieth century, general education requirements had been quite substantially reduced at most of America's top fifty schools (as defined by their *US News* rankings). According to the NAS study, around the time of the First World War, virtually all American colleges required students to undertake course work in English composition, foreign languages, history, literature, philosophy, the social sciences, natural sciences, and mathematics. Such requirements remained the norm as recently as the 1960s, though in many instances the number of credit hours students were required to complete in each area had been reduced.

By the 1990s, however, as though following the script of the well-known novella *I Am Legend*, what had once been the humanistic norm had become the rare exception. By the 1990s, barely a third of the fifty schools in the NAS sample required English composition; only 14 percent required a literature course; 4 percent required philosophy; 34 percent required a natural science course; only 12 percent required a traditional mathematics course, though another 32 percent mandated "quantitative reasoning," taught outside the math department. Even schools, like Harvard and Chicago, that maintained core liberal arts requirements cut the number of hours and in other ways reduced the scope of the requirement.[19] This trend has continued to the present day.[20] At one state university, where degree programs in classics, German, French, and other humanities subjects were eliminated, the president declared that subjects like these are, "stuff that you don't need."[21]

Former Harvard dean Harry Lewis and others have argued correctly that students from working-class backgrounds, in particular, come to college for the purpose of acquiring skills that will lead quickly to jobs. These students, though, probably do not realize that the vocational curriculum to which they are directed ensures that they will leave college with skills that will almost certainly limit them to the blue collar or lowest rungs of the white-collar ladder. Skilled blue-collar workers are certainly needed, but, given a choice, some students might find that the other "stuff" might enhance their lives and life chances.

Research

In the realm of research, faculty tend to take the view that ideas and discoveries should be broadly disseminated through peer-reviewed publications and presentations at professional meetings. Some professors, to be sure, are interested in the possibility of profiting from their discoveries. Some have even accepted bribes and kickbacks from pharmaceutical companies and other corporate interests in exchange for biased or even false reporting of research findings.[22] Most professors, though, are more concerned with the process of discovery and the professional recognition that comes from developing new ideas in the laboratory, in the library, or at a computer terminal, and see any pecuniary gain to themselves as incidental to their main goals. University administrators, on the other hand, view faculty research mainly as a source of revenue for the institution and are not particularly entranced by its intellectual merits except when commissioning puff pieces for the alumni magazine. Administrators seek to profit from faculty research in two ways. The first is grant income and overhead; the second is revenue from patents and licenses.

Administrative Overhead

Typically, especially in the sciences, faculty research is supported by grants from federal agencies like the National Science Foundation, private foundations such as Ford or Hughes, major corporations, or, in some instances, wealthy individual donors. For faculty members in the sciences, whose work may require millions of dollars in equipment and a host of personnel, research grants are absolutely essential, and the process of applying for such grants is virtually a full-time activity. In many labs, the most senior professor spends much of his or her time writing grant proposals while supervision of the actual work in the lab is left to more junior faculty or postdoctoral fellows.

For major research universities, income from grants, especially grants from federal agencies, can amount to hundreds of millions of dollars ever year. Grant income pays for professors' salaries, graduate students' stipends, laboratory supplies and equipment, and the other costs connected with research and scholarship. Chemists or biologists who are unsuccessful in securing funding for their grant proposals must generally close their labs and try to help their graduate students and fellows find other positions.

Before the advent of the professional administrator, some of these individuals might have finished their careers helping to manage the university's affairs. At the same time, on every campus there are superannuated but famous professors whose signatures on grant proposals virtually guarantee showers of dollars from the federal government. These individuals are treated with great respect, though they are never allowed near potentially dangerous laboratory equipment.

Grant dollars are usually divided into two categories—those awarded for "direct costs" and those designated to pay indirect costs or "overhead." The term "direct costs" refers to the dollars to be actually spent for the equipment, supplies, and salaries directly related to the research endeavors for which funding has been awarded. Indirect costs or "overhead" refers to the portion of every grant allocated to compensate the university for the use of its offices, libraries, computer systems, and general resources such as water and electricity by grant recipients.

In the case of federal grants, the overhead rate is fixed by an agreement negotiated between the school and the federal government. Top research universities receive a rate of more than 60 percent. That means that if a faculty member is awarded $1 million by a federal agency for his or her project, the university will bill the government for an additional $600,000 for its indirect costs. In the case of grants from nongovernment donors, the overhead rate is usually negotiable, but the university will turn away intellectually worthy grants if it believes that the overhead rate is too low to make the project financially worthwhile for the institution.

Most universities have a grants office, often called the office of "sponsored programs," or the like, which nominally exists to help faculty identify and apply for grant funding. In reality, the main function of this office is to serve as the administration's tax collection agency. Sponsored programs negotiates with donors and makes certain that overhead is collected. At some universities, the office of sponsored programs audits the uses of grants—especially federal grants—to make certain that faculty members do not use grant funds for purposes inconsistent with those stated in their approved grant proposals. Official university authorization and sponsorship is regarded by most granting agencies as a necessary safeguard against the misuse of funds by grantees.

But while sponsored programs may watch the faculty's expenditure of funds covering direct costs, it does not audit the use of overhead funds by administrators. This would be a difficult task since these funds, almost by definition, can be applied toward the general expenses of the university so long as the expenditures can, in some general way, be seen as relevant to supporting the research endeavors specified in the grant. Thus, some portion of the school's utility bills, staff costs, maintenance and repair costs might, in a general sense, be seen as legitimate expenditures of overhead dollars. Unfortunately, some university administrators view these overhead dollars as a general slush fund that can be used for whatever purposes they deem appropriate. This administrative perspective has led to a number of abuses in recent years.

One of the best-known cases of misuse of grant dollars was discovered at Stanford University in 1990. Stanford is an important research university, and its scientists are awarded tens of millions in federal funds every year. Stanford's overhead rate in 1990 was more than 78 percent, among the highest rates in the nation. Suspicious of Stanford's overhead charges, federal auditors examined the school's billing practices. Among their discoveries was that grant overhead had been used to pay for improvements to the university president's residence. These included installation of an antique commode and cedar lined closets. Federal research dollars were also used to pay for the daily delivery of flowers to the president and the maintenance of a university-owned yacht. The university agreed to refund $3.4 million to the government and to change its accounting practices.[23] One federal auditor estimated that over the course of the previous decade, Stanford might have collected as much as $185 million in inappropriate overhead charges from the federal government, though this figure was vigorously disputed by the university.

The Stanford case is by no means an isolated one. In recent years, a number of major universities have been forced to return millions of dollars in federal overhead payments after auditors found that administrators had used the money for inappropriate purposes. The roster includes NYU, which returned $15 million; Thomas Jefferson University, forced to return $12 million; Florida International, $27 million; Yale, $5.6 million; Texas, $12 million; University of California, $3.9 million; Northwestern, $5.5 million; and University of South Florida, $4 million. These and other universities denied any wrongdoing and asserted that the government was applying improperly strict standards to their use of overhead dollars. University administrators view restrictions on overhead spending as "unfunded mandates."[24] Some administrators apparently cannot see why it was wrong to spend overhead dollars for flowers and antique commodes.

Professors understand that universities must recover whatever costs they might incur as a result of the faculty's research activities. Faculty, however, are already required to cover the direct costs of their research, including salaries, equipment, supplies, materials, and so forth, from their grant funds. Hence, they regard the high levels of overhead charged by universities as a form of double taxation that diverts dollars that might pay for research. The high rate charged for overhead, moreover, far exceeds the value of the services the institution actually provides to support research activities. One year after Stanford was forced to repay overhead funds it had used for commodes and flowers, the university proposed a new overhead rate of 76 percent on federal grants—a percentage university administrators claimed barely covered the schools indirect costs. Well, antique commodes are expensive. As Stanford chemistry professor James Collman observed about the administration's stance, "It shows a lot of chutzpah."[25]

The faculty's attitude toward administrative overhead is another illustration of the difference between professorial and administrative perspectives. The faculty thinks that the university exists to further its research agenda and believes that every possible dollar should be spent in its laboratories or other research venues. For administrators, on the other hand, the purpose of faculty research is to enrich the university. Administrators view research projects as instruments that generate income in the form of overhead. As every faculty member has learned, research grants that are not deemed sufficiently profitable in terms of overhead dollars, will be turned down by the university whatever arguments might be made for their intellectual merits. Generally speaking, faculty research must not only pay for itself, but is expected to produce the handsome surplus needed to pay for administrative salaries and other expenses.

Intellectual Property

A second way in which administrators seek to profit from professorial research is through income derived from inventions, scientific discoveries, and other forms of intellectual property originating from the ideas and laboratory work undertaken by faculty members. The realm of intellectual property law is complicated and involves many issues. We will be concerned only with two sets of questions. The first is the ability of universities to profit from the work of its faculty members and the second is the right of universities to profit from faculty research funded by federal agencies with taxpayer dollars.

As to the first of these issues, the main way in which universities seek to profit directly from faculty research is through patent assignment. Under U.S. law, patents are generally granted to actual inventors, not their employers. Inventors who happen to be employed by some corporation, institution, or agency are still entitled to patent their own discoveries unless they were employed for the specific purpose of developing the particular device or process in question.[26] Thus, under the law, a university professor who created a patentable device or process in the course of his or her general research activities, would be entitled to claim the patent, with the university retaining what is called a "shop right," the right to use the device in its own laboratories or classrooms without being obligated to pay royalties or fees.[27]

The right of employees to patent the results of their work can be transferred to their employers by contract. And, many corporations set as a condition of employment for their engineers and scientists, that any patentable discoveries they might make in the course of their work will belong to the employer. Traditionally, universities did not seek to compel faculty members to sign away their patent rights. In recent years, however, most schools have sought to tap this potential source of income by claiming ownership of the faculty's patentable research. Most universities have patent policies, which are incorporated into their faculty handbooks or other employment agreements, giving the institution the right to patent products produced using the school's facilities and resources. In order to encourage faculty to pursue research that might lead to patentable products, most schools offer faculty inventors a share of any eventual profits generated by their discoveries. Typically, university patent policies award faculty members about one-third of any profit derived from their patented products with the school retaining the remainder. Under these policies, too, professors are required to disclose to university administrators any patentable discoveries and to cooperate with administrators in their efforts to patent and commercialize the resulting product.

Prior to 1980, universities were seldom interested in patents and most faculty members were far more eager to publish than to protect their research findings. Indeed, many of America's most important industries are based on technologies developed in university laboratories through research funded entirely or in part by the federal government by researchers who had little or no interest in profiting financially from their work. As a result, many of the foundations of the computer industry, the software industry, the biotechnology industry, and others moved directly from university laboratories into the public domain.[28]

In 1980, however, spurred in part by university lobbyists, Congress enacted the Bayh-Dole Patent and Trademark Act, which brought about a major change in the way in which universities viewed the research being conducted on their campuses. Under the terms of the act, universities were permitted to take owner-ship, via the patent process, of products or processes discovered by university researchers using federal grant dollars. The nominal purpose of the act was to accelerate the pace of technological inno-vation by giving universities a financial incentive to commercial-ize discoveries made in their laboratories. The presumption was that schools would patent promising products and license their development and use to private firms. These firms, it was said by the act's proponents, would have an incentive to invest in commer-cial applications, an incentive that had been lacking when the products of university laboratories were in the public domain and could be used by anyone. Hence, the act would reduce the time interval between the process of discovery and the public availabil-ity of important new products and processes.

As initially drafted, the act contained a "recoupment" provision that would have required universities to pay the federal govern-ment a percentage of the income derived from patenting products developed with federal grant funds. Senator Harley Kilgour (D–WV) said recoupment was necessary to "prevent a giveaway of the fruits of publicly-funded research."[29] An intense lobbying cam-paign by research universities, however, resulted in the elimina-tion of this provision and, as enacted, Bayh-Dole, indeed, awarded schools the fruits of publicly funded research conducted in their laboratories. As a result, research universities became, in effect "triple dippers." First, universities benefit directly from the grant funds won by their scientists. These funds pay salaries, graduate stipends and other costs that would otherwise be borne by the institution. Second, as we saw above, universities collect a hefty sum, in the form of indirect cost recovery, on top of every dollar of grant money. Third, thanks to Bayh-Dole, universities are in a position to patent and profit from the discoveries made in their laboratories, even though the research that produced these discov-eries was funded by the tax-paying public.

Universities moved quickly to take advantage of Bayh-Dole by establishing technology licensing or technology transfer offices to monitor and commercialize faculty research. Technology transfer offices were rare prior to Bayh-Dole—only twenty-five were known to exist—but within twenty-five years of the act's signing, some 3,300 such offices had sprung up on university campuses, with some schools boasting several offices to supervise research in different areas.[30] These offices are somewhat misnamed. There role is less to transfer technology than to transfer power over the dissemination of science and technology from researchers to administrators. Perhaps a more accurate label might be the university "technology control office."

Nominally, university technology transfer offices function to bring together scientists engaged in promising work with commercial enterprises that might have the capabilities and resources to bring resulting products to market. In reality, the administrators charged with fostering such relationships seldom have enough experience in either the scientific domain or the corporate world to connect the two. Usually, technology transfers take place when a university scientist is approached by his or her corporate counterpart who read about the work in a scientific publication or heard a presentation at a scientific meeting. In terms of actually bringing discoveries from the laboratory to the eventual beneficiary, the technology transfer office mainly handles the administrative details after an agreement is initiated.[31]

In point of fact, technology transfer offices usually thwart more than promote the transformation of laboratory research into useful technologies. The administrators who direct these offices usually instruct faculty members to continually review their work for possibly marketable products before they discuss their theories or findings with colleagues outside the university. Since publication places a product in the public domain, professors are told always to file provisional patent applications before publishing a paper or presenting their work in the form of papers at scientific conferences.[32] The effect of such rules is to slow the process through which ideas developed by one set of scientists are brought to the attention of others who might incorporate them into their own work. And, to the extent that universities surround the work of their scientists with thickets of patents, the upshot can be what Heller and Eisenberg call a scientific "anticommons" in which ideas and concepts that in the public domain might spur discovery and innovation are zealously guarded by the institutional owners who value income more than innovation.[33]

According to Law Professor Mark Lemley, such an anticommons has indeed developed in the field of nanotechnology, where universities have patented a significant percentage of the products and processes considered to be the basic building blocks of the industry, including carbon nanotubes, semiconducting nanocrystals, light-emitting nanocrystals, atomic force microscopes, and so forth.[34] These patents present real and potential legal impediments to innovation in the field. In this way, taking advantage of Bayh-Dole, universities threaten to become obstacles to, rather than centers of intellectual innovation.

Some faculty members, to be sure have always sought to profit financially from their research and will, indeed, seek opportunities to evade university rules and patent their own discoveries.[35] As noted above, however, most professors are more interested in publishing than patenting and value recognition in their field more than financial reward. Most would agree with the chemical engineering professor who said, "I think the thing that is valued the most [by members of the faculty] is a high-quality scientific publication."[36] Before the advent of the university technology transfer office, relatively few professors gave much thought to claiming legal ownership of, as opposed to scientific recognition for, their work. They were eager to publish their work and allow it to enter the public domain, where they would receive credit in the form of an enhanced academic reputation.

With the establishment of patent policies and the creation of technology transfer offices, universities have turned into standard procedure something that had been previously the practice of a few scientists who happened to be a bit more greedy than their fellows. Administrators, in effect, institutionalized scientific avarice. Professors find the university technology transfer process irritating because it slows the publication and dissemination of research findings. But the real victims of the process are members of the general public who must now pay twice for whatever benefits arise from university research. Taxpayers must first pay for the research. Then they pay again when some firm that has purchased a license from the patent-holding university markets the resulting product and charges a hefty fee for its use.

One often-cited example is the anticancer drug, Taxol, which was developed by Florida State University (FSU) scientists who received nearly a half-billion dollars in funding from the National Institutes of Health (NIH). FSU licensed the drug to a pharmaceutical company, Bristol-Myers Squibb (BMS), which, after spending a good deal of its own money on required testing, development, and marketing, was able to generate nearly $10 billion dollars in revenues from worldwide sales of the drug. Ironically, among BMS's main customers was the U.S. government. The federal government's Medicare program paid BMS nearly $700 million for Taxol prescriptions between 1994 and 1999 alone. Thus, American taxpayers paid FSU to develop the drug and then paid BMS for the drug's use.[37] FSU, for its part, profited from the NIH's research grants and, again, from the licensing fees paid by BMS, which eventually totaled nearly $400 million. One might say that FSU administrators and BMS executives worked together to plunder the public treasury.

Unfortunately, the Taxol case is not an isolated example. In another often-cited case, to take just one of many, the Scripps Research Institute, which had already been awarded some $700 million in federal funding for the next ten-year period, signed a $30 million contract with Sandoz, a European pharmaceutical company, which would give the company the right to license any products developed by Scripps during the same ten years.[38] In effect, Scripps sold Sandoz the right to profit from research for which U.S.

taxpayers (via their government) had already agree to pay hand-somely. The Scripps case is a bit different from many similar instances only because an outcry in Congress forced the institute to cancel the agreement with the pharmaceutical company.

Again, some scientists are personally avaricious and endeavor to profit financially from their discoveries. Most, however, are more focused on scientific discovery and professional reputation more than money. Through technology transfer offices, though, the administrators, not the scientists, are in charge of the dissemination of knowledge. And university administrators are all institutionally avaricious. To administrators, scientific discoveries are not important for their own sake. Rather, they are sources of millions of dollars, even hundreds of millions of dollars in potential overhead and licensing fees. The fact that the processes generating this revenue represents a form of triple dipping, a de facto plunder of taxpayer funds and, ultimately, may create a scientific anticommons, slowing the discovery and dissemination of ideas, is of no concern to university administrators. In the all-administrative university, revenue is far more important than research.

Administrative Priorities

The priorities of the all-administrative university emerge most clearly during times of economic crisis when administrators are forced to make choices among spending options.[39] As noted above, like professors, most administrators will aver that the mission of the university is the production and dissemination of knowledge through teaching, research, and other programs. Yet, when forced by economic circumstances, like those that developed in the United States in 2009–10, to make major spending cuts, administrators will relegate teaching and research to secondary roles and focus instead on the institution and particularly on the preservation of administrative jobs and perquisites. Some administrators, indeed, appear to see hard times as an opportunity to enhance administrative power on their campuses.

The sharp economic downturn that followed America's 2008 financial crisis led to substantial declines in revenues for virtually all of America's colleges and universities. State schools saw their appropriations slashed by as much as 10 percent while donations to private colleges and universities dropped off sharply.[40] As endowments dropped in value, schools saw substantial declines in their investment income. And, at the same time, students, and their financially hard-pressed parents, requested considerably more help paying tuition than had been the case in previous years. Almost every institution, even Harvard, America's wealthiest school, was compelled to make substantial cuts in its expenditures.

What cuts did university administrations choose to make during these hard times? A tiny number of schools took the opportunity to confront years of administrative and staff bloat and moved to cut costs by shedding unneeded administrators and their brigades of staffers. The most notable example is the University of Chicago's Pritzker School of Medicine, which in February 2009 addressed a $100 million budget deficit by eliminating fifteen "leadership positions," along with 450 staff jobs, among other cuts.[41] In announcing the cuts, the medical school's dean apologized for eliminating jobs during a time when employees would have difficulty securing new positions. The dean declared, however, that his action was necessary in the face of the school's large budgetary shortfall. In another part of the same letter, however, the dean declared that spending in those areas that were part of the school's "core missions," which he defined as research and patient care, would be increased, not cut. Thus, the school planned to continue construction of a new multimillion-dollar hospital pavilion that would allow Chicago to expand its research activities and work in "leading-edge" medical and surgical procedures. The dean also emphasized that faculty would not be affected by the planned budget cuts. Chicago's message was clear. Administrators

and staffers were less important than teaching, research, and—
since this involved a medical school—patient care. If the budget
was to be cut, this would be done by thinning the school's administrative ranks, not by reducing its core efforts.

Unfortunately, few if any, other colleges and universities copied
the Chicago model. Facing budgetary problems, many schools
eliminated academic programs, and announced across-the-board
salary and hiring freezes, which meant that vacant staff and faculty positions, including the positions of many adjunct professors,
would remain unfilled until the severity of the crisis eased. For
example, the University of Texas at Austin decided to save money
by cutting its language requirement.[42] Florida State eliminated
its anthropology program as well as math and science education,
geography, and management information systems. Oregon State
dropped computational physics, American studies, and five other
undergraduate majors. Michigan State eliminated forty-nine degree programs including classics and statistics. The University of
Iowa announced plans to drop American studies, comparative literature, classics, and statistics. The list goes on and on.[43] In 2010,
the University of California announced plans to save money by
developing online undergraduate degree programs to potentially
replace conventional programs.[44] In principle, online courses
require less investment in physical plant and fewer professors,
but do not reduce the need for administrators. This makes them a
perfect solution to any school's financial problems.

Schools announcing hiring and salary freezes for both faculty
and staff included Cornell, Texas, Bowling Green, Middlebury,
New Mexico, Villanova, Maryland, University of Nevada, the University of Hawaii, and hundreds of others. Such across-the-board
freezes might seem fair and equitable. Adoption of this equitable
principle, however, ignores the fact that failing to fill a vacant faculty or adjunct faculty position means fewer and larger classes,
less faculty-student contact and less research. Freezing vacant
administrative posts, on the other hand, merely means that fewer
individuals will be available for staff meetings, that administrative

retreats will not be well attended, and that some delays might be encountered in the long-range planning process. Adopting the principle of the across-the-board freeze declares that preserving schools' bloated administrative and staff ranks is as important as protecting teaching and research.

And that is, of course, precisely what many university administrators believe. Administrators and staffers are, in the view of many, if not most, university officials, more important than the school's students, faculty, classrooms, and laboratories. Take Florida State, which, as we saw above, has been cutting programs and laying off faculty in the face of a putative financial crisis. FSU, according to its Web site, employs numerous senior administrators—vice presidents, associate vice presidents, deans, associate deans, and so forth—supported by a large staff. One staffer in the provost's office, according to the school's Web site, "Prepares batches so documents can be scanned and electronically filed into Cyberdocs, and assigns a file name and document type for later retrieval." Another, "Serves as primary requestor and receiver for the Offices of the Provost and the President."[45] Perhaps this might be seen by some as a radical notion, but it seems to me that if the provost and president could learn to do their own requesting and receiving (this might entail learning to use the telephone), the need for still more faculty layoffs and program cuts might be reduced. Just a thought.

Or, take the steps announced by Brandeis University administrators. In January 2009, Brandeis announced that because of a budget crisis it planned to close its art museum and sell its excellent collection. In May 2009, the university announced that because of the continuing financial crisis it would suspend payments to the retirement accounts of faculty and staff members.[46] A quick look at the Brandeis Web site reveals that the school employs, in addition to a president, an executive vice president, an associate vice president, a provost, three senior vice presidents, two assistants to the president, an executive assistant to the president, an assistant to the executive assistant to the president, and an assistant to the assistant to the president, as well as the usual coterie of deans and deanlets. It may not have occurred to the school's officials, but the paintings and pensions might be saved if the university's bloated bureaucracy was trimmed just a bit. Couldn't the assistant to the president and executive assistant to the president share an assistant?

Perverse administrative priorities were even more in evidence at a number of schools that actually raised administrative salaries or, in other ways, opted to spend more money on administrative services while cutting expenditures on teaching and research in the face of budget deficits. For example, in January 2009, facing $19 million in budget cuts and a hiring freeze, Florida Atlantic University awarded raises of 10 percent or more to top administrators, including the school's president.[47] In a similar vein, in February 2009, the president of the University of Vermont (UVM) defended the bonuses paid to the school's twenty-one top administrators against the backdrop of layoffs, job freezes, and program cuts at the university. The university president, Daniel Fogel, asserted that administrative bonuses were based on the principles of "extra pay for extra duties" and "pay for performance." The president rejected a faculty member's assertion that paying bonuses to administrators when the school faced an enormous budget deficit seemed similar to the sort of greed recently manifested by the corporate executives who paid themselves bonuses with government bailout money. Fogel said he, "shared the outrage" of those upset at corporate greed, but maintained there was a "world of difference" between the UVM administrative bonuses and bonuses paid to corporate executives.[48] He did not specify what that world might be.

In the meantime the president of Washington State University, Elson Floyd, accepted a $125,000 pay raise, bringing his 2009 salary to $725,000 per year, soon after announcing that financial circumstances required the school to freeze hiring.[49] At another university that had just announced a large budget deficit and mandated salary and hiring freezes, the outgoing president was feted by the board of trustees at a gala, 350-person dinner, to which trustees, senior administrators, alumni, donors, and other notables—but no students or faculty—were invited. The dinner, which might as well have been held on the promenade deck of the *Titanic*, featured musical performances, videos, and a lounge area with hundreds of Chinese newspapers and a tea set to recognize the president's many trips to China. No wonder university spending was frozen. Chinese tea sets can be quite expensive. Later, this same university placed restrictions on the use of copy paper by graduate students. I wonder if the Chinese newspapers could be recycled.

Even this example of administrative *chutzpah* was outdone by the University of Tennessee president John Petersen. In response to $75 million in state budget cuts, Peterson announced a moratorium on new programs; froze all hiring, renovations, furniture and equipment purchases, and nonessential travel; and initiated a process to review all academic programs to identify areas that might be cut. At the same time, though, Petersen also announced the appointment of former head football coach, Philip Fulmer as a special assistant to the president. Fulmer, who would be paid $12,500 per month, would be tasked with "enhancing and developing strategic relationships on behalf of UT."[50] Clearly, at least to this university administrator, strategic relationships take precedence over academic programs.

Crisis and Opportunity

Some resourceful university administrators saw the recent financial crisis as an opportunity more than as a problem. The rules of all colleges and universities allow administrators to exercise extraordinary powers in times of financial exigency. The meaning of exigency is a matter of some dispute. The American Association of University Professors (AAUP) defines exigency as an imminent financial crisis that threatens the survival of an institution. The courts, however, have declared that an institution's governing board can reasonably determine that the school faces exigent circumstances if it is running deficits and facing a "state of urgency." Bankruptcy need not be imminent.[51]

If a board determines with reasonable cause that exigent circumstances exist, the board and the school's senior administrators are essentially empowered to govern by decree. Each school's rules and procedures are different, but emergency powers may include suspension of faculty self-governance procedures, the power to summarily reorganize or eliminate academic programs and departments, and the power to abrogate faculty tenure contracts.[52] Recall that the president of Tulane University saw Hurricane Katrina as an opportunity to declare financial exigency and to brush aside faculty resistance to his campuswide reorganization plan. A mere recession may not have the dramatic punch of a Category 5 hurricane, but a recession's sustained havoc lasts longer and can provide clever administrators with more opportunities to circumvent and disempower the faculty. Some schools, as we saw above, have sought to institute emergency procedures even without a formal declaration of financial exigency.

Late in 2008, administrators on a number of campuses, even without formal declarations of financial exigency began using the emerging financial crisis to institute reorganization plans while delimiting the faculty's role in campus governance. At the University of South Florida, for example, administrators instituted a sweeping campuswide reorganization plan without consulting the faculty.[53] Claiming that their efforts were a necessary response to a $52 million budget gap, the administration reorganized colleges, eliminated programs, and left unclear whether some tenure-track faculty whose departments had disappeared would remain in a tenure track. The faculty senate is now working with administrators to lay out procedures for faculty consultation in future reorganization planning.

In Tennessee, the chancellor of the board of regents, Charles Manning, issued a new "business model" for the state's universities and community colleges. The model mandated sweeping changes in colleges' procedures and organization to accommodate a projected 20 percent cut in state funding over a two year period. Among the highlights of the chancellor's money-saving plan was a proposal to increase the use of adjuncts rather than full-time faculty and to offer students a tuition discount if they agreed to, "work online with no direct support from a faculty member."[54] Presumably this would entail some form of autotutorial. While the faculty was not formally consulted in the planning process, Manning asked professors for "a summary of your thoughts," about the proposal. Unfortunately, given the financial emergency, the board was unable to wait for all these summaries to arrive before beginning its work on Manning's initiatives. At any rate, those faculty members who did provide timely replies were apparently unsympathetic to the idea that money could be saved by simply allowing students to teach themselves in online courses without professors. Manning characterized faculty opposition to his plan as "extreme."[55]

Given the projected length and severity of the nation's economic downturn, it seems more than likely that administrators will find new opportunities to declare financial distress or even exigency, silence the institutions of faculty governance, and restructure schools according to their own lights. Given administrative priorities, it seems clear that such restructuring would not improve the quality of teaching and research at those school unfortunate enough to fall victim to emboldened administrators. Tennessee Chancellor Manning has given us a glimpse of what some administrators might do if given the opportunity. Eliminate the professors—let the students teach themselves. Perhaps the savings could be plowed back into administrative salaries and bonuses. What a perfect university!

The All-Administrative University: An Institution with an All-Administrative Mission

From the faculty's perspective, teaching and research are the main purposes of the university. The institution exists to promote these ends. From the perspective of many university administrators, however, teaching and research are merely instrumental endeavors. They are undertaken in order to draw customers (aka students) and research funds to the university. Hence, to administrators, the content of the curriculum makes little difference so long as the school's offerings are attractive to fees-paying customers. And, as to research, the main administrative goal is to maximize the flow of overhead and licensing dollars into the school's coffers, even if the process ultimately hampers rather than enhances academic research endeavors.

What is the ultimate purpose of these administrative efforts? Administrators say their goal is to strengthen their institutions in order to better equip them to pursue their teaching and research missions. If, however, we focus on what administrators do, rather than what they say, a different picture emerges. What administrators do with a good many tuition and research dollars is to reward themselves and expand their own ranks. At most schools, even midlevel administrators are now paid more than all but the senior professors in the professional schools, and considerably more than professors in the arts and sciences. And, as we saw in chapter 1, administrative growth has outpaced faculty growth everywhere, from the elite private schools to more proletarian public institutions. Over the past decade, to name but a few examples, the University of Virginia increased the size of its faculty by 15 percent while enlarging its administrative ranks by 28 percent; at Stanford the faculty grew by 15 percent while the number of administrators increased by 34 percent; at the University of Massachusetts, a school constantly facing budget problems, the faculty grew by only 5 percent, but despite budgetary shortfalls the number of administrators increased 25 percent; at Yale the number of professors actually declined 4 percent but the number of administrators, nevertheless, increased by 25 percent.[56]

Another recent study showed that between 1997 and 2007, the number of administrative and support personnel per one hundred students had increased dramatically at a number of schools—103 percent at Williams College; 111 percent at Johns Hopkins; 141

percent at Lynn University; 325 percent at Wake Forest University; and 351 percent at Yeshiva University. Though it showed an increase of only 97 percent between 1997 and 2007, Vanderbilt still ranks first in the absolute employee to student ratio. On Vanderbilt's Nashville campus 11,395 students enjoy the services of 7,339 deanlets and staffers. By contrast, the 11,345 students attending Yale suffer and surely receive an inferior education under the guidance of only 3,919 administrators.[57] Harvard, Chicago, and Princeton students were even more deprived of the chance to interact with deanlets and should demand tuition refunds.

These numbers do not merely indicate an enormous shift of resources away from teaching and research, they also signal a continuing transfer of power from the faculty to the administration even at top schools. With ever-growing legions of deanlets and deanlings at their command, senior administrators increasingly have the capacity to circumvent the faculty, seize control of programs, oversee research activities, and meddle in the curriculum. The result will be a continuing erosion of educational quality and research productivity. In the all-administrative university, the students will teach themselves and the results of publicly funded research will be sold to the highest bidder. Faculty members with the temerity to question this state of affairs will, no doubt, be cited for demonstrating a shameful lack of civility.

7

What Is to Be Done

PROFESSORS, TAKEN AS a group, are far from perfect. They can be petty, foolish, venal, lazy, and quarrelsome. Nevertheless, at its best, the university is a remarkable institution. It is a place where ideas are taken seriously; where notions that are taken as givens elsewhere are problematized; where what has seemed to be reality can be bent and reshaped by the power of the mind.

The university is also a vitally important social institution. Chief Justice Warren, quoted in chapter 2, said American society would "stagnate and die" without free scholarly inquiry. In truth, society would not die, but it would become more stagnant without the philosophical and scientific concepts that are conceived and debated on university campuses. In the sciences, university laboratories continue to be a source of ideas that promise not only to improve established technologies but, more important, to spark the development of new technologies. This is why the Bayh-Dole Act and its encouragement of patent thickets and an anticommons in the scientific realm is potentially so destructive.

In the humanities, the university is one of the few institutions to encourage and incubate new visions and modes of thought. Where else are smart people paid primarily to think and rewarded for thinking things that haven't been thought before? The university, moreover, is a bastion of relatively free expression and, hence, one of the few places where new ideas can be discussed and sharpened. The old left, new left, neocons, and neoliberals of recent years all had their roots in academia. Political impulses that changed American life, including the "new politics movement," the peace movement, civil rights movement, feminist movement, gay rights movement, environmental movement, the conservative legal movement, and a host of others were nurtured, if not launched, on university campuses. And why not? The university is a natural center of ideological ferment and dissent. The recipe is a simple one. Take large numbers of young people, add a few iconoclastic faculty members, liberally sprinkle with new ideas, place into a Bohemian culture, and half bake. The result is almost certain to be a welter of new ideas. Some will challenge and displace conventional wisdom, while others will disappear. The faculty, to be sure, has its own ideological perspectives, but most professors enjoy debate and ideological contestation. Faculty members who think some of their colleagues are narrow minded probably have not spent much time in the world outside the campus, where those who hold unconventional views are reflexively regarded as misguided, outlandish, kooky, or worse. Off the campus, instead of debate, the holder of unconventional ideas is likely to be greeted with incredulity or hostility.

It is because it is such a unique institution that it is so important to save the university from its deanlets. But the rescue mission is belated and not certain to succeed. The blight of the all-administrative university is spreading from campus to campus, from the community colleges to the private research universities, as deanlets copy one another's best practices, expand their already bloated administrative ranks, and use financial crises to further erode the autonomy of the faculty. More schools will sell bits and pieces of research, along with their art museums, to the highest bidder and adopt vocational curricula with courses taught online by contingent faculty. Those inspired by Chancellor

Manning's visionary plan (a new best practice?) may be embold-ened to do away with the faculty altogether and to encourage the students to teach themselves.

But, if it is not too late, I do have some thoughts on what might be done to slow the onward march of the all-administrative uni-versity. As is true of many malignant growths, there is no guaran-tee that chemotherapy or even radical surgery will cure the condition, but treatment may offer some hope of remission and a productive life for the patient until a more effective therapy can be identified. And, in the absence of a single definitive medical regi-men, a combination of several therapies may be required. Accord-ingly, my proposed therapeutic regimen includes a variety of medicines and procedures that should be administered by or to board members, the media, faculty members, alumni, students and parents, and, lastly, administrators themselves.

The Board

On any given campus, the only institution with the actual power to halt the onward march of the all-administrative university is the board of trustees or regents. The board selects the school's president, must approve the school's budget, and, at least for-mally, exercises enormous power over campus affairs. If it so desired, the board could halt or even scale back the expansion of managerial numbers and authority on its campus.

To be sure, many board members serve for social reasons or out of a sense of loyalty to the institution and are loathe to become involved in governance issues. Yet, precisely those trustees who do have a sense of loyalty to the colleges and universities from which they graduated should want to prevent those institutions from sinking into the ever-expanding swamp of administrative mediocrity. Board members interested in this problem may find data on their own campuses in the April 24, 2009, *Chronicle of Higher Education* and the 2009 report of the Center for College

Affordability and Productivity cited by the *Chronicle* article. The *Chronicle* article, cited above, presents data on the ratio of management and staff members per student for a number of schools in 2007, as well as changes in that ratio between 1997 and 2007 for the twenty public and private schools whose managerial ranks have expanded most during this period.

Administrative and staff numbers have increased everywhere, but managerial inflation at some schools has been truly astonishing. Indeed, the trustees of Yeshiva University, Wake Forest, Lynn, Johns Hopkins, and Williams College—the five schools exhibiting triple-digit growth in their employees per one hundred students ratio—should ask very, very tough questions at the next board meeting. I venture to predict that the answers they are likely to receive will consist mainly of lies and evasions. I have found that when questioned on this point, senior administrators will claim that increases in managerial ranks are the result of federal and state mandates and other factors beyond their control. Board members should not accept this explanation. If government mandates are to blame, then what explains the enormous variation among schools in the number of managers and staffers they employ? For example, why does Vanderbilt employ sixty-four staffers for every one hundred students when Emory manages with a still grossly inflated thirty-four, and the University of Wisconsin makes do with only seventeen deanlets per one hundred students? Perhaps the government was picking on Vanderbilt and compelled it to hire all the stray deanlets it could find at local unemployment offices.

Thankfully, most of America's top universities and colleges—Harvard, Princeton, MIT, Chicago, Stanford, Amherst, Swarthmore—are not among the schools reporting the highest administrator to student ratios. That several well-regarded schools, including my own, have recently been received into the pantheon of the most administratively bloated, bodes poorly for them and for American higher education. As I observed in chapter 1, numbers do not tell the whole story. Most deanlets, left to themselves, are content to wile away their days meeting and retreating. They represent a growing cost to the university but do not appear to be an immediate threat to its management or academic priorities. But, appearances are deceiving. New numbers create new possibilities. The existence of large numbers of deanlets gives ambitious senior administrators the tools with which to manage the university with minimal faculty involvement and to impose their own programs and priorities on the campus. Like other potentially destructive instruments, armies of staffers pose a threat by their very existence. They may seem harmless enough at their tiresome meetings but if they fall into the wrong hands, deanlets can become instruments of administrative imperialism and academic destruction.

On my own campus, a rapid increase in staffers under our previous president was quickly followed by a series of administrative initiatives including the creation of a new business school with no faculty consultation, the CUE commission designed to enhance administrative control of undergraduate education (discussed in chapter 1), an effort to impose mandatory "civility" training on the faculty, and so forth. Having expanded his administrative army, the president was prepared to make war on the faculty and to expand his administrative power. The availability of the instrument did not cause the result, but it made the result possible. On a foundation of managerial bloat our president sought to erect the all-administrative university. And so it may come to pass at other currently excellent but managerially bloated schools as well.

Given the danger, I would strongly recommend that boards truly concerned with maintaining the quality of their schools compel university administrators to shift spending priorities from management into the real business of the university—teaching and research. A 10 percent cut in staff and management ranks would save millions of dollars but would have no effect whatsoever on the operations of most campuses. The deanlets would never be missed; their absence from campus would go unnoticed. A 20 percent or larger cut would begin to be noticed and have the beneficial effect of substantially reducing administrative power and the ongoing diversion of scarce funds into unproductive channels. With fewer deanlets to command, senior administrators would be compelled to turn once again to the faculty for administrative support. Such a change would result in better programs and less unchecked power for presidents and provosts. Part-time faculty administrators tend to ask questions, use judgment, and interfere with arbitrary presidential and provostial decision-making. Senior full-time administrators would resent the interference, but the university would benefit from the result. Moreover, with fewer deanlets to pay and send to conferences and retreats, more resources might be available for educational programs and student support, the actual purposes for which parents, donors, and funding agencies think they are paying.

Trustees interested in trimming administrative fat might be wondering just how to evaluate their own school's level of administrative bloat. As a benchmark, trustees should compare their own school's ratio of managers and staffers per hundred students to the national mean, which is currently an already inflated 9 for private schools and 8 for public colleges. If the national mean is 9 deanlets per student at private colleges, why does Vanderbilt need 64? Why does Rochester need 40 and Johns Hopkins 31? The national mean for public colleges is 8, so why does the University of Illinois at Chicago employ 25 and the University of Washington 24 deanlets per student? Management-minded administrators claim to believe in benchmarking, so they should not object to being benchmarked. If I were a board member at one of the administratively top-heavy schools, I would want to know why my school employed three or four or five or six times more deanlets than the national average—an average which has, itself, increased more than 30 percent during the past decade. After listening to the various administrative evasions likely to be offered in response to this question, I would want to begin work on a firm plan for reducing the size of my school's bureaucracy. That would be a far more useful strategic plan than the vacuous vision of excellence usually produced by administrators.

In its work and investigations, the board would benefit greatly from regular communication with the faculty. To be effective, the board needs sources of information other than the school's official propaganda organs and the administrative skits presented to them at meetings. As an aside, I have often thought that administrators should be forced to shut down the various propaganda sheets in which they tout their virtues and heroic achievements to all who will listen. I have a feeling that the main result of all the self-puffery is to give administrators an incredibly inflated sense of their own worth. This is a phenomenon social psychologists call *self-persuasion*, and may help to explain why initially self-effacing college presidents are so often transformed into egomaniacs. But, even if the board won't shut down all the *Campus Chronicles* and *Gazettes* and *Pravdas* of the academic world, trustees should, at least, know that, like their old Soviet counterparts, these managerial rags are generally filled with fibs and distortions. Institutional channels of conversation with the faculty would help those administrators interested in campus governance separate fact from administrative fiction.

In addition, if they are to be effective, boards must police themselves with tough conflict-of-interest rules. Board members and companies in which they have significant financial interests should not be permitted to do business with the school. Federal conflict-of-interest law addresses issues of overcharging stemming from insider dealing. The problem, however, with business relationships between boards and university administrators is not that the school will pay too much for goods and services. The problem is one of power rather than money. As we saw earlier, board members who profit from their relationship with the university will not provide effective oversight of its administration. Unfortunately, boards everywhere include members whose insurance firms, construction companies, food service enterprises, and the like do business with the school. Such board members cannot possibly provide proper managerial oversight. Perhaps, a strict conflict-of-interest rule would discourage many persons from undertaking board service. So be it. A former Cornell provost once told me that the university had two types of board members—those who were committed to the university's interests and those merely interested in profiting from their relationship with the university. We should welcome the former and discourage the latter. Otherwise, those trustees who want to do good will be blocked by those who merely want to do business.

Lastly, boards should be wary of university administrators who spout managerial jargon. University administrators aping last year's management argot provide comic relief for the faculty, but their underlying purpose is not amusing. What all management theories have in common is an effort to impose order and hierarchy on an institution. Even those theories that provide a place for employee involvement see this as a way of pacifying underlings with the appearance of consultation. Through their management speak, administrators are asserting that the university is an institution to be ruled by them. Shared governance, faculty power, tenure, and so forth have no place in management theory. In fact, I have observed that the most vigorous proponents of MBO, TQM, PPBS, and the other forms of neocorporate gibberish are often the same individuals who would prefer to do away with faculty influence and tenure if they could. Wouldn't the university be better managed and more efficient if its employees wielded no power? I suppose that the influence of the faculty, tenure in particular, does complicate decision making and protect some lazy and ineffectual professors. I would submit to university boards, however, that the absence of faculty influence would empower the truly incompetent.

The Media

Some boards might not be eager to tackle the problem of administrative ineptitude and bloat. The questions that I encourage board members to ask would not be well received by college presidents and would likely spark sharp conflicts among board members and between the board and senior administrators. Most board members did not sign on to engage in unpleasant struggles.

Boards would be emboldened to ask the right questions by appropriate media coverage. In particular, the various publications that rate and rank colleges—*USNews* is the most important—should take account of administrative bloat in their ratings. After all, a high administrator-to-student ratio means that the school is diverting funds from academic programs to support an overgrown bureaucracy. I am certain that if Vanderbilt or Duke or Hopkins or Rochester or Emory or any of the other most administratively top-heavy schools lost a few notches in the *USNews* rankings because of their particularly egregious administrative bloat, their boards would be forced to ask questions. Administrators might prevaricate or might, as is often the case, attempt to report false numbers to *USNews*. Nevertheless, adverse consequences for schools' rankings, which have implications for enrollments and revenues, would almost certainly compel trustees to take a hard look at their managerial ranks.

The Faculty

A major burden of resisting administrative encroachment falls on the faculty, which unfortunately is not well prepared to defend its interests. Professors teach classes, spend time with students, and work in their laboratories, the library, and their computer terminals. They present papers at conferences and submerge themselves in dusty archives. While many faculty members make time for administrative tasks, some view attendance at meetings and participation in the institutions of faculty governance as a waste of time. Thus, some professors contribute to the disempowerment of the faculty.

I remember that one of my most distinguished colleagues at Cornell, Theodore J. Lowi, for a time refused to attend any meetings and made a point of always working on a book while others met to discuss departmental and university issues. After two years of boycotting meetings, Lowi published a very nice book on the presidency, which was very well received by reviewers. He cheerfully pointed out that he had written virtually the entire book during hours when he was not present at meetings. Most colleagues agreed that Lowi had done the right thing and mentally kicked themselves for having wasted their own time while he engaged in productive scholarship. I confess to sometimes having the same attitude. After a torturous year on a university governing board, I was asked if I was interested in becoming a candidate for another term. I replied that if offered a choice between another year of service and a year of incarceration at the Abu Ghraib prison, I would have to give the matter some thought.

Lowi and I were both right and wrong. We were right in thinking that teaching and scholarship were far more important than administrative service. We were wrong, however, in succumbing to the temptation to shirk administrative service. While we worked on our books and taught our classes, our universities hired dozens of new vice provosts and associate provosts and hundreds of new deanlets. Administrators used our absence and the absence of some of our colleagues to strengthen their own managerial capabilities and their continuing capacity to circumvent and marginalize the faculty.

But, as I observed in chapter 1, in addition to having other things to do, a reason that members of the faculty are reluctant to spend time on matters of campus governance is their perception that most of the established institutions of faculty governance have no real power.[1] On many campuses, as we saw above, administrators feel free to ignore or even disband faculty senates and councils if they seek to thwart administrative ambitions. Recall that the RPI faculty senate was disbanded by a provost who did not like its composition and that the Brandeis senate was ignored when it objected to the administration's violation of university rules in the Hindley case. Lack of faculty enthusiasm for administrative matters is as much a consequence as a cause of the growing power of university administrators.

The one institution, of course, that administrators cannot ignore is the board of trustees. For this reason, the faculty should seek the creation of one or more positions on the board to be held by faculty members. This proposal, to be sure, is not novel. Faculty members were represented, but not allowed to vote, on the Cornell Board of Trustees as early as 1916.[2] And, students of educational governance, even including one prominent, if iconoclastic, ex-administrator, the former University of Michigan president James Duderstadt, have for years been suggesting that faculty be included on university boards.

Despite this history, few schools today provide faculty seats on their boards. Indeed, many more colleges and universities have established student seats on their boards than currently permit faculty representation.[3] The reason is simple. Administrators fear the creation of direct lines of communication between the faculty and the board. Typically, university and college administrators present the board with a rosy picture of campus life and, of course, their own accomplishments. Readers of the various administrative propaganda organs will probably have a sense of what the trustees are told at their meetings. The administration is wise; the faculty loyal and grateful; the students well scrubbed and hardworking; the vision articulated by the strategic plan moving ever closer to realization; and so forth. During every board meeting, the campus is transformed into a Potemkin village and readied for the administration's dog and pony show.

Students may have radical ideas and preferences but are usually not in a position to know much about the operations of the university and are, hence, unlikely to be able to present facts that would embarrass administrators or raise questions about their integrity. Anyway, to the board, the students are just kids. Members of the faculty, on the other hand, often do know facts that might contradict administrators' claims. Perhaps the much-ballyhooed new computer system is an expensive disaster. Perhaps the new graduate school of business is a foolish and hopeless endeavor rather than a brilliant and novel approach to business education. Members of the faculty know these and many other administrative secrets that the president, provost, and other top administrators do not want publicly asserted at board meetings. Trustees loyal to the school's administration may also not wish such matters to be stated in public. Hence, as Harvard education professor Richard Chait once wrote, many trustees and college presidents "are apprehensive that regular, two-way communication between faculty members and board members . . . would undermine administrative authority."[4]

Probably, such communication would, indeed, undermine administrative authority—which is why the faculty must insist that it take place. A pertinent example was related to me by a colleague from a prominent east coast university. One evening, he was giving a talk to an alumni group in another city. At the reception that followed his lecture, he was approached by one of the school's trustees, who happened to live in that city. The trustee, whom he knew casually, took him aside and out of earshot of the "minder" from the development office who usually accompanies faculty speakers, asked him what professors thought about the university's president. As is the case on most campuses, the institution's various propaganda organs, perhaps receiving stylistic inspiration from the North Korean press, touted the president as an academic and intellectual giant and a Renaissance man beloved by employees, venerated by the students and respected by the faculty.

In point of fact, according to my informant, many employees believed the president to be short-tempered and vindictive, more than a few students thought he was a stuffed shirt, and some members of the faculty resented what they saw as his indifference to the school's academic quality, and mused about defacing the president's heroic portrait in the university club. When my informant bluntly reported these opinions to the inquiring trustee, the latter smiled and said he was not surprised. Indeed, he said, he personally shared these views but had been reluctant to criticize a president who appeared to be so well regarded on the campus. Perhaps if some institutional mechanism had existed for communication between trustees and the faculty, a false impression might have been corrected earlier and several serious problems more fully addressed by the board. By the way, faculty representatives on the board should be elected by the faculty rather than appointed by the administration. On every campus there are several sycophantic faculty members on whom administrators rely when they need to pretend that they have consulted with the faculty. These are the sorts of individuals whom administrators like to appoint to boards and, for that reason alone, should not be accepted by the faculty.

Professorial representation on the board is only one vehicle of resistance to administrative encroachment. Whether professors sit on the board or not, the faculty must be wary of the several administrative ploys discussed in the foregoing chapters. On many campuses administrators have hijacked the language of equal opportunity, diversity, inclusion, and so forth, for their own purposes. Administrators believe that the faculty will be reluctant to oppose initiatives labeled as efforts to expand equal opportunity or to promote diversity and will often use this language to describe proposals that, if brought to fruition, would give administrators more control over faculty hiring and promotion and reduce the faculty's role in campus governance. I have noticed on my campus that because of their own political principles and commitments, professors can be taken in by administrative demands that they agree to undergo civility training or harassment counseling or other humiliating forms of reeducation by the human resources thought police. Faculty members need to train themselves to look past the camouflage provided by the nominal purposes of these initiatives and see them clearly as efforts by the administration to bring the faculty to heel. Administrators will always seek to use our principles against us. These efforts should be resisted even though administrators and some credulous colleagues will declare that such opposition indicates a lack of proper political commitment.

Similar wariness is appropriate with regard to the current administrative push for "outcomes assessment." On almost every campus, administrators are declaring that the university or college as an institution needs to develop tools and tests to measure the impact of educational programs on its students. Often, administrators cite demands by accrediting agencies and even the federal government as justification for the imposition of an assessment regime. As in the case of equal opportunity, no one could be opposed to making certain that educational programs are maximally effective. The question is who will be in a position to develop the assessments, to interpret their results, and to recommend subsequent action. Currently, these decisions are in the hands of the faculty. In every class, professors and other teachers develop examinations and assignments, grade the results, and recommend further action to the students. At a more collective level, academic departments evaluate their curricula and the effectiveness of their programs.

What's wrong with this system? From a pedagogical perspective, nothing is wrong. From an administrative perspective, though, what's wrong is that the current system empowers the faculty. The established system of outcomes evaluation leaves the faculty in control of the students, the classroom, and the curriculum and as a result delimits administrative power on the campus. So long as teaching is solely in the hands of the faculty, professors can and will claim a privileged position in the university hierarchy as the group that creates and provides the service that is the school's ultimate reason for being. To the extent, however, that administrators are able to contest this claim, they are calling into question the primacy of the faculty on the college or university campus. The push for outcomes assessment is, at its heart, an effort to transfer control over course content, curriculum planning, and the evaluation of what students have learned from the faculty to committees of deanlets on which the faculty might be represented.

In their effort to destroy the ultimate bastion of faculty authority, administrators have allied themselves with various accrediting agencies. Historically, these agencies have been able to bully community colleges but have been treated with polite contempt by major universities, especially the top tiers of private research universities. The Harvards of the world hardly fear loss of accreditation—accreditors know that the credibility of their agencies could not survive confrontations with such schools. Yet, at a number of major universities, including my own, some administrators have warned the faculty of serious problems with our accreditors if we do not succumb to demands for the introduction of assessment regimes. I would submit that the faculty should not be fooled by these warnings and should vigorously resist administrators' demands. As I observed in an earlier chapter, testing is a form of control. Professors exercise authority when they control testing and evaluation; administrators hope to relocate that authority by wresting control of the process from the professors.

Before leaving the faculty portion of my proposed therapeutic regimen, I must observe that it is time for the professorate to take some especially bitter medicine itself, and support the curtailment or elimination of many PhD programs. As is well known, every year many more individuals are awarded doctoral degrees than can possibly find full-time employment in America's colleges and universities. Many of the recipients of these degrees join the growing army of adjunct faculty members who seek to eke out a living by teaching courses, sometimes at several schools, for low salaries and without benefits while continuing to search for full-time employment. Most, especially in the humanities, will never find regular academic positions. Unfortunately, for the academic prestige they confer and cheap labor they provide, many universities continue to support doctoral programs in academic areas where few of their students can ever hope to find jobs. The end result is disappointment for thousands of bright students and the creation of a contingent faculty commanded by college administrators. This is an area where in regular two-way communication, members of the faculty and university boards might discover a formula for abating this unacceptable state of affairs.

Alumni and Other Donors

Administrators often assert that they hope to give alumni a sense of greater involvement in and even ownership of the university. What administrators mean, of course, is that they want alumni to contribute more money to the university. As part of every school's fund-raising effort, the university development office establishes alumni boards, councils, and organizations designed to inveigle loyal alumni and transform their nostalgia into cash.

Alumni who contribute to their schools are to be commended. Alumni seldom have hidden agendas. For most, the goal is to contribute to the educations of their successors. For precisely this reason, alumni and other prospective donors should be wary of development officers and university officials seeking unrestricted gifts. If they want their dollars to be used wisely, donors should consider earmarking their contributions for particular programs, centers, or organizations within the university. As a number of recent controversies have revealed, even money donated for a specific purpose can be diverted by enterprising administrators.[5] Unrestricted dollars, though, will almost certainly flow into the coffers of the deanlets and improve the quality of food served during administrative retreats more than the quality of the education offered by the school.

Parents and Students

One day I was walking across the Hopkins campus with a colleague, the chair of the Political Science Department, when we smelled popcorn. We followed our noses to a large meeting room, where huge quantities of popcorn were being prepared. Overwhelmed by gluttony, we asked if we could have some popcorn. We were rebuffed and told that all the popcorn was needed for the "yield reception" that was to begin within the hour. A yield reception is a social event organized by the admissions office for students who have been accepted to the following year's freshman class. These prospective students, along with their parents, are invited to the campus for what is usually called, "admit weekend," in an effort to convince them to enroll. Virtually every school has its own version of this event. In addition to popcorn, students and parents usually attend panels and meet faculty members and others associated with the school.

My colleague and I expressed some surprise. Political science is a popular undergraduate major and he had not been contacted to participate or find another professor who might participate in a faculty panel. Curious, we contacted other departments and, finally, the dean of arts and sciences, a vacationing biology professor, to find out if they knew anything about the weekend's planned events. The faculty members we contacted, and even the dean, were puzzled at not even having been notified by the admissions office that admit weekend had been scheduled. Further inquiries revealed that the weekend's activities included panels devoted to discussions of finances, housing, dining, equal opportunity, health services, and a number of other useful but ancillary topics. Not a single panel had been organized on academic topics, and not a single faculty member had been invited to take part in this weekend effort to recruit students. The admissions office seemed to think that students came to Hopkins to work with deanlets and to eat our great food.

I was annoyed but not shocked since I had encountered a similar situation at Cornell some years earlier. I am also happy to report that administrative changes were made and subsequent admit weekends at least acknowledged that we had a faculty and that, when not busy studying with the deanlets, students might take classes and work with faculty members. I have often advised parents who found themselves at admit weekends or similar events with no academic content to complain loudly and vehemently to the school's administrators and to consider sending their kid to a different school. The school they are visiting might be exactly as it presents itself—an all-administrative university.

Once they matriculate, students have only one real power—the power to choose among courses, advisers, curricula, and major fields. Students should, if possible, avoid the student life curriculum promoted by and taught by administrators. These classes are a waste of time and their lessons quickly forgotten. Choose a liberal arts major, and take classes in philosophy, language, economics, history, politics, science, math, and literature. Their relevance may not be immediately apparent to you or your parents, but you will not regret the choice. Your choices will also force the deanlets—always customer friendly—to stop trying to destroy the curriculum.

Administrators

At every college and university there are excellent, talented, hard-working administrators. But, there are too many administrators, and large numbers have little to do besides attend meetings and retreats and serve as agents of managerial imperialism. At one time, most administrative tasks were handled by faculty on a part-time or temporary basis. Even today, some professors undertake administrative duties on a part-time basis, as I do. Some deans and other higher-ranking administrators intend to return to the faculty after their administrative stints are up. Generally speaking, short-term or part-time faculty administrators are to be preferred to professional administrators. Faculty administrators are usually committed to the primacy of the university's academic mission; the latter too often are not. The former have no particular interest in administrative aggrandizement; the latter find it too easy to confuse the mission of the university with the interests of its bureaucracy.

Can What Is To Be Done, Be Done?

I am convinced that my proposed remedies, if adopted, would at least slow the spread of administrative blight in higher education. The trouble, though, with prescribing remedies for social problems is that the existence of the problem often precludes acceptance of the cure. University administrators do not want faculty members elected to the board of trustees. Board members who do business with the university do not want conflict of interest rules to be strengthened. Members of the faculty do not want to take time away from their research and teaching to handle administrative chores and contest administrative aggrandizement.

In the 1980s version of *Star Trek*, the leader of the part-human, part-machine "Borg," who represent the expansion of bureaucracy and the demise of individualism, always said, "You will be assimilated, resistance is futile." Perhaps the Borg were correct. Perhaps the professorate will join the other professions assimilated into the expanding white-collar proletariat. Even the once-proud and seemingly invincible physicians have been defeated by a Borg-like coalition of bureaucrats, insurance peddlers, and drug pushers and assimilated into their dark machinery. But, if resistance is futile, it remains essential. The university can be a marvelous institution—well worth protecting from the deanlets and Borg.

Notes

PREFACE

1. Jeffrey Brainard, Paul Fain, and Kathryn Masterson, "Support-Staff Jobs Double in 20 Years, Outpacing Enrollment," *Chronicle of Higher Education*, April 24, 2009, 1.

CHAPTER 1

1. Peter Schmidt, "Under Multiple Assaults, Academic Freedom Is Poorly Defended, Scholars Warn," *Chronicle of Higher Education*, June 26, 2009, A12.
2. Henry Rosovsky, *The University: An Owner's Manual* (New York: W.W. Norton, 1990), 13.
3. American Council on Education, Center for Policy Analysis, *The American College President* (Washington, DC: ACE, 2007), 53–54.
4. Julianne Basinger, "4 Years after a Scandal, a President Steps Down," *Chronicle of Higher Education Online*, March 5, 2004, http://chronicle .com/article/4-Years-After-a-Scandal-a/30708.
5. Julianne Basinger, "In a Surprise, Cornell Chief Steps Down," *Chronicle of Higher Education Online*, June 24, 2005, http://chronicle.com/article/In-a-Surprise-Cornell-Chief/20306.
6. Lisa Foderaro, "New School Faculty and President Remain at Odds," *New York Times* February 21, 2009, A24.
7. Tom Palaima, "NCAA Panel Disses the Faculty," *InsideHigherEd.com*, November 27, 2006, http://www.insidehighered.com/views/2006/11/27/palaima.

8. Leon Jaroff, "Tempest in Tallahassee," *Time.com*, January 27, 2005, http://www.time.com/time/columnist/jaroff/article/0,9565,1021206,00 .html.

9. Alan Finder, "At One University, Tobacco Money Is Not Taboo; It's a Secret," *New York Times*, May 22, 2008, 1.

10. American Association of University Professors, "Academic Freedom and Tenure: University of Dubuque." *Academe: The Bulletin of the AAUP*, Vol. 97, Issue 5 (September–October 2001): 62–73. http://www.aaup .org/AAUP/programs/academicfreedom/investrep/2001/dub.htm.

11. Report of an AAUP Special Committee, "Hurricane Katrina and New Orleans Universities," May–June 2007, 89.

12. "Hurricane Katrina," 104.

13. *University of Buffalo Reporter* 30, no. 18 (June 28, 1999): 1.

14. Scott Jaschik, "Outsourcing the Faculty," *InsideHigherEd.com*, May 17, 2005, http://www.insidehighered.com/layout/set/popup/ news/2005/05/17/delstate.

15. Benjamin Ginsberg, *The American Lie: Government by the People and Other Political Fables* (Boulder, CO: Paradigm Publishers, 2007), 67.

16. Amy Cowles, "Wanted: A Few Good Advisers," *Hopkins Gazette*, February 24, 2003, 7.

17. Leah Maniero, "Five Years out, Some CUE Goals Remain Unmet," *The Johns Hopkins News-Letter*, April 24, 2008, 1.

18. John A. Douglas, "Shared Governance at the University of California," Center for Studies in Higher Education, Research and Occasional Paper Series, March 1998.

19. Thomas Tighe, *Who's In Charge of America's Research Universities?* (Albany: State University of New York Press, 2003), 45–46.

20. Brandeis University, "Faculty Senate Minutes," February 9, 2006.

21. "Faculty Inter-Action," July 2006, 1.

22. Scott Jaschik, "Division at RPI," *InsideHigherEd*, April 28, 2006, http:// www.insidehighered.com/news/2006/04/28/rpi.

23. "Faculty-Governance Fracas," *Chronicle of Higher Education*, September 28, 2007, A9.

24. Donna Euben, "Some Legal Aspects of Collegial Governance," *Presentation Made to the 2003 AAUP Governance Conference*, Indianapolis, Indiana, October 11, 2003, 4.

25. *Florida Memorial College*, 263 NLRB 1248 (1982), *enforced*, 820 F.2d 1182 (11th Cir. 1987). Discussed in Euben, "Some Legal Aspects," 3.

26. Stephen Ambrose, *Eisenhower: Soldier and Patriot* (New York: Simon and Shuster, 1990).

27. Barbara R. Bergmann, "Bloated Administrations, Blighted Campuses," *Academe*, November–December, 1991, 12.

28. Center for Policy Analysis, American Council on Education *The American College President* (Washington, DC: 2007), 9.

29. Joseph Rago, "Mr. Rodgers Goes to Dartmouth," *The Wall Street Journal*, September 1, 2007, A7.

30. Alec MacGillis, "In UM System, More Administrators, Higher Pay," *The Baltimore Sun*, April 2, 2003, D1.

31. MacGillis, "In UM System," D1.

32. Bergmann, "Bloated Administrations," 15.

33. Scott Jaschik, "Administrator's Salaries Are Up 3.5%," *InsideHigher-Education.com*, February 20, 2006, http://www.insidehighered.com/news/2006/02/20/cupa.

34. "Median Salaries of College Administrators," *Chronicle of Higher Education*, August 31, 2007, 21.

35. Jonathan D. Glater, "More College Presidents in Million-Dollar Club," *New York Times*, November 12, 2007, A11.

36. "Compensation of Presidents of Private Institutions," *Chronicle of Higher Education* November 16, 2007, B21.

37. Audrey Williams June, "Why Presidents Are Paid so Much More Than Professors," *Chronicle of Higher Education*, November 16, 2007, B12–13.

38. National Center for Educational Statistics (NCES), "Digest of Educational Statistics: 2006," Table 228.

39. William Waugh Jr., "Issues in University Governance: More 'Professional' and Less Academic," *Annals of the American Academy of Political and Social Science* 585 (January 2003): 89.

40. Francis E. Rourke and Glenn E. Brooks, *The Managerial Revolution in Higher Education* (Baltimore: Johns Hopkins University Press, 1966), 4.

41. Calculated from NCES, "Digest," Tables 345, 348, 353, 354.

42. Jeffrey Brainard, Paul Fain, and Katherine Masterson, "Support-Staff Jobs Double in 20 Years, Outpacing Enrollment," *Chronicle of Higher Education*, April 24, 2009, 1.

43. Sam Dillon, "Share of College Budgets for Recreation Is Rising," *New York Times*, July 10, 2010, A13.

44. Johns Hopkins University, Krieger School of Arts and Sciences, Visiting Committee Report, Spring, 2010.

45. Rourke and Brooks, *Managerial Revolution*, 5.

46. Kenneth Andersen, "Anatomizing Bloat," *Academe*, November–December, 1991, 20–24.

47. Bergmann, "Bloated Administrations,"13.

48. Paul Basken, "A Year Later, Spellings Report Still Makes Ripples," *Chronicle of Higher Education*, September 28, 2007, 1.

49. Richard Ohmann, "Historical Reflections on Accountability," *Academe Online* 86, no. 1 (January–February 2000), http://aaup.org/AAUP/pubsres/academe/2000/JF/Feat/ohma.htm.

50. Freeman A. Hrabowski III, "Getting the Faculty On Board," *InsideHigherEd.com*, June 23, 2006, http://www.insidehighered.com/views/2006/06/23/hrabowski.

51. See, for example, Terra Community College, "Annual Report on Assessment of Student Learning," http://www.terra.edu/about/assessment/results.asp.

52. William Niskanen, *Bureaucracy and Representative Government* (Chicago: Aldine, 1971), ch. 4.
53. Anthony Downs, *Inside Bureaucracy* (Boston: Little Brown, 1967), ch. 9.
54. See Richard Vedder, *Going Broke by Degree: Why College Costs Too Much* (Washington, DC: AEI Press, 2004), 45.
55. Calculated from NCES, "Digest," Table 346.
56. *Chronicle of Higher Education*, December 19, 2007, C60.
57. *Chronicle of Higher Education*, December 19, 2007, C59.
58. *Chronicle of Higher Education*, December 19, 2007, C72.
59. Downs, *Inside Bureaucracy*, 93–95.
60. Brainard, Fain and Masterson, "Support-Staff Jobs Double in 20 Years," A16.

CHAPTER 2

1. North Central College, "Minutes of the President's Staff Meeting," October 10, 2006.
2. Purdue University, "Minutes of the Administrative and Professional Staff Advisory Committee Meeting," July 12, 2006.
3. Owens Community College, "Minutes of the Process Management Steering Committee," November 2, 2006.
4. President's welcoming address, Chicago State College, Summer 2005 Administrative Retreat, July 29 and July 30, 2005.
5. Ibid.
6. David Allen and Larry Calhoun, "Administrative Retreats: A New Twist to Avoid Administrative Isolation," *American Journal of Pharmaceutical Education* 70, no. 6 (December 15, 2006).
7. Adam Emerson, "College Financial Aid Administrators Meet on Lenders' Dime," *Tampa Tribune Online*, May 24, 2007. Available at http://news.tbo.com/news/metro/MGBZFF0P22F.html.
8. Paul Fain, "Vision for Excellence," *Chronicle of Higher Education*, October 5, 2007, A26.
9. Fain, "Vision for Excellence."
10. Francis Rourke and Glenn Brooks, *The Managerial Revolution in Higher Education* (Baltimore: Johns Hopkins University Press, 1966), ch. 3.
11. Sar Levitan and Diane Werneke, *Productivity Problems: Prospects and Policies* (Baltimore: Johns Hopkins University Press, 1984), ch. 3.
12. American Council on Education, Center for Policy Analysis, *The American College President* (Washington, DC: ACE, 2007), ch. 7.
13. University of Illinois Strategic Plan, updated September 22, 2007.
14. Brian Mason, "College Sets Seven Year Agenda," *The Lafayette Online Edition*, October 19, 2007.
15. Doug Lederman, "Southern Illinois Chancellor Forced Out," *InsideHigherEd.com*, November 9, 2006, http://www.insidehighered.com/layout/set/popup/news/2006/11/09/siu.
16. Ashan R. Hampton, "EWC Sues Sacs over Accreditation Loss, Top Administrator Arrested," *University Faculty Voice*, March 9, 2005.

17. "A Special Report," *Chronicle of Higher Education* 50, no. 35 (May 7, 2004): A12–13.
18. Don Phillips and Richard Morin, "Amtrak Subsidy Support Strong, Survey Shows," *Washington Post*, August 5, 2002, 9.
19. "A Special Report."
20. Center for Aid to Education, 2007 VSE Survey. www.cae.org.
21. "Harvard Alumni and Friends Contribute $651M in Fiscal Year 2008," *Harvard Gazette Online*, September 11, 2008. http://www.news.harvard.edu/gazette/2008/09.11/11-gifts.html.
22. Milton Mayer, *Young Man in a Hurry: The Story of William Rainey Harper, First President of the University of Chicago* (Chicago: University of Chicago Alumni Association, 1957). Also, John W, Boyer, *Broad and Christian in the Fullest Sense: William Rainey Harper and the University of Chicago* (Chicago: The College of the University of Chicago, 2005).
23. Michael J. Worth, *New Strategies for Educational Fund Raising* (Westport, CT: Praeger, 2002), 26.
24. Worth, *New Strategies*, 33.
25. Worth, *New Strategies*, 27.
26. Ronald G. Ehrenberg, *Tuition Rising: Why College Costs So Much* (Cambridge: Harvard University Press, 2002), ch. 1.
27. Stanley Aronowitz, *The Knowledge Factory* (Boston: Beacon Press, 2000), 135.
28. Ehrenberg, *Tuition Rising*, 46.
29. Craig Karmin, "Ivy League Endowments Finally 'Dumb,'" *The Wall Street Journal* June 30, 2009, C1.
30. Ford Foundation, Advisory Committee on Endowment Management, "Managing Educational Endowments" (New York, 1969).
31. Donald Frey, "University Endowment Returns Are Underspent," *Challenge* 45, no. 4 (July/August 2002): 109–21.
32. Tamar Lewin, "College Presidents Defend Rising Tuition, But Lawmakers Sound Skeptical," *New York Times Online*, September 9, 2008, http://www.nytimes.com/2008/09/09/education/09college.html.
33. Lewin, "College Presidents," 2008. Hoping to forestall future congressional concern, several of the wealthiest schools, led by Harvard, subsequently announced that they would significantly increase financial aid to middle-class parents.
34. Adam Smith, *The Wealth of Nations* (New York: Random House, 1937), book 5, ch. 1.

CHAPTER 3

1. Robert Birnbaum, *Management Fads in Higher Education* (San Francisco: Jossey-Bass, 2000).
2. Birnbaum, *Management Fads*.
3. Roderick Kiewiet and Matthew D. McCubbins, *The Logic of Delegation* (Chicago: University of Chicago Press, 1991).

4. Anthony Downs, *Inside Bureaucracy* (Boston: Little Brown, 1967), 77–78.

5. Downs, *Inside Bureaucracy*, 77.

6. James Q. Wilson, *Bureaucracy* (New York: Basic Books, 1989), 60.

7. Harold Seidman, *Politics, Position, and Power*, 5th edition (New York: Oxford University Press, 1998), 129.

8. Paul Starr, *The Social Transformation of American Medicine* (New York: Basic Books, 1984).

9. Wilson, *Bureaucracy*, 369–70.

10. Andrew J. Bacevich, *The New American Militarism* (New York: Oxford University Press, 2005), ch. 2.

11. Margaret Turner Warwick, "Professional Values—Thoughts for Discussion," Royal College of Physicians, December 10, 2004. http://www.rcplondon.ac.uk/pubs/books/docinsoc/docinsoc.pdf.

12. John Brehm and Scott Gates, *Working, Shirking, and Sabotage* (Ann Arbor: University of Michigan Press, 1997).

13. George Stigler, "The Theory of Regulation," *Bell Journal of Economics and Management Science* 2, no. 1 (1971): 3–21.

14. Donald Campbell, *Interests: Motivation and the Economics of Information* (New York: Cambridge University Press, 2006).

15. Anne Bennett Swingle, "HopkinsOne Gets Real," *Dome* 55, no. 9 (November 2004).

16. Johns Hopkins University Administrative Bulletin, Post SAP Upgrade Edition, May 2010.

17. Steven Pinker, *How the Mind Works* (New York: W.W. Norton, 1997), 493.

18. Harry Jaffe, "Ben Ladner's Years of Living Lavishly," *Washingtonian.com*, 2006, http://www.washingtonian.com/articles/people/1714.html.

19. Jaffe, "Ben Ladner's Years."

20. Susan Kinzie and Valerie Strauss, "$500,000 in Ladner Spending Itemized," *Washington Post*, September 22, 2005, A01.

21. Jodi S. Cohen, "Ex-CSU Chief Oks $18,000 Book on . . . Self," *Chicagotribune.com*, August 7, 2008, http://articles.chicagotribune.com/2008-08-07/news/0808061321_1_chicago-state-university-illinois-house-leadership.

22. James Duderstadt, *Intercollegiate Athletics and the American University* (Ann Arbor: University of Michigan Press, 2003), 109.

23. Bruce Lambert, "New York Regents Oust 18 Trustees from Adelphi U," *New York Times*, February 11, 1997, B1.

24. Julianne Basinger, "Boards Crack Down on Members Insider Deals," *Chronicle of Higher Education*, February 6, 2006, 1.

25. Basinger, "Boards Crack Down."

26. Craig Gima, "Regents Blast UH Housing Bid," *Honolulu Star Bulletin*, February 20, 2004, 1.

27. Basinger, "Boards Crack Down."

28. Josh Margolin and Ted Sherman, "How UMDNJ Became a Patronage Pit," *Newark Star-Ledger*, April 4, 2006, 1.

29. Margolin and Sherman, "How UMDNJ Became a Patronage Pit."
30. "Former Alabama Postsecondary Chancellor Agrees to Plead Guilty," *WSFA 12 News, Birmingham, Alabama*, http://www.wsfa.com/global/story.asp?s=7768327&ClientType=Printable.
31. Patricia Sabatini and Len Boselovic, "MBA Mystery in Morgantown: Questions Raised over How WVU Granted Mylan Executive Her Degree," *Pittsburgh Post-Gazette*, December 21, 2007, D1.
32. Douglas Belkin and Carrie Porter, "Two Trustees Quit in Illinois Admissions Scandal," *The Wall Street Journal*, August 6, 2009, A5.
33. Clifford Marks and Nathan Strauss, "With House Divided, HMI Spun Off," *The Harvard Crimson*, February 21, 2008, 1.
34. Clifford Marks and Nathan Strauss, "The Contentious Rise of HMI," *The Harvard Crimson*, February 20, 2008, 1.
35. Marks and Strauss, "With House Divided."
36. "Trustees: More Willing Than Ready," *Chronicle of Higher Education*, May 11, 2007, A11–21.
37. U.S. Department of Education, Office of Inspector General, "Two Former Tufts Employees Indicted for Stealing Nearly $1 Million from University," Investigation Report, July 1, 2008.
38. Doug Lederman, "Tangled Web at Wesleyan," *InsideHigherEd*.com, January 6, 2010, http://www.insidehighered.com/news/2010/01/06/wesleyan.
39. Kelly Field, "The Selling of Student Loans," *Chronicle of Higher Education*, June 1, 2007, A15–18.
40. Gadi Dechter, "Aid Official at Johns Hopkins Is Suspended: Payments to Financial Services Chief from Loan Company Probed," *Baltimoresun.com*, April 10, 2007, http://articles.baltimoresun.com/2007-04-10/news/0704100016_1_frishberg-preferred-lenders-student-loan-xpress.
41. Mary-Jo Kranacher, "DeFrauding the Halls of Academe," *Fraud Magazine*, March/April, 2005.
42. Karen Grassmuck, "What Happened At Stanford," *Chronicle of Higher Education Online*, V.37, no.35. May 15,1991, A25–27.
43. C. J. Hughes, "Ex-Dean Accused of Forcing Students to Work as Her Servants," *New York Times*, October 1, 2010, A18.
44. Skip Cauthorn, "Wasteful Spending at UT," *Nashville City Paper*, August 14, 2003, http://nashvillecitypaper.com/content/city-news/wasteful-spending-ut.
45. *Chronicle of Higher Education*, News Blog, "Jury Finds Texas Southern U Retaliated against Former Students," August 2, 2008, http://chronicle.com/news.article/4924/jury-finds-texas-southern-university.
46. U.S. Department of Education, Office of Inspector General, "Former Director of Admissions of Touro College and Others Indicted," Investigation Report, July 16, 2007.
47. Marisha Agha, "Former UCR Administrator Pleads," *Press-Enterprise, Jan.9, 2011*. http://www.pe.com/localnews/inland/stories/PE_News_Local_D_webchiu07.24bc85c.html.

48. *WSFA 12 News*, January 24, 2008, http://www.wsfa.com/Global/story .asp?S=7768327.

49. Stephanie Strom, "Report Sketches Crime Costing Billions: Theft from Charities," *New York Times Online*, March 29, 2008, http://www .nytimes.com/2008/03/29/us/29fraud.html.

50. Peter Panepento and Paul Fain, "Insider Deals Are Common among Nonprofit Boards, Study Finds," *Chronicle of Higher Education*, July 6, 2007, 1.

51. "Boise Attorneys Eiguren, Miller Reach Agreement With Idaho State Bar," *Idaho Business Review.com*, March 30, 2007.

52. Patrick Healy, "Goldin Said to Question Trustees' Ties to BU Deals," *BostonGlobe.com*, October 31, 2003, http://www.boston.com/news/ education/higher/articles/2003/10/31/goldin_said_to_question_trustees_ ties_to_bu_deals/.

53. Julianne Basinger, "Boards Crack Down on Members Insider Deals: Recent Scandals Trigger New Scrutiny of Trustees," *Chronicle of Higher Education Online*, February 6, 2004, http://chronicle.com/ article/Boards-Crack-Down-on-Members/13659/.

54. Erin Jordan, "Regents Ties Stir Concerns at U of I: Critics Fear Insurers Could Be Affecting Presidential Search," *Des Moines Register Online*, November 29, 2006, http://www.nicholasjohnson.org/BlogStuf/ regents/ejdr1129.html.

55. Thomas Bartlett, "President Accused of Plagiarism Will Resubmit His Dissertation for Review," *Chronicle of Higher Education Online*, August 31, 2007, http://chronicle.com/article/President-Accused-of/39487.

56. Thomas Wanat, "College President Resigns after His Resume Is Questioned," *Chronicle of Higher Education Online*, February 2, 1996, http://chronicle.com/article/College-President-Resigns/95575/.

57. Eric Hoover and Sierra Millman, "Shocking Admission," *Chronicle of Higher Education*, May 11, 2007, A45–46, http://chronicle.com/article/ Shocking-Admission/18011/.

58. Jeffrey Selingo, "Ex-Official at 2-Year College in Florida Accused of Falsifying Grades and Degrees," *Chronicle of Higher Education Online*, February 17, 1998.

59. "Former U. of Louisville Dean Faces Fresh Allegations," *Chronicle of Higher Education*, September 19, 2008, A16.

60. David Glenn, "Education Dean's Fraud Teaches U. of Louisville a Hard Lesson," *Chronicle of Higher Education*, June 12, 2009, 1.

61. Paul Fain, "Chancellor Hire at U. of Wisconsin at Parkside Resigns Amid Criminal Probe," *Chronicle of Higher Education*, June 24, 2008, http://chronicle.com/article/Chancellor-Hire-at-U-of/41208.

62. Doug Lederman, "Plagiarism Mystery," *InsideHigherEd.com*, June 5, 2006, http://www.insidehighered.com/layout/set/popup/ news/2006/06/05/wesley.

63. Paula Wasley, "Moving On," *Chronicle of Higher Education*, November 2, 2007, A5.

64. Fox Butterfield, "Dean Apologizes for Plagiarizing Part of Boston U. Commencement Speech," *New York Times Online*, July 6, 1991, http://www.nytimes.com/1991/07/06/us/dean-apologizes-for-plagiarizing-part-of-boston-u-commencement-speech.html.

65. Thomas Bartlett, "Missouri Dean Appears to Have Plagiarized a Speech by Cornel West," *Chronicle of Higher Education Online*, June 24, 2005, http://chronicle.com/article/Missouri-Dean-Appears-to-Have/12743.

66. "Report Finds University President Plagiarized," *New York Times Online*, March 18, 2004, http://www.nytimes.com/2004/03/18/nyregion/metro-briefing-connecticut-hartford-report-finds-university-president.html?fta=y.

67. Jonathan Margulies, "President of N.Y.'s Hamilton College Steps Down amid Controversy over Speech," *Chronicle of Higher Education Online*, October 2, 2002, http://chronicle.com/article/President-of-NYs-Hamilton/116644/.

68. Stacey Stowe, "University President Is Accused of Plagiarizing an Article," *New York Times*, March 12, 2004, D1.

69. Brian Martin, "Plagiarism: A Misplaced Emphasis," *Journal of Information Ethics* 3, no. 2 (Fall 1994): 36–47.

70. Gavin Moodie, "Bureaucratic Plagiarism." *Campus Review* 3, no. 10 (March 25–31, 1993): 10–19.

71. William Thornton, "Another Plagiarism Accusation Hits JSU Chief," *The Birmingham News Online*, August 9, 2007. A subsequent investigation, organized by the president, found that the former director of the school's news bureau was entirely at fault in the matter. http://tripatlas.com/Jacksonville_State_University.

CHAPTER 4

1. For critiques of academic liberalism, see Dinesh D'Souza, *Illiberal Education* (New York: Free Press, 1991); David Horowitz, *Indoctrination U* (New York: Encounter Books, 2007); and Roger Kimball, *Tenured Radicals* (New York: Harper, 1990).

2. Neil Gross and Solon Simmons, "The Social and Political Views of American Professors," *Working Paper*, September 24, 2007, http://www.wjh.harvard.edu/~ngross/lounsbery_9-25.pdf.

3. Johns Hopkins University Office of News and Information, "News Release: University Statement on Investigation of Fraternity," October 30, 2006.

4. Andy Guess, "Sending in the Class Monitor," *InsideHigherEd.com*, November 9, 2007, http://www.insidehighered.com/news/2007/11/09/brandeis.

5. Heather MacDonald, "Victimology 101 at Yale," *The Weekly Standard*, March 16, 2009, 14.

6. Jon B. Gould, *Speak No Evil: The Triumph of Hate Speech Regulation* (Chicago: University of Chicago Press, 2005), 90.

7. Robert McCaughey, *Stand Columbia* (New York: Columbia University Press, 2003), chs. 15 and 19.

8. Stuart Taylor and K. C. Johnson, *Until Proven Innocent* (New York: St. Martin's, 2007).

9. Robin Wilson, "Notoriety Yields to Tragedy in Iowa Sexual-Harassment Cases: After 2 Suicides, Colleagues Question University's Role," *Chronicle of Higher Education*, February 20, 2009, A1.

10. Jerome Karabel, *The Chosen* (Boston: Houghton-Mifflin, 2005).

11. D'Souza, *Illiberal Education*, 205.

12. Richard Bradley, *Harvard Rules* (New York: HarperCollins, 2006).

13. "Henry Louis Gates Jr. to Continue at Harvard," *Harvard University Gazette*, December 5, 2002.

14. "Henry Louis Gates Jr. to Continue at Harvard."

15. Marcella Bombardieri, "Harvard's Gates to Step Down as Department Head," *The Boston Globe, boston.comNews*, April 16, 2005, http://www.boston.com/news/education/higher/articles/2005/04/16/harvards_gates_to_step_down_as_department_head/.

16. *Journal of Blacks in Higher Education*, June 22, 2008.

17. Timothy Williams, "In West Harlem Land Dispute, It's Columbia vs. Residents," *New York Times*, November 20, 2006.

18. Matthew Schuerman, "Mr. Bollinger's Battle," *The New York Observer*, February 18, 2007.

19. Daniel Amzallig and Joshua Chambers, "CU Responds to Strike Demands," *Columbia Spectator online edition*, November 13, 2007, www.columbiaspectator.com/2007/11/. . ./cu-responds-strike-demands.

20. Charles V. Bagli, "Court Bars Land Takeover for Columbia Campus," *The New York Times*, December 4, 2009, 1.

21. Charles Bagli, "Victory for Columbia in Eminent Domain Suit," *The New York Times*, June 25, 2010, A27.

22. University of Rochester, "Diversity at the University," http://www.rochester.edu/diversity/faq.html.

23. Damon A. Williams and Katrina C. Wade-Golden, "What Is a Chief Diversity Officer?" *InsideHigherEd.com*, April 18, 2006, http://www.insidehighered.com/workplace/2006/04/18/williams.

24. Pauline Keyes, "New Paradigms for Diversifying Faculty and Staff in Higher Education: Uncovering Cultural Biases in the Search and Hiring Process," *Multicultural Education*, Winter 2006.

25. Alan Contreras, "Affirmative Inaction," *InsideHigherEd.com*, July 21, 2006, http://www.insidehighered.com/views/2006/07/21/contreras.

26. Lisa M. Portugal, "Diversity Leadership in Higher Education," *Academic Leadership Online*, February 12, 2007, http://www.academicleadership.org/article/Diversity_Leadership_in_Higher_Education.

27. Anne Bromley, "Faculty Diversity Rising: Search Committees Required to Have EOP Training," *Inside UVA Online*, August 26, 2005, http://www.virginia.edu/insideuva/2005/14/diversity.html.

28. University of California, Berkeley, "Efforts of the Faculty Equity Office: October 2001 to April 2002," www.universityofcalifornia.edu/faculty-diversity/efforts-faculty-equity-office.pdf.
29. Contreras, "Affirmative Inaction."
30. Keyes, "New Paradigms."
31. Johns Hopkins University, "Feedback Needed on Equity, Civility and Respect Recommendations," May 5, 2008.
32. Peter Brownfield, "Administration Deals Blow to Campus Censorship," *FoxNews.com*, September 2, 2003, http://www.foxnews.com/story/0,2933,96252,00.html.
33. Harvey A. Silverglate, "Memorandum to Free Speech Advocates," University of Wisconsin, January 26, 1999.
34. Peter Berkowitx, "Academia Goes Silent on Free Speech," *The Wall Street Journal*, October 17, 2009, A13.
35. Gould, *Speak No Evil*, 90–91.
36. Posted by Adam Kissel on June 24, 2008, http://thefire.org/article/9453.html.
37. Alan Kors and Harvey Silverglate, *The Shadow University* (New York: Harper, 1999), 150.
38. Kors and Silverglate, *The Shadow University*, 152.
39. Kors and Silverglate, *The Shadow University*, 167.
40. Kors and Silverglate, *The Shadow University*, 11.
41. Kors and Silverglate, *The Shadow University*, ch. 1.
42. Kors and Silverglate, *The Shadow University*, ch. 1.
43. 315 U.S. 568 (1942).
44. Donald A. Downs, *Restoring Free Speech and Liberty on Campus* (New York: Cambridge University Press, 2005), 59.
45. Kent M. Weeks and Joel D. Eckert, "Student Civility," *Lex Collegii* 29, no. 4 (Spring 2006): 2.
46. Kors and Silverglate, *The Shadow University*, 10.
47. Foundation for Individual Rights in Education, "Spotlight on Speech Codes 2007," 11.
48. Johns Hopkins University, "Principles for Ensuring Equity, Civility and Respect for All," 2006.
49. 526 U.S. 629 (1999).
50. Weeks and Eckert, "Student Civility," 3.
51. Dorothy Rabinowitz, "American Politics Aren't Post-Racial," *The Wall Street Journal*, July 7, 2008, A13.
52. In California, state law requires private institutions to obey the First Amendment. The courts, however, have been equivocal in their application of the state's statute. David Bernstein, *You Can't Say That* (Washington, DC: The Cato Institute, 2003), 65–66.
53. Andy Guess, "Maybe He Shouldn't Have Spoken His Mind," *Inside-HigherEd.com*, January 11, 2008, http://www.insidehighered.com/news/2008/01/11/valdosta.
54. Gould, *Speak No Evil*.

55. Kenneth L. Marcus, "Higher Education, Harassment and First Amendment Opportunism," *William & Mary Bill of Rights Journal* 14, no. 4 (April 2008): 1025.
56. Frederick Schauer, "First Amendment Opportunism," in Lee Bollinger and Geoffrey Stone, eds., *Eternally Vigilant: Free Speech in the Modern Era* (Chicago: University of Chicago Press, 2003), 176.
57. Jodi Wilgoren, "Life 101: Useful Skills for College and Beyond," *The New York Times*, October 15, 1999.
58. Steve Bradt, "College Adds 'Life Skills' to Its Curriculum," *Harvard University Gazette Online*, March 22, 2007.
59. University of Delaware Office of Residence Life, *Diversity Facilitation Training*, August 14 and 15, 2007. Presented by Dr. Shakti Butler.
60. Angela Schaeffer, "Freshman Book Discussion Yields Rich Insights," *Johns Hopkins University Arts and Sciences Magazine* 5, no.1 (Fall/Winter 2007).

Chapter 5

1. Richard Hofstadter and Walter Metzger, *The Development of Academic Freedom in the United States* (New York: Columbia University Press, 1955), ch. 8.
2. *Sweezy v. New Hampshire*, 354 U.S. 134 (1957).
3. 364 U.S. 479 (1960).
4. 385 U.S. 589 (1967).
5. William A. Kaplin and Barbara Lee, *The Law of Higher Education*, 4th ed. (New York: Wiley, 2007), 249.
6. 574 US 410 (2006).
7. Scott Jaschik, "Not So Free Speech in Campus Governance," *InsideHigherEd.com*, March 24, 2008, http://www.insidehighered.com/news/2008/03/24/garcetti.
8. Scott Jaschik, "Loss for Whistle Blowers," *InsideHigherEd.com*, April 23, 2007, http://www.insidehighered.com/layout/set/popup/news/2007/04/23/vila. Also, Peter Schmidt, "Professors' Freedoms under Assault in the Courts," *Chronicle of Higher Education*, February 27, 2009, A1.
9. Scott Jaschik, "Faculty Speech Rights Rejected," *InsideHigherEd.com*, December 23, 2009, http://www.insidehighered.com/news/2009/12/23/sadid.
10. See the case of *Brown v. Armenti*, 247 F.3rd 69 (3rd Cir. 2001).
11. Richard Hiers, "Institutional Academic Freedom or Autonomy Grounded upon the First Amendment: A Jurisprudential Mirage," *Hamline Law Review* 30, no. 1 (Winter 2007): 1ff.
12. John LaNear, "The Misreading of Sweezy: How Justice Powell Mistakenly Created Institutional Academic Freedom," *West's Education Law Reporter*, May 18, 2006, 501–25.
13. *Urofsky v. Gilmore*, 216 F.3rd at 410 (4th Cir. 2000).

14. J. Peter Byrne, "Constitutional Academic Freedom after Grutter: Getting Real about the 'Four Freedoms' of a University," *University of Colorado Law* Review 77, no. 4 (Fall 2006): 929–53.

15. Alan K. Chen, "Bureaucracy and Distrust: Germaneness and the Paradoxes of the Academic Freedom Doctrine," *University of Colorado Law Review* 77, no. 4 (Fall 2006): 955.

16. Amy Gutman, *Democratic Education* (Princeton: Princeton University Press, 1987), 176.

17. Mitchell Stevens, *Creating a Class* (Cambridge, MA: Harvard University Press, 2007), 149.

18. Alan Finder, "Decline of the Tenure Track Raises Concerns at Colleges," *New York Times*, November 20, 2007, 1.

19. Hofstadter and Metzger, *Development of Academic Freedom*, 217.

20. Hofstadter and Metzger, *Development of Academic Freedom*, 330.

21. Hofstadter and Metzger, *Development of Academic Freedom*, 252–53.

22. Hofstadter and Metzger, *Development of Academic Freedom*, 258.

23. Upton Sinclair, *The Goose-Step: A Study of American Education* (Pasadena, CA: Published by the Author, 1923). Kessinger reprint edition.

24. Thomas E. Will, "A Menace to Freedom: The College Trust," *Arena* 26 (September, 1901). Quoted in Hofstadter and Metzger, *Development of Academic Freedom*, 420–21.

25. Orin L. Elliott, *Stanford University: The First Twenty-Five Years* (Stanford, CA: Stanford University Press, 1937), 343–44. Quoted in Hofstadter and Metzger, *Development of Academic Freedom*, 439.

26. Sinclair, *The Goose-Step*, 156–57.

27. Hofstadter and Metzger, *Development of Academic Freedom*, 424.

28. Christopher J. Lucas, *American Higher Education*, 2nd ed. (New York: Palgrave Macmillan, 2006), 205.

29. Hofstadter and Metzger, *Development of Academic Freedom*, 444.

30. Hofstadter and Metzger, *Development of Academic Freedom*, 478.

31. American Association of University Professors, "Report of the Committee on Academic Freedom and Academic Tenure," December 31, 1915.

32. Quoted in Lucas, *American Higher Education*, 206.

33. Quoted in Hofstadter and Metzger, *Development of Academic Freedom*, 483.

34. Quoted in Hofstadter and Metzger, *Development of Academic Freedom*, 484.

35. James Fishman, "Tenure and Its Discontents: The Worst Form of Employment Relationship Save All of the Others," *Pace Law Review* 21 (Fall 2000): 159–63.

36. 3 Call 587 (1790).

37. M. M. Chambers, *The Colleges and the Courts* (Boston: Updike, 1941).

38. *Ward v. The Regents of Kansas State Agricultural College*, 138 Fed. 372 (1905).

39. Hofstadter and Metzger, *Development of Academic Freedom*, 486.
40. John Thelin, *A History of American Higher Education* (Baltimore: Johns Hopkins University Press, 2004), 70.
41. Thelin, *A History*, 158.
42. National Center for Educational Statistics (NCES), "Digest of Educational Statistics, 2006," Table 174.
43. Morris Bishop, *A History of Cornell* (Ithaca, NY: Cornell University Press, 1962), 241.
44. A. W. Coats, "The Origins of the Chicago 'Schools'?" *The Journal of Political Economy* 71, no. 5 (October 1963): 488.
45. Edward H. Cotton, *The Life of Charles W. Eliot* (Boston: Small, Maynard & Co., 1926), 196.
46. Laurence Vesey, *The Emergence of the American University* (Chicago: University of Chicago Press, 1965),360.
47. Thelin, *A History*, 133.
48. Thorstein Veblen, *The Higher Learning in America: A Memorandum* (New York: Kessinger reprint edition), ch. 3.
49. Vesey, *Emergence of the American University*, 326.
50. Vesey, *Emergence of the American University*, 327.
51. Adolf Berle Jr., *Power without Property* (New York: Harcourt, Brace, 1959).
52. Bishop, *A History of Cornell*, 238.
53. Cotton, *The Life of Charles W. Eliot*, 190.
54. Bishop, *A History of Cornell*, 240.
55. Bishop, *A History of Cornell*, 240.
56. Richard Storr, *Harper's University* (Chicago: University of Chicago Press, 1966), 334.
57. Vesey, *Emergence of the American University*, 322.
58. Walter Rogers, *Andrew D. White and the Modern University* (Ithaca, NY: Cornell University Press, 1942), 150–55.
59. Hofstadter and Metzger, *Development of Academic Freedom*, 497.
60. Hofstadter and Metzger, *Development of Academic Freedom*, 502.
61. Michael Rosenthal, *Nicholas Miraculous* (New York: Farrar, Straus and Giroux. 2006), 234.
62. Hofstadter and Metzger, *Development of Academic Freedom*, 488.
63. Ellen W. Schrecker, *No Ivory Tower* (New York: Oxford, 1986).
64. Walter Metzger, "Academic Tenure in America: A Historical Essay," in *Faculty Tenure: A Report by the Commission on Academic Tenure in Higher Education* (San Francisco: Jossey-Bass, 1973), 155.
65. Roger Baldwin and Jay Chronister, "What Happened to the Tenure Track?" in Richard Chait, ed., *The Questions of Tenure* (Cambridge, MA: Harvard University Press, 2002), 131.
66. David Glenn, "When Tenured Professors Are Laid Off, What Recourse?" *Chronicle of Higher Education*, October 2, 2009, A12.
67. Scott Jaschik, "Layoffs without Financial Exigency," *InsideHigherEd. com*, March 2, 2010, http://www.insidehighered.com/news/2010/03/02/

exigency. Also, Doug Blackburn, "FSU Layoffs of Tenured Faculty Cause a Stir," *Tallahassee.com*, February 19, 2010.

68. Jaschik, "Layoffs."

69. Mary Burgan, *What Ever Happened to the Faculty?* (Baltimore: Johns Hopkins University Press, 2006), ch. 8.

70. Arthur Schafer, "Biomedical Conflicts of Interest," *Journal of Medical Ethics* 30 (2004): 8–24.

71. Schafer, 17.

72. Scott Jaschik, "Students Fail—and Professor Loses Job," *InsideHigherEd.com*, May 14, 2007, http://www.insidehighered.com/news/2008/05/14/aird.

73. Scott Jaschik, "Academic Freedom Violations Found at Hunter," *InsideHigherEd.com*, May 13, 2007, http://www.insidehighered.com/news/2008/05/13/hunter.

74. Scott Jaschik, "Prior Restraint on Speech?" *InsideHigherEd.com*, July 26, 2006, http://www.insidehighered.com/layout/set/popup/news/2006/07/26/fredonia.

75. Scott Jaschik, "The Phantom Professor," *InsideHigherEd.com*, May 11, 2005, http://www.insidehighered.com/news/2005/05/11/phantom.

76. Jonathan Travis, "Academic Censored and Threatened," *University World News*, June 7, 2009, http://www.universityworldnews.com/article.php?story=20090604192259634.

77. Alan Finder, "Decline of the Tenure Track Raises Concerns at Colleges," *New York Times*, November 20, 2007, 1.

78. Benjamin E. Hermalin, "Higher Education Boards of Trustees," in Ronald Ehrenberg, ed., *Governing Academia* (Ithaca, NY: Cornell University Press, 2004), 28–48.

79. Elka Jones, "Beyond Supply and Demand: Assessing the Ph.D. Job Market," *Occupational Outlook Quarterly* (Winter 2003).

80. Audrey Williams June, "A Philosopher Stirs Up the World of Adjuncts," *Chronicle of Higher Education*, May 23, 2008, 1.

81. Kinley Brauer, "The Tenure Crisis at Minnesota," Organization of American Historians, 1996. http://www.oah.org/pubs/nl/96nov/brauer1196.html.

82. Stanley Aronowitz, *The Knowledge Factory* (Boston: Beacon Press, 2000), 67.

CHAPTER 6

1. Sheila Slaughter and Gary Rhoades, *Academic Capitalism and the New Economy* (Baltimore: Johns Hopkins University Press, 2004), 1.

2. Clark Kerr, *The Uses of the University*, 5th ed. (Cambridge: Harvard University Press, 2001), 66.

3. Stanley Aronowitz, *The Knowledge Factory* (Boston: Beacon Press, 2000).

4. Daniel Golden, *The Price of Admission: How America's Ruling Class Buys Its Way into Elite Colleges—and Who Gets Left Outside at the Gates* (New York: Crown, 2007).

5. Aronowitz, *The Knowledge Factory*, ch. 6. Also, David L. Kirp, *Shakespeare, Einstein, and the Bottom Line* (Cambridge, MA: Harvard University Press, 2003).

6. http://www.college.columbia.edu/core.

7. http://www.stjohnscollege.edu/.

8. http://collegecatalog.uchicago.edu/liberal/curriculum.shtml.

9. http://my.harvard.edu/icb/icb.do?keyword=core.

10. Ronald L. Baker, "Keystones of Regional Accreditation: Intentions, Outcomes and Sustainability," in Peter Hernon and Robert Dugan, *Outcomes Assessment in Higher Education* (Westport, CT: Greenwood, 2004), 1.

11. Joan S. Stark and Lisa R. Lattuca, *Shaping the College Curriculum* (Needham Heights, MA: Allyn & Bacon, 1997), 360. See also Harry R. Lewis, *Excellence without a Soul: How a Great University Forgot Education* (New York: Public Affairs Press, 2006), ch. 8.

12. http://www.bls.gov/opub/ooq/2007/winter/art01.pdf.

13. http://www.iseek.org/education/liberalarts.html.

14. Austin Doherty et al., "Developing Intellectual Skills," in Jerry Gaff, ed., *Handbook of the Undergraduate Curriculum* (San Francisco: Jossey-Bass, 1997), 170–189.

15. http://northhall.blogspot.com/2005/09/kurt-schmidt-why-are-liberal-arts.html.

16. Will H. Corral and Daphne Patai, "An End to Foreign Languages, an End to the Liberal Arts." *Chronicle of Higher Education*, June 6, 2008, http://chronicle.com/article/An-End-to-Foreign-Languages/20912.

17. Quoted in Aronowitz, *The Knowledge Factory*, 135.

18. Kirp, *Shakespeare, Einstein*, 36.

19. National Association of Scholars, "The Dissolution of General Education," http://www.nas.org/polReports.cfm?Doc_Id=113.

20. Victor E. Ferrall Jr., "Can Liberal Arts Colleges Be Saved" *Insidehighered.com*, February 11, 2008, http://www.insidehighered.com/views/2008/02/11/ferrall.

21. Quoted in Andrew Hacker, "The Truth about the Colleges," *New York Review of Books*, November 3, 2005, 53.

22. For example, see David Armstrong, "U.S. Probe Focuses on Emory Doctor's Ties to Glaxo," *The Wall Street Journal*, February 26, 2009, A6. Also, Marcia Angell, "Drug Companies and Doctors: A Story of Corruption," *New York Review*, January 15, 2009, 8–12.

23. Anthony Depalma, "Stanford to Alter Its Accounting of Overhead on Research Grants," *New York Times*, July 23, 1991, A9.

24. Jeffrey Brainard, "Have Federal Constraints on Reimbursing Overhead Gone Too Far?" *Chronicle of Higher Education*, August 5, 2005, 1.

25. "Despite Furor over Research Fees, Stanford Plans Similar Rate Again," *New York Times*, July 5, 1991. http://query.nytimes.com/gst/fullpage.html?res=9D0CE7DC113DF93.

26. Steven G. Poskanzer, *Higher Education Law* (Baltimore: Johns Hopkins University Press, 2002), 43.
27. Poskanzer, *Higher Education Law*, 43.
28. Mark A. Lemley, "Patenting Nanotechnology," *Stanford Law Review* 58 (November 2005): 613ff.
29. Ron A. Bouchard, "Balancing Public and Private Interests in the Commercialization of Publicly Funded Medical Research: Is There a Role for Compulsory Government Royalty Fees?" *Boston University Journal of Science and Technology Law* 13 (Summer, 2007): 173.
30. Lorelei Ritchie de Larena, "The Price of Progress: Are Universities Adding to the Cost," *Houston Law Review* 43 (Spring, 2007): 1412.
31. De Larena, "The Price of Progress," 1413.
32. Clifton Leaf, "The Law of Unintended Consequences," *Fortune*, September 9, 2005, 250.
33. Michael A. Heller and Rebecca S. Eisenberg, "Can Patent Deter Innovation? The Anticommons in Biomedical Research," *Science* 280 (1998): 698.
34. Lemley, "Patenting Nanotechnology," 613.
35. De Larena, "The Price of Progress," 1402.
36. Slaughter and Rhoades, 114.
37. De Larena, "The Price of Progress," 1426.
38. De Larena, "The Price of Progress," 1428.
39. See Harvey Silverglate, "Let's Cut the Administrative Fat," December 10, 2008, http://www.mindingthecampus.com/originals/2008/12/after_years_of_fat_our.html.
40. Kathryn Masterson, "Recession Tempers the Usual Optimism in College Fund-Raising Offices," *Chronicle of Higher Education* January 9, 2009, A16.
41. "A Message to Alumni from Dean James Madara," February 10, 2009, Also, Mike Colias, "U of C Hospital to Cut $100M," *Chicago Business*, Jan. 9, 2009. http://www.chicagobusiness.com/apps/pbcs.dll/article?AID=9999200032567#axzz1AYTs2fP0.
42. Simmi Aujla, "At Texas Flagship, Budget Cut May Translate into Less Language Study," *Chronicle of Higher Education*, October 9, 2009, A8.
43. David Glenn and Peter Schmidt, "Disappearing Disciplines: Degree Programs Fight for Their Lives," *Chronicle of Higher Education*, April 2, 2010, 1.
44. Josh Keller and Marc Parry, "U. Of California Considers Online Classes or Even Degrees," *Chronicle of Higher Education*, May 14, 2010, 1.
45. http://provost.fsu.edu/staff/.
46. Tamar Lewin, "Brandeis Halts Retirement Payments," *New York Times*, May 22, 2009, A12.
47. Scott Travis, "Florida Atlantic University Faculty, Administration at Odds over Salary Increases," *South Florida Sun-Sentinel.com*, January 12, 2009, http://www.tcpalm.com/news/2009/jan/12/some-question-employee-salary-increases-fau/.

48. Jon Reidel, "President, Faculty, Staff, Students Discussed Budget Cuts at February 26 Forum," The University of Vermont, University Communications, February 27, 2009, http://www.uvm.edu/~uvmpr/?Page=News&storyID=13740.

49. http://www.kxly920.com/global/story.asp?s=8972788. WSU "President Floyd Gets Pay Raise to $725,000." *Seattle Times, Aug. 29, 2008.* http://seattletimes.nwsource.com/html/localnews/2008147000_webswuprez29m.html. After being criticized in the local media, Floyd announced that he would actually take a pay cut of $100,000, but only after his pay raise began, so that he would still receive a net raise of $25,000. Dan Hansen, "WSU President Takes A Pay Cut," *SpokesmanReview. com.* http://www.spokesmanreview.com/breaking/story.asp?ID=17882.

50. Chloe White, "Petersen Suspends New Programs, Defends Fulmer's Appointment," *Knoxville News Sentinel*, December 10, 2008, http://w.w.w.knoxnews.com/news/dec/10/hiring-freeze-om-at-ut/?

51. Poskanzer, *Higher Education Law*, 226–27.

52. American Association of University Professors, "Financial Exigency, Academic Governance, and Related Matters (2004)," http://www.aaup.org/AAUP/comm/rep/finexg.htm.

53. Robin Wilson, "Downturn Threatens the Faculty's Role in Running Colleges," *Chronicle of Higher Education*, February 6, 2009, A1.

54. Wilson, "Downturn Threatens," A7.

55. Wilson, "Downturn Threatens," A7.

56. Silverglate, "Let's Cut."

57. Jeffrey Brainard, Paul Fain, and Kathryn Masterson, "Support-Staff Jobs Double in 20 Years, Outpacing Enrollment," *Chronicle of Higher Education*, April 24, 2009, A1.

CHAPTER 7

1. Courtney Leatherman, "Higher Education under Siege," *Chronicle of Higher Education*, January 30, 1998, A1.

2. William H. Cowley, *Presidents, Professors and Trustees: The Evolution of American Academic Government* (San Francisco: Jossey-Bass, 1980), 96–97.

3. Thomas J. Tighe, *Who's in Charge of America's Research Universities?* (Albany: State University of New York Press, 2003), 74.

4. Richard Chait, "Trustees and Professors: So Often at Odds, So Much Alike," *Chronicle of Higher Education*, Aug 4, 2000, A6.

5. John Hechinger, "Big-Money Donors Move to Curb Colleges' Discretion to Spend Gifts," *Wall Street Journal*, September 18, 2007, B1.

Index